PICTURES of jesus
in the Stories He Told

Other books by David B. Smith

Bats, Balls & Altar Calls
Bucky Stone series
Finding Waldo
More Than Amazing Grace
Music Wars
Time of Terror, Time of Healing

Visit the author at his Web page:

www.davidbsmith.com

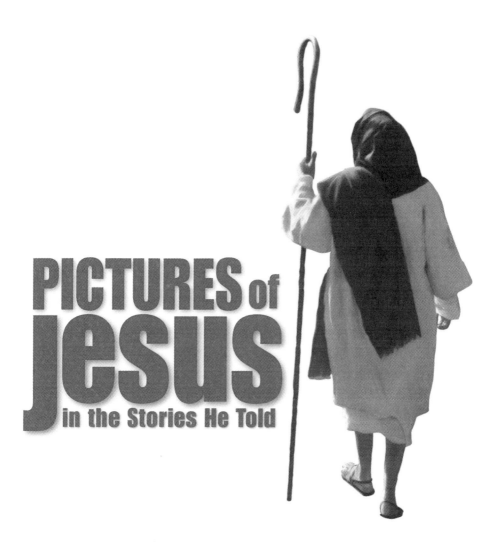

PICTURES of JESUS
in the Stories He Told

DAVID B. SMITH

Pacific Press® Publishing Association
Nampa, Idaho
Oshawa, Ontario, Canada
www.pacificpress.com

Cover design by Gerald Lee Monks
Cover design resources from sermonview.com
Inside design by Aaron Troia

The author assumes full responsibility for the accuracy of all facts and quotations as cited in this book.

Unless otherwise noted, all Bible quotations are from the HOLY BIBLE, NEW INTERNATIONAL VERSION®. Copyright © 1973, 1978, 1984 by International Bible Society. Used by permission of Zondervan Publishing House. All rights reserved.

Bible quotations marked KJV are from the King James Version of the Bible.

Scripture quotations marked *Clear Word* are from *The Clear Word Bible: A Paraphrase to Nurture Faith and Growth.* Copyright © by Jack J. Blanco, 1994.

Scripture quotations from *The Message.* Copyright © by Eugene H. Peterson, 1993, 1994, 1995, 1996, 2000, 2001, 2002. Used by permission of NavPress Publishing Group.

Scriptures quoted from NKJV are from The New King James Version, copyright © 1979, 1980, 1982, Thomas Nelson, Inc., Publishers.

Scriptures quoted from TLB are from *The Living Bible,* copyright © 1971 by Tyndale House Publishers, Wheaton, IL. Used by permission.

You can obtain additional copies of this book by calling toll-free 1-800-765-6955 or by visiting http://www.adventistbookcenter.com.

Library of Congress Cataloging-in-Publication Data:
Smith, David B., 1955-
  Pictures of Jesus : in the stories he told / David B. Smith.
     p. cm.
  ISBN 13: 978-0-8163-2507-8 (pbk.)
  ISBN 10: 0-8163-2507-3 (pbk.)
  1. Jesus Christ—Parables. I. Title.
  BT375.3.S65 2011
  226.8'06—dc23
                                                          2011022738

11 12 13 14 15 • 5 4 3 2 1

Contents

Chapter 1 7
Diary of a Prodigal Father

Chapter 2 25
Buying a Farm From Jed Clampett

Chapter 3 43
Saints to My Right, Sinners to My Left

Chapter 4 61
Bedrock or Jell-O for the Foundation

Chapter 5 79
When to Pull the Weeds

Chapter 6 96
The Lady Who Won a Million Bucks

Chapter 7 115
The Cost of Saving Private Ryan

Chapter 8.. 132
I Can't Afford Your Free Tuxedo

Chapter 9.. 148
Year-End Report of the Ten Mutual Funds

Chapter 10.. 168
A Really High-Paying Temp Job

Chapter 11.. 184
The Good Guy From the Bad Neighborhood

Chapter 12.. 202
The Girls Who Missed the Wedding

Notes 220

Chapter 1

DIARY
of a Prodigal Father

He is so angry that he can hardly see straight. In fact, he's red-in-the-face furious at the entire world. I'm talking about a little guy named Calvin, superhero of the late, great cartoon strip *Calvin and Hobbes*. Creator Bill Watterson for a number of years delightfully captured the thought processes of this wild little boy whose vivid imagination conjured up the tiger Hobbes, out of a stuffed toy.

But in this particular strip, Calvin is fuming. When bedtime comes—always too soon, of course—he asks his dad, "Why can't I stay up late? You guys can!"

And there's no answer. "It's not fair!" he cries out to the world in general, his screaming mouth filling up the entire cartoon frame.

"Well." Dad casually clears his throat. "The world isn't fair, Calvin." As if that fixed anything.

And the scowling rebel stalks off, his shoulders sagging. "I know," he admits, still spitting nails in his frustration. "But why isn't it ever unfair in my favor?"[1]

If any part of God's Word came with a guarantee to make a person angry, it would be the parables of Jesus. They reek of unfairness! They're absolutely loaded with undeserved favors: people finding treasures they didn't earn, bad boys getting to come back home, guys working one hour and being paid for the entire day. "The first shall be last, and the last shall be first." If you're the kind of person who has a built-in sense of fairness and justice and you believe the maxim "a day's pay for a day's work," then the parables of Jesus Christ are a collection of stupid stories designed to make you see red. And that's all there is to it. They're awful.

My cousin Pastor Morris Venden was so struck by this unfairness that he wrote an entire book a number of years ago titled *Parables of the Kingdom*. And he comments openly about the upside-down mentality of God's kingdom. "The kingdom of heaven is on the gift system—the kingdoms of earth are based on merit and on earning your own rewards. The kingdom of heaven offers service for others as the highest privilege—the earthly kingdoms seek service *from* others as evidence of highest honor. The heavenly kingdom works through the freedom of love—the kingdoms of earth use force to accomplish their goals."[2]

Venden's first sentence says it all. "The kingdom of heaven is on the gift system." Over and over again, these frustrating stories tell us that many, many wide-eyed people are going to get something good—something they don't deserve. When all the redeemed walk through the pearly gates into heaven, there will be quite a number of "thieves on crosses"—people who get into heaven at the very last second, who didn't do a single thing to merit even a hanky, let alone a glorious robe of victory. They don't deserve a torn and tattered tent, let alone a mansion beyond all imaginings. And yet here we are, standing on a sea of glass, when we should be down in a much warmer and more unpleasant climate.

Now, the good news is that these strange *Twilight Zone* stories are aggravating and irritating only until you're the person who receives these undeserved treats. Our little friend Calvin howled out in his anger. "Why isn't it ever unfair in *my* favor?" And in all these stories told by Jesus, the unfairness comes pouring into our own front doors, in our favor every time.

The story that has to be the epitome of all the Bible's "unfair" parables is "The Diary of the Prodigal Father." Oh, I know that in the Bible, it's the "prodigal son." But as we read and ponder this incredible vignette, we find to our amazement that the dad was the most prodigal, not the son.

This famous story is found in Luke 15. The characters are a dad and two sons—the older son and the famous one who ran off. He's the prodigal son. And here's how Jesus tells the story to His spellbound audience: "The younger [son] said to his father, 'Father, give me my share of the estate.' So he divided his property between them" (verse 12).

Right away this is very strange. When does a son generally inherit the family ranch? Not until Dad has passed away, of course. So this son, underneath the narrative line, is saying a couple of things. First of all: "I can't wait!" And really he's saying to Dad, "I wish you were dead. I don't like being your son; I don't like living here; I want out."

Here's the irony—and of course, this lands on your doorstep and mine. How often do God's people, His sons and daughters, decide they don't want that relationship any longer? "I'm leaving," we say to ourselves. "God, You leave me alone, and I'll leave You alone too. Because I want out of here." And yet with the very same breath, we tell God that we want an inheritance from Him. We want the family fortune: money, good health, prosperity, a college education, a new car, a wardrobe, and all the rest—*from God.* We say to Him, "Give me this and this and this and this—and then I'm going to leave." And, wonder of wonders, just like in this story, a loving Dad goes along with such an incredibly selfish demand. He gives wicked people, rebellious earthlings who want to travel out of His jurisdiction, the family fortune!

Have you seen fabulously wealthy people on the evening news, who were very clearly living lives separate from their heavenly Father? And yet they were wearing on their bodies the beautiful clothes God blessed them with resources to buy. Every breath they were taking was a gift from God; the beating of their hearts was God's present to them, an inheritance. And without so much as a "thanks a lot," they headed to Beverly Hills and the land of many parties.

And so does this bad boy of Luke 15. This dad gives his boy what he wants: his half of the family fortune. And just a few days later, son number two does what he intended: he packs up and leaves. In fact, the Bible describes his departure this way: "Not long after that, the younger son got together all he had, set off for a distant country and there squandered his wealth in wild living" (verse 13).

There's an understated permanence to this whole expedition. First of all, the math of the real world says this: once you get the inheritance from Pop, that's it, man. You've got it. There's no more where it came from. You get your share and you leave, and there's no coming back, *because you already got your share.* That's the math of our world. And this boy leaves home with that understanding. He's not just going on a three-day, two-night junket to Las Vegas for a quick bit of fun. He's leaving forever. The Bible says he "got together *all he had.*"

In the real world, the story would end right there! In our terms, in our math, it would. You run away from home, you lose your money, you pawn your car, you go broke, and that's it. But in these parables of Jesus, everything is upside down. Where a story would usually end, this one is just getting started. Where normal math would say, "You're busted, mister," this story goes in an entirely different direction. No wonder a recent bestseller by Philip Yancey entitled *What's So Amazing About Grace?* has this for a chapter title "The New Math of Grace."

As this young man flees toward the digital billboards of Sin City, we notice something very wonderful. A person of this world might very well head off to a far country, determined that he's through with God. I mean, through! And he says so! "Father, I'm leaving and I'm not going to be back." His plane ticket is one-way, and so is his mind-set and the jut of his jaw.

Pastor George Vandeman tells how in his youth he actually shook his fist at heaven. "Leave me alone!" he shouted at God. "Holy Spirit, go away! And don't come back!" Here was another young rebel who got on the bus for what he was absolutely sure was a one-way ride to the devil's Disneyland. But sometimes our God holds that return ticket stub in His hand and just doesn't say anything for quite a long while.

So the young man gets to the faraway country and proceeds to spend his dad's fortune in loose living. He quickly blows the entire bundle on booze and babes and blackjack and bubbly wine. And again, this is his father's money he's spending. Dad gave him some wonderful gifts, and he spent them in Las Vegas.

Here's one lesson for us immediately. Every time we waste a talent or drop a dollar where we shouldn't, do we remember that it was a gift from a loving Father? Right now at this moment, you might be a rebel on your own journey. But every ability you have—your earning power, your personality, your skills and talents, your friendships—those are all gifts God has given you. At the moment you may be spending them unwisely; the inheritance you were given might be going right into the dealer's tray at the roulette wheel. God gave you gifts, and you wasted them. Shame on you and shame on all of us.

Where have all the friends gone?

A disquieting article titled "Heaven's Gatekeepers" appeared in *Newsweek* about a decade ago. Several New Age authors had really hit the big time, and their books on the topic of communicating with spirits were riding high on the *New York Times* bestseller charts. And one in particular, *Talking to Heaven,* suggests that people are pretty much guaranteed eternal life, no matter who or what they might have believed in here on earth. Supposedly, the spirits of our departed friends and relatives are all around us. The book tells of a grieving mother who comes to the author for comfort and asks him to contact the spirit of her dead little girl. "I see figures on the wallpaper," he says. "Yes. She's talking about . . . rabbits. The bunny rabbits." And the mother almost weeps for joy: yes, there were rabbits on the wallpaper in her little girl's room.

In this same article, a very thought-provoking assertion is made. "[This author] holds out the promise of eternal life after death without the necessity of believing in Jesus or in anything else beyond the grasp of an average dog or cat."

And he goes on to assert that everyone, I mean, everyone, including Adolf Hitler, will be in heaven. He mentions Hitler by name as being a person who will be saved in heaven.[3]

This is quite a distance removed from the parable of the prodigal son; and yet, this New Age claim of eternal life is familiar to a lot of us. In Jesus' story was a young man who repudiated his father. "Dad, I want your money," he said. "But I don't want you. I don't want to be your son; I don't want any relationship with you. Nothing but half of your estate. And then I'm out of here."

Again, this kid took off—in his mind, permanently—chartered a limousine to a faraway land, and then proceeded to live a life of profligacy, spending his father's money. He wouldn't take Dad, but he would take Dad's money—and he was certainly very happy to spend Dad's money.

Right here in the story is where many of us find ourselves. Everything we have came to us from God. Our money, our abilities, our health, our friends, our homes, all of our comforts, every meal we eat. The Bible talks over and over about how all good gifts come from God. "Every good and perfect gift is from above" (James 1:17), is one example.

And yet we find in the human race a strong proclivity to spend those gifts, not just apart from God, but in active defiance of Him and in opposition to His kingdom. We almost use His money to fund the rebel, anti-heaven campaign. As these New Age superstars suggest, a person can live life without God, either making millions on the talk-show circuit, or maybe even feeding the fires of the Auschwitz ovens, and still get an inheritance of eternal life from God.

Using a bit of a Las Vegas motif reminds me of an old comedy paragraph from Bill Cosby, who once addressed a ballroom of vacationers and gamblers in one of Glitter Gulch's hotels. And he pointed out how many of them would spend their entire weekend out in the casino playing cards at the 21 tables, praying to God. "Oh, God, give me an eight. Give me a five. Give me a ten for this double-down." And then he scolded, tongue-in-cheek, "And ain't none of you going to then go to church Sunday morning. Not if you're winning." In other words, they had this prodigal-son attitude: Take God's money and His blessings . . . and then do your own thing.

Just a few pages before this Luke 15 parable, we find another of God's principles enumerated for us to consider. Have you received gifts and talents from God?

Of course you have. We all have. We owe God everything, and the more gifted a person might be, the more he or she owes, according to Luke 12:48: "From everyone who has been given much, much will be demanded; and from the one who has been entrusted with much, much more will be asked."

That's actually the tagline to more than one of Jesus' parables, but considered in this story right here, it reminds us of the fact that we all are in this adventure together. We all are that runaway son. We all are spending, one way or another, a fortune a loving Parent has given to us.

The lesson for us is this: let's live in relationship with the Father who gave us these gifts. We'll return to this idea in chapter 6, the parable of the unforgiving servant. But so often people pray to this distant Father, and they really do want an answer. But they don't want anything more than the answer. They don't want the God who provides the answer. They might pray for healing; they might beg Heaven for a mate or for a job. It might even be a pretty good prayer, an unselfish prayer—healing for a child or for a friend. They might pray for forgiveness of sins, for guilty feelings to be removed. Even Judas Iscariot once cried out in desperation, "I have sinned!" But it's still a prayer with the most important part clipped off: they don't want a relationship. They don't want anything more than the return package in the mail. They want a kind of free New Age eternity without a life lived in devotion to Jesus Christ, without a surrendered heart.

But now back to this son. Very quickly the money runs out. The merry-go-round stops spinning. And isn't that true of all of Satan's promises? "I'll give you knowledge," he said to Eve. And true, she did learn about a few new things: thorns, pain, sorrow, her first son killing her second one. And then she died herself. "I'll give you fun," he says to people today. And there is fun out there in Lucifer's playground. Champagne glasses clink together, and pretty girls offer their services to someone who's spending God's fortune in Satan's kingdom. But when the fortune runs out, so does the fun. King Solomon once lamented, "I tried everything. I had everything and I tried everything. And it was all vanity. Meaningless. Unfulfilling." That man had three hundred wives and seven hundred girlfriends, but couldn't find fulfillment. And that's the eventual discovery of every prodigal son or daughter.

As we keep reading here in Luke 15:14, we learn that two things hit the prodigal son all at once. Not only does his money run out, but a famine hits. And our young hero hadn't planned for either of these events. But right here we discover yet another contrast between the math of the world and the math of God's kingdom. Because here on earth, on Tropicana Boulevard in Las Vegas, people are connected to each other by what? By a man's bankroll. For nights on end, this boy's existence was flavored by one expression: "Drinks are on me." He had friends because the drinks were on him. People were connected to him because of money. That's how the world operates. Politicians vote the way lobbyists suggest because six-figure campaign contributions are much appreciated and because golf junkets on private jets are kind of fun. We go to work for a company because they agree to pay us. We hang around with certain people because they have things we like or because their presence makes us feel important. We're kind to our aging relatives because we know they have wills and sports cars and mountain cottages to give away. These are the strands that connect us to one another; this is the mathematics of a sinful race. And this young man found out with a vengeance that in Sin City, A always leads to B. Money leads to friends; no money leads to no friends. And when he got down to his last quarter, all of his so-called friends crossed the street to another casino. That's the fundamental math equation in Satan's textbook.

So the prodigal son finds himself having to work for a living. Which, once you've departed from the kingdom of God, is the way of the world too. That's Economics 101 here on planet Earth: when there's a famine going on and you've run out of Daddy's money, you get a job, Buster. Any job you can get. This is salvation by works of the most fundamental sort.

And this young man, now reduced to wearing rags, bums a classified section out of a trash can and finds that the only job listings have to do with feeding pigs. That's right! This kid, born and raised as an orthodox Jew, now has to feed the most unclean animal of all. He's a pig-keeper, and soon he's so hungry he's tempted to eat the pigs' food, the pods from the carob trees. Things are that bad.

In the King James Version, verse 15 says, "And he went and joined himself to a citizen of that country; and he sent him into his fields to feed swine."

The Greek word *kollaō,* which gives us "joined himself to," actually can mean "to glue together" or "join" or "to cleave to." In essence, this starving young man now has to basically sell himself off as a slave to the owner of the pig farm, this citizen of a faraway country. He's a slave now! Where once he lived in freedom with Dad, having access to all of Dad's love and wealth and wisdom, now he's a slave to someone in the enemy camp. More of Satan's math—where a person trades in freedom for slavery, the holdings of heaven for the leftover scraps of a pig's dinner.

So far the equation is holding up about as expected. But the whole story's about to turn upside down with one wake-up call.

Heaven's wake-up calls

The National Geographic book *Everest: Mountain Without Mercy* describes how a pathologist named Beck Weathers was lost on the world's highest mountain in the killing season of May 1996. A number of climbers were already dead, and he was lying comatose in the snow just 350 yards away from Camp Four. Another climber, Yasuko Namba, lay nearby; the rest of his party had struggled through the horrific blizzard winds back to their tents.

It was the evening of May 10 when he and the others got lost on the South Col. The next morning, with the winds abating just a bit, a couple of climbers managed to stagger out to where the two lost climbers were lying in the snow. To their surprise, the two were still breathing, but just barely. Neither one had much of a pulse; their eyes were glazed over, their limbs frozen. With heavy hearts, the climbers decided that it just wasn't possible to even try to rescue them. The scant resources of oxygen and human strength they had left had better be reserved for stronger climbers. "It was a classic case of triage," one wrote later.

It wasn't long before Namba finally breathed her last. And yet for hours this Texan, Beck Weathers, lay there in the snow, completely comatose. Then all at once, for some reason no one can explain, something flickered on in his brain. He "came to." Somehow a light went on and he regained consciousness. He stared at this odd blue object, which he suddenly realized was his own completely frozen hand. And he slowly grew aware of where he was: near the top of Everest with no one around. He finally recognized that, as he put it later, the cavalry wasn't about to come get him; if he was going to be saved, he would have to get up and walk back through his almost snow-blinded condition into camp. Which is precisely what he did. In a feat of courage still legendary with climbers of the world's tallest peaks, this stubborn doctor figured out by wind currents which way it was to the tents. And like a mummy in a horror movie, he slowly shuffled through the blizzard and into the camp of safety. He later lost both hands, one forearm, and a nose . . . but he's alive and well these many years later.[4]

And it's that moment of "coming to" which ties into Jesus' parable of the prodigal son. Beck Weathers can't explain it. Normally he should have just slowly lapsed into unconsciousness and then a peaceful death. But right when he needed a jolt of some kind, it was provided there at twenty-six thousand feet. Something or Someone said to him, "Wake up."

In Luke 15, this young rebel has gotten to a similar point. Lost on the mountain. In his case, he was lost on the pig farm. And it wasn't just a case of being out in the middle of nowhere; this boy has simply gone into a moral stupor. For months, perhaps years, he'd been so blind that he couldn't see what was what. He had left what was good, and ran off to sample that which was bad. He left safety for danger; security for risk, God for Satan. True love for false. Real friends for phony ones. A full table for starvation.

And now here are six wonderful words found in Luke 15:17: "When he came to his senses . . ."

In the King James Version, it says, "And when he came to himself . . ."

All through God's Word, we find this shuddering moment replayed over and over. King Solomon had it hit him after years of being in a moral stupor of concubines and idolatry. His father, King David, was jolted right off his throne when a prophet named Nathan pointed a finger in his face and said, "Thou art the man!" Saul, later to be the apostle Paul, was breezing along the road to Damascus, his conscience stuck in neutral, when a bright light from heaven knocked him off his horse of spiritual complacency.

In this Bible parable, Luke 15 doesn't say anything about the father's intervention at this point. Dad is simply waiting back home, going out to the mailbox each day and looking down the road for his son. But I'd like to suggest that in the real story, which is you and me, that moment of "coming to our senses" is one that is caused by the Father every time. We don't wake ourselves up. Just as God sent the prophet Nathan with that forceful wake-up call to an adulterous king, He jolts this prodigal son. "That's enough," He says. "Wake up!"

Through what means does a heavenly Father wake us? He does have His prophets: men and women whose warnings are direct communiqués from heaven. How many of us have been reading in our Bibles, when all at once a verse leaped out at us and gave a strong spiritual pinch. And after we said, "Ouch!" we fell on our knees and thanked God for putting that verse there specifically for us. Has that happened to you? It certainly has happened to me—many times. And I didn't enjoy it, but I thank God that He has caused me to "come to my senses." Often when writing a sermon, the messages I've shared, which were written and intended for others, turned around and became God's loving missive for me instead.

God also uses His own Holy Spirit as an active agent to wake up comatose climbers on the Mount Everest of the spiritual journey. And I believe He uses even heaven-sent trials and hard times, if necessary, to jar a man, or an entire nation, to repentance.

Many years ago, when I was a scriptwriter at the Voice of Prophecy radio ministry, someone brought in a letter expressing a most unusual sentiment. It was from a man named Terry, and from the look of the envelope and the return address, we could tell that this envelope was from a prisoner. Sure enough, inside there was a three-page letter from an inmate in the California Department of Corrections. But here's the sentence that made everyone sit up straight. "Prison has been a great and wonderful experience for me."

And maybe we say, "What! He likes it in there? Is this guy on the psych ward?" No, because here's how he finished that sentence. "Prison has been a great and wonderful experience for me . . . and I thank God for His loving chastisement."

Most of his three-page letter was filled with praise to Christ and Bible verses. But there was just a tiny and humble glimpse into his former life. And it almost sounds word-for-word like the story of the prodigal son. He wrote about "the self-destructive life that I lived once I hit the big city with its mountain-high buildings, late nights, wild parties, and dark alleys. And oh! we must not forget the stones . . . crack [cocaine]. How could I sink so low? By resisting the call of God over and over again. I ran right into the open arms of the devil."

Now this rescued man was a vibrant, witnessing, born-again Christian, praising God that he was in prison! Praising God that somehow there went off a heavenly wired lightbulb in his brain. And like that prodigal son, he had an illuminating moment after which he smacked himself in the head and asked himself, *Where have I been? What could I have been thinking? Why was I so foolish? All at once I realize what I could have had!*

It's painful reality that most people have fallen clear down to the bottom before this coming-to-the-senses moment. If we think there's any way, any way at all, to survive on our own, we're going to do it. We have to be feeding the pigs, so to speak, or down to our last nearly empty oxygen canister on Everest, before we realize that we've run out of options. The son in this story doesn't think about going home until he's completely given up on himself. He has no money left. No food. No earning power. No friends. He's in a pit and absolutely cannot get a toehold.

And finally he says to himself in verses 17–19, "How many of my father's hired men have food to spare, and here I am starving to death! I will set out [The King James says, "I will arise."] and go back to my father and say to him: Father,

I have sinned against heaven and against you. I am no longer worthy to be called your son; make me like one of your hired men."

Right here is just the clearest picture of the human response. This is giving up without really giving up! He has a little speech planned, and some things in it are right. "I have sinned." That's for sure true. "I'm not worthy to be your son." That's even more true; after all, he's used up the inheritance that would be his by rights. He's depleted the family tank of "sonship." So he knows he's in bad shape. According to the math of this world, he's down to zero and below. He's well down in the negative numbers.

And yet, what's his plan? "I'll go home and work! I'll qualify to be a servant! I'll at least earn some food and maybe a warm bed. I know I can't be a son anymore; that option is lost to me. But I still have a strong body; I can get a job at Dad's place and earn a day's pay for a day's work." So this broken-down guy surrenders about the way most of us do. "I'm helpless," we admit. "But maybe I'm not *completely* helpless. I still have some earning power with God. I can come back to Him and do some odd jobs around the house, maybe at least get into the servants' quarters, and then take it from there."

So he starts out. But this young man's about to receive the new-math explosion of his life.

A party in Traverse City, Michigan

And on the jacket of Philip Yancey's *What's So Amazing About Grace?* reviewer Brennan Manning writes, "[This is] the crown jewel of all [Yancey's] books." And then comes this warning: "If you read the chapter, 'The Lovesick Father,' and do not weep for joy, I suggest you check your pulse . . . or make an appointment with your mortician."

And then Yancey tells his story, of how a young girl in Traverse City, Michigan, decides that Dad is stupid and home is stupid and church is stupid, and she wants to leave for the big city. So she does. She runs away, goes to Detroit, and ends up making a living the same way many other homeless girls do. A guy with a big car—"The Boss"—gets her all set up with a nice penthouse suite, with room service and limo rides and men who pay handsomely for the tricks she knows. But drugs wear down her body, and soon, with the dark circles under her eyes, she can't command the same prices as before. The next day The Boss throws her out, and things get harder and harder. Soon she's sleeping on metal grates outside department stores through a hard Detroit winter.

And finally she has the Beck Weathers moment of coming to her senses. "Maybe I'll go home," she says to herself. So she calls, but gets just the answering machine. "Dad, Mom, it's me," she says. "I was wondering about maybe coming home. I'm catching a bus up your way, and it'll get there about midnight tomorrow. If you're not there, well, I guess I'll just stay on the bus until it hits Canada."

So she rides. And she rides. And she practices over and over the speech: She's sorry. She's been so foolish. Can you ever forgive me? And as the bus gets closer, her heart is pounding. *What if they never even got the message? What if they're not there?* The bus rolls into the Traverse City terminal, and she realizes that the next fifteen minutes will decide her life. And it's pure terror for her. According to the math of the world, she ought to get nothing. Zip. And she knows it. No forgiveness, no welcome back, no making up for how she's slapped everyone in the face. *Is that how it will be? Or will Dad be there?*

Here's the finish to the story, in Yancey's own words:

"She walks into the terminal not knowing what to expect. Not one of the thousand scenes that played out in her mind have prepared her for what she sees. There, in the concrete-walls-and-plastic-chairs bus terminal in Traverse City, Michigan, stands a group of forty brothers and sisters and great-aunts and uncles and cousins and a grandmother and great-grandmother to boot. They're all wearing goofy party hats and blowing noise-makers, and taped across the entire wall of the terminal is a computer-generated banner that reads 'Welcome home!' Out of the crowd of well-wishers breaks her Dad. She stares out through the tears quivering in her eyes like hot mercury and begins the memorized speech, 'Dad, I'm sorry. I know . . .' He interrupts her. 'Hush, child. We've got no time for that. No time for apologies. You'll be late for the party. A banquet's waiting for you at home.' "[5]

End of story. But right here, you and I can simply get out the biggest trash bin we can find and throw into it every math textbook we can find. Every book about philosophy. Every book about sensible business principles. Every calculator that says that two and two is four. Every diary in which a record is kept of someone else's wrongs. Every scorecard, every set of scales where things ought to balance. And we just keep throwing out and throwing out because this strange and wonderful story of the prodigal son just *turns the universe upside down*!

Because here's a kid who deserves nothing. Nothing! He already got his share! And he used it up! He burned his account down to zero! And he staggers home, knowing full well that he deserves zero in return. His only hope is to perhaps receive minimum wage, $7.25 an hour, working on Dad's farm. He doesn't even deserve that after all the "I hate yous" he shouted on his way out.

But here in verse 20 we discover the new math of heaven: "While he was still a long way off, his father saw him and was filled with compassion for him; he ran to his son, threw his arms around him and kissed him." And now comes the foolish speech. "The son said to him, 'Father, I have sinned against heaven and against you. I am no longer worthy to be called your son' " (verse 21). But the father said to the son, "Shut up. Just shut up." Actually, I added that part. Here are verses 22–24, though: "But the father said to his servants, 'Quick! Bring the best robe and put it on him. Put a ring on his finger and sandals on his feet. Bring the fattened calf and kill it. Let's have a feast and celebrate. For this son of mine was dead and is alive again; he was lost and is found.' "

Now, math-wise, this is a stupid story. Psychology-wise, this is a stupid story. I imagine even the late Dr. Benjamin Spock would say, "That is a stupid story." But here is the mathematics of heaven! A kid uses up half the family fortune, but Dad takes him back and restores him to a whole new fortune. Not as a servant, not as a prison parolee with a record to live down. He's back as a son!

In *Parables of the Kingdom,* Venden points out the symbolism in all three of the dad's gifts. The boy says, "I have sinned." And he receives a rich robe to cover the shame of his rags, his sins. He says, "I'm not worthy to be your son." But the dad doesn't even hear him; he immediately gives the boy his signet ring to wear, a symbol of reinstatement in the family. The boy, hardly able to get in a word edgewise, says, "Dad, wait. Let me just be a servant." But before he can finish the sentence, Dad hands him a brand-new pair of shoes; and of course, in that Judean culture, the servants and slaves didn't wear shoes; they went barefoot. Only a trusted son would have shoes on. This father gives his son the very gifts that demonstrate the wonderfully strange, different mathematics of heaven, God's equation of grace.[6]

Maybe you've been wondering about this chapter title, "Diary of a Prodigal Father." Isn't it the son who was the prodigal? Is this a typo? I sometimes like to reminisce about a classic Hollywood line from the old film *Jerry Maguire.* A young man who has basically spurned his wife finally comes to his senses. *How could I have been so foolish?* he wonders. *She loved me so much and I didn't realize! I will arise . . . and go home to her.*

And at the house he tries to find her in the crowd. "Hello? Hello? I'm looking for my wife." And he begins this long prodigal-son speech: "I was so foolish. I need you. Please forgive me. Please take me back." And he goes on for about three minutes, until Dorothy cuts him off. "Just shut up," she says very softly. Then, just like the dad in this story, she adds, "You had me at 'hello.'" She throws out the old math of revenge and divorce and I-want-so-much-alimony, and says to the man she loves with such an incredible love, "Jerry, shut up with your foolish, unnecessary speech. Because you had me at 'hello.'"

And so who is it who is the prodigal? Do you know what *prodigal* really means? It refers to wild, reckless, wasteful, lavish spending. Giving profusely. Abundantly overflowing generosity. Which the son in this story certainly did during his Las Vegas days. But how much more "prodigal" is the dad . . . in how much he loves! After frittering away half the family fortune, the son who returns is handed the keys to the bank again! Talk about prodigal! Talk about excessive! This is truly the story of the prodigal dad.

And every one of us is in this story. We've all taken the inheritance down to zero. Not one of us has anything good in us to recommend us to the Dad we rejected. Oh, we may still have a few dollars left of good deeds and obedience and so-called loyalty left in our pockets. But the Bible teaches that we're all sinners. We've all wandered away. And we've all dreamed of making a comeback in our own power, or at least getting hired on as servants next time even if not sons and daughters.

And maybe this very moment in time is God's way of waking you up. You can't even get home by yourself, but Dad has a return ticket for you. And it absolutely does not matter what you've done. A hundred sins, a million, a billion. Small or big. White lies or huge lies. Small sins or vile offenses. It doesn't matter. Pile them up as high as you can; it doesn't matter. Make a list as long as the Constitution; it doesn't matter. Because the math of heaven, the grace of God, the prodigal love of the Father simply throws it all out. You start with your speech, and God tells you to stop. He's not interested in that. He just wants to get started with the robe and the ring and the shoes and the party.

There's one more thing about the math of Heaven: They seem to be able to afford an awful lot of parties.

Oops! We haven't spent any time thinking about the older brother.

A wrong turn to India

In order to bring him into the tale, I have to get up my courage to tell you today about a very foolish man. I know that sounds crude, but wait until you hear about him.

His name is Dr. Paul Brand. He is a devout Christian believer who took a nasty and ill-advised detour down the wrong road.

Dr. Brand got his degree in medicine in the year 1946, right after the end of World War II. And he was talented, no doubt about that. He's written some good bestsellers and had a noteworthy career. But right there at the start, he just plain and simple made a wrong choice. Instead of starting up a lucrative practice in London, he got suckered into traveling back to the land of his birth and working in a hospital in Vellore, India.

Unfortunately, his family couldn't come with him for six months. So he was in the middle of nowhere all by himself. Second, in 1946, the hospital in Vellore wasn't exactly the Johns Hopkins Medical Center. He lived in a tiny little cubicle, taking baths by dipping a ladle into the water and then splashing it on himself. And then there was the heat. A hundred and ten degrees, all day, every day. Just breathing made a person sweat, he confessed later.

Could he just switch on the air conditioning? Not in 1946, he couldn't. Nothing was air conditioned in Vellore, even in the operating room. In fact, with the risk of infection, he and his fellow surgeons and nurses didn't even dare to have fans going. So they would stand there, dripping wet with perspiration, doing one operation after another. Between each patient, they would go outside, step out of their sopping-wet gowns, change into dry ones, and then head right back into the sauna for another operation. And this was for twelve-hour days.

In that kind of a climate, you really needed to drink at least six quarts a day, but Brand found that when he did so, he would break into a horrible "prickly heat" rash. Which, if you scratched at it, would turn into boils and infection. A fellow doctor advised him that if he cut back on the drinking, he would develop kidney stones instead. So that was the choice: kidney stones or painful rash. And most of the medical people endured bouts of dysentery, hepatitis, influenza, and a tropical disease called dengue, more commonly referred to as "break-bone fever," because for about a week a person felt as if every bone in his or her body were broken.

So that's the choice this foolish, misguided doctor made. Instead of practicing medicine in Beverly Hills, he was out there in Vellore, "working for Jesus." That was what his missionary spirit had led him to do.

As we think about the mathematics of God's kingdom and this story of the prodigal son, how does the older brother fare? All of the math in this story works against the older brother too. His younger brother takes half the family inheritance, goes to a faraway place, and spends it like a drunken sailor. Then when he comes home, Dad simply rewrites the will so that he's back in it with a whole new inheritance. He scores twice! Meanwhile, this older brother, who had stayed on the farm, working away year after year, obeying the rules, toeing the mark, gets nothing. Oh, he got the regular inheritance, but he had that coming anyway. But as he points out to his father, he'd never been given so much as a goat so he could have a little barbecue party with his friends.

Several of these stories Jesus tells have a common theme where someone is a chump. In this story, it's definitely the older brother. In another of Jesus' parables, some guys work for the master in the vineyard all day—speaking of 110 degrees—and then get the exact same pay as those who just worked for one hour right at quitting time.

So we surmise that these are the people who have served God the whole way. It's hot out there in the blazing sun of the mission field . . . and these men and women put in sixty-hour weeks for perhaps fifty years of service. And then they die, perhaps of amoebic dysentery, and get a tiny little grave marker out in Bangladesh, while their counterparts are soaking in Southern California Jacuzzis.

Peter, the disciple of Jesus, finally noticed that there were two kinds of people who were going to get into Jesus' kingdom. People like himself, who put in a whole lifetime of work and obedience, and then people like this prodigal son. And contrary to some of the jokes you read in Christian magazines these days about who got to heaven and got a big mansion and who got there and had to sleep in a little chicken coop, Jesus Christ never talked about bigger houses for the faithful few who served for years and years. And so finally Peter asked Him that very question. "Hey!" he protested. "We've left everything to follow You! What's in it for us?" In other words, if Calvary's gift of grace puts every single believer on the golden streets of the kingdom, then where's the extra reward for the older brother? For the missionary to India? For the person who works for God his entire life, instead of just slipping in under the wire like the thief on the cross?

I think we find some biblical understanding here by considering some of the characters we haven't addressed yet. And those are the servants of this estate owner. They live right there on the property, but they're not sons; they are working merely for a wage. They put in forty hours a week, punching a clock, wearing their uniforms, protected by the company's Delta Dental health plan, and once a week they get a check. Now, there's nothing wrong with this kind of a relationship, but it's not the same thing as being a son.

Remember that when the prodigal son first thought of coming home, he had no inkling that he might get to be a son again. But he might get to stay out back in the servants' quarters, where there was heat in the winter, air conditioning in the summer, and three good meals a day, and that Blue Shield health plan. And he knew, deep down, that his father—former father, really—was a decent employer: fair, honest, reasonable. Working for Dad—actually, he would probably have to call him Mr. Jones now—wouldn't be that bad. Compared to feeding these pigs, anyway. And that's what he went back hoping to receive: the relationship of an employee.

When you think about it, the older son was actually more like an employee than a son too. He obeyed, but he didn't enjoy it. He followed the rules, but didn't love the rule giver. He stayed on the farm because it was comfortable and because it was the status quo. And frankly, he stayed on the farm because he knew that he, too, had an inheritance coming. For him, those were the true "wages." If he put in his time until Dad died and the entire farm was deeded to him, it'd be a lot more than minimum wage. So it was worth staying. Deep down, this guy was a glorified employee who just happened to have the same last name as the boss.

Morris Venden makes this observation: "The elder brother was a 'good liver.' But it isn't much fun being good in the way he was good. That kind of good living will put ulcers in your stomach and lines on your face, because badness held in check is not goodness, and never will be."[7]

Some of us run the risk of being servants instead of sons too. Let me confess to you because I spent a number of years getting a paycheck every two weeks from the church. I was paid from heaven's storehouses. I paid my rent and my grocery bill with money that, in a way, went through heaven's financial savings-and-loan. And frankly, it would be rather easy—and surely a great tragedy—to begin to think of that form of service, that work for God, as just that: work. A medium-paying job for a fifty-five-year-old man. A career in which God is the boss and not the Father, an employer rather than a Friend.

The older brother in this parable betrays his feelings with a nasty little remark in verse 30. He's angry about Dad giving his younger brother a robe and a ring and a feast, and he says so. But notice his language: "When this son of yours who has squandered your property with prostitutes comes home, you kill the fattened calf for him!"

Notice. Not "my brother." No, it's "this son of yours." This older brother doesn't even consider that he's in the family. Dad is an employer, not a father.

And he certainly doesn't claim this renegade as his brother.

But this story lifts up for us the joys of sonship. When you love your Dad, really love Him, then it's wonderful to be with Him in His vineyard. The longer the better! The more you get to serve with Him, the more rewarding! Wouldn't you rather have the whole day with this wonderful Father than just the last hour? Better, don't you think, to work a whole lifetime in joy for Jesus than just the last fifteen minutes like the foolish thief on the cross? Really, who's the lucky one? The older brother enjoyed—or should have enjoyed—a full lifetime of secure and rewarding fellowship, ministry partnership, with such a wonderful and generous Dad.

We return to the story of Dr. Paul Brand, who made the "dumb" decision to go work in the steamy town of Vellore, India. Many years later he described the experience: "Never had I felt so challenged and fulfilled. Some people look upon expatriate doctors in Third World countries as self-sacrificing heroes. I know better. Most are having the time of their lives."[8]

For Dr. Paul Brand, the heat and the mosquitoes and the sores and the endless surgeries were a mosaic of joy, because he was working for God and with God. Foolish? By the world's math, of course. Measured by heaven's yardstick, the man was a genius.

Chapter 2

BUYING A FARM
From Jed Clampett

(Guest Testimony: Jeremiah Clampett)

I was readin' in the Good Book the other day, me and my missus, and I got myself to that story in the book of Matthew. Along around chapter 13, I think it was, and old number thirteen wasn't never unlucky for me, Jeremiah Clampett. Although I must say, those folks who put our family story on the TV never did get it right. But right where I get to that business about the farmhand who finds a big pot of treasure in a field, I slap that Bible down and I say to Mayella Sue—that's my little woman—"Wife," I says, "that there's *my* story! I'll be a skinned coon if that ain't exactly how it happened to me and Brother Jed."

Now, folks, you all know how that song goes. A Mr. Paul Henning made himself a few dollars offen that tune, I must say. But it goes along like, "Come 'n listen to my story 'bout a man named Jed. Poor mountaineer barely kept his family fed." Well, that was sure enough true for both Jed and me. We were so far out in the woods that roads got littler and littler and finally just ran up trees. And sometimes supper was up *in* that tree. But that business of Jed shooting at some food, and having oil come out—you remember, "bubblin' crude"—didn't happen that way at all. But you just hush for a spell, and I'll tell you how it really came to be.

See, Jed and I had our little forty acres right next to each other. Truth be told, he had about twenty-five, and me fifteen. Him bein' the big brother. And most of the time, we got along just dandy-good, 'cept when that nephew boy o' ours, Jethro, got into trouble. Boy was the dumbest excuse for a human bein' I ever did see. He was a few mules short of a pack, if you take my meanin'. But me and Jed, we were in one of our not-speakin' spells that summer. It got to the point where I had to watch out lessen Granny would take a shotgun to me just lettin' my shadow land on their blessed property.

Well, anyhows, one day our little pet goat, Buzzard, jumps the fence over onto Jed's place. So, after makin' sure Granny and Elly Mae aren't within range, I mosey on over the fence and aim to fetch him back.

And all at once, right next to Jed's old persimmon tree, I step down and say to myself, "Boy, this soil here is softer 'n that brain of Jethro's if I do say so myself." Real wet and soggy-like. Fact is, I pretty near sank down to my ankles in the goo and ruined my six-dollar boots I got down at Woolworth's. "What in tarnation is big-brother Jed doin' with this piece of worthless dirt?" I says to myself.

Well, sir, didn't take me but two shakes of a lamb's tail to put two and two together and figure me out that Jed Clampett, my own flesh and blood, is sitting himself on a oil well deluxe. I mean, that soggy ground was a dead giveaway. Don't know how he missed it. But I stamp around there, still watchin' out for Granny, and pretty soon say to myself, "Boy, there's enough black gold here to fill Turtle Lake two, three times at least."

So I go back home and I'm so excited I can't hardly chew my corn at lunch. Mayella Sue thinks I've got me a case of the vapors or somethin', keeps hoverin' over me like a vulture on a church steeple. "You look like you seen an *apparition,*" she tells me. And I've got my mind hummin' away, thinking how I can get that soggy land away from Jed.

Well, sir, let me tell you, I played it as cool as Granny's huckleberry ice cream, which was about the only edible thing that woman ever made. But I went on over to Jed's that very night and said to him, "Brother of mine, it's time you and me buried the hatchet. I'm right ashamed of the feudin' I started. Want you to forgive me and let bygones be bygones." I about bygoned myself to death, tellin' him how much I loved him. Then, when he got all misty-eyed, I said to him, "But now I got a favor to ask, Jeddy-boy."

"What?" he says.

"That corner piece of land," I tell him. "That corner that tucks into my fifteen acres."

"Yes, sir," he says. "What of it?"

"Why don't you sell it to me?" I says. "All these years it's been Jed twenty-five, and Jeremiah just fifteen. Now, I don't mind, and Mayella Sue don't mind neither. But that corner runs into my property, and means our fences are all crooked over there. You sell me two acres, that makes it Jed twenty-three, and little brother'd have seventeen. Plus"—now this was hard to get out, but I said it without chokin'—"I give you any amount you ask. Name your price."

Well, he gets a look on him like a calf that had three suppers in one evening. "That old spot by the persimmon tree?"

"The very one," I tell him. "Sell me them two acres, and I'll go to meet my Maker a happy man. Amen."

Well, Jed knows how to drive a hard bargain, even with his own kinfolk. He didn't take but two bites of huckleberry ice cream before sayin' to me, "Six hundred dollars."

"Six hundred?" I act to be surprised even though my heart is just poundin' away. "Now, Jed, that's for the whole two acres. Right? Six hundred twice would be highway robbery without the guns."

And my older brother saw his opening right there. Fact, I think what I said put it in his head. " 'Course I meant six hundred per acre," he said. "Six for one, and a grand plus two for the whole thing. 'Course, if you don't want it . . ."

Well, I pretended to gasp and swaller my tongue and let my eyes stick out like June bugs. But when I said, OK, it was a deal, he gave me a look like he'd just taken me on a one-way ride to Fool's Market. "Well, dogie," he said, like you've always seen on them TV shows. And I thought, *You're the dogie goin' to stay on the farm. It's Little Brother who's goin' to be sellin' out and movin' to Beverly. Hills, that is.*

But first I had to get me a stash of twelve hundred dollars. Mayella Sue and I had just a hundred and fifty of egg money we'd put in a tomato can out back. So I started rustlin' and hustlin'. We had three cows. I sold two of 'em. Five goats, I auctioned off four. And when I was still short four hundred, I went right into town and sold the Studebaker. Didn't get but three hundred seventy-five dollars for it and had to hitchhike home, but I knew I could borrow twenty-five dollars from Cousin Lester, and sure enough, I went over to Jed's that very night with the whole whoppin' twelve hundred bucks in the pocket of my overalls. He signed the paper to the two acres, grunting and chuckling to himself like he'd just jumped me four times in checkers.

So the land was mine. My wife thought I'd gone clean daft out of my head: no cows, no chickens, no car. Just two more acres of scrub brush, dirt, and a dead persimmon tree. And by the way, just one more little detail. I had me an oil well, which, as you all know, I up and fetched off to the O.K. Oil Company over in Tulsa. They collected them some samples, and then, pretty as you please, gave me the total sum of twenty-five million dollars. Yes, sir. Mr. John Brewster shook my hand, called me Mr. Clampett, how do you do, and handed over the check hisself. Twenty-five million dollars. You can buy yourself a whole lot of huckleberry ice cream, I told Granny, as she screamed and cursed about how it was the most dad-blasted betrayal she'd ever heard of in her entire life.

So we moved right out of there and got us a mansion at 516 Crestview Drive, Beverly Hills. They didn't add the 90210 till later, but the surroundings were just the same, believe you me. Swimmin' pools, movie stars. And Mr. Milburn Drysdale of the Merchant Bank of B. H. livin' right next door to us.

Well, I was like a hog in heaven 'cept for one thing. I felt real low about what I'd done to my brother Jed. I mean, twenty-five million minus a thousand two is a whole lot of stealin'. Some nights I couldn't sleep even in them satin sheets the maid always put there in the master bedroom suite. My conscience was bitin' me like a flock of March mosquitoes. And I finally says to Mayella Sue—or, as the hired help here call her, Yes, Ma'am, Mrs. Clampett—"What say we telegraph old Jed and his family, and give them back half that Texas tea money? There's enough black gold here for them and us too." And danged if she didn't say, yes, that'd be all right. She reckoned she could squeak by on twelve-and-a-half million dollars if she had to.

So Jed and all his kin came out to Californy too—in that truck you seen on your TV sets. Moved in right next to us at 518 Crestview. That's the right address, by the way; you can look it up on Elly Mae's trivia Web site if you got a scratchin' urge to do so.

So I was at peace in my mind again. Jed gave me a big hug and 'bout the biggest "Well, dogie" I ever heard when he saw the size of his new swimmin' hole. Granny fired up the stove and made some possum stew, and Jethro started right in with his Hollywood adventures, wantin' to be a movie director and a double-aught spy and all the other tomfool things you saw in nine seasons of Filmways Presentations plus reruns on Nick at Night.

So it's just like Reverend Scooter used to say in Bug Tussle back home. That diggin'-fer-treasure-an'-hidin'-it-back-up story's in the Bible fer sure, but so is that bit about doin' unto others. Amen, and pass the collection plate, 'cause the Clampett brothers got more 'n egg money to put in now.

Is it OK to swindle Circuit City?

So what is Jesus saying in this delightfully quirky story? If you spot the Hope diamond at a yard sale, sticker-price of fifteen dollars, or that *Titanic* "Heart of the Ocean" necklace, mismarked down to seven bucks, is it appropriate to buy it? The way Jesus tells this classic parable, a shrewd man finds buried treasure in someone else's field and then quietly rips off the owner.

It reminds me of a more recent story about a kid named Tom. He was pretty much like any boy living life on the Mississippi River right after the Civil War. Nickels and dimes were few and far between, especially when you were living with your aunt. St. Petersburg was a very ordinary little village, and there just wasn't a lot of money. But all of a sudden, the possibility of hidden treasure landed on his doorstep, and Tom and his childhood friend were faced with the possibility—in fact, the driving obsession—of having just tons of money in their pockets.

"He had never seen as much as fifty dollars in one mass before," writes the narrator of his story, "and he was like all boys of his age and station in life, in that he imagined that all references to 'hundreds' and 'thousands' were mere fanciful forms of speech, and that no such sums really existed in the world. He had never supposed for a moment that so large a sum as a hundred dollars was to be found in actual money in anyone's possession. If his notions of hidden treasure had been analyzed, they would have been found to consist of a handful of real dimes and a bushel of vague, splendid, ungraspable dollars."[1]

If you remember back to your literature classes, you remember that Tom Sawyer and Huckleberry Finn made their way into the cave after the death of Injun Joe, and came out with a whole booty of treasure. And by the time Aunt Polly and everyone else gaping at the gold coins finished counting it, the two boys had themselves something like twelve thousand dollars.

Mark Twain finishes up the saga like this: "The Widow Douglas put Huck's money out at six per cent, and Judge Thatcher did the same with Tom's at Aunt Polly's request. Each lad had an income, now, that was simply prodigious—a dollar for every weekday in the year and half of the Sundays. It was just what the minister got—no, it was what he was promised—he generally couldn't collect it. A dollar and a quarter a week would board, lodge, and school a boy in those old simple days—and clothe him and wash him too, for that matter."[2]

And as the old classics always point out, "They lived happily ever after." With six thousand bucks to his credit, even the Widow Douglas was glad that she had "snaked [Huck Finn] in out of the wet."[3]

Well, I would be the last person in the world to accuse one Mr. Samuel Clemens of literary theft, but the fact is that at least the germ of this gold-in-the-cave story comes right out of an even older volume, and that's the book of Matthew, chapter 13. There's a day of storytelling from the backseat of a boat on the Sea of Galilee, with hundreds of people sitting on the shore listening, and Jesus is able to match Mark Twain story for story, yarn for yarn. But then, after the crowds have packed up and gone home, He has another little trilogy of stories for just the inner circle, the disciples. And here's His own buried-treasure tale, which lasts just one verse.

"The kingdom of heaven," He says, for the fourth time that day, "is like treasure hidden in a field. When a man found it, he hid it again, and then in his joy went and sold all he had and bought that field" (verse 44).

Well, that makes sense. Even though I had my tongue firmly planted in cheek with my bootleg remake of *The Beverly Hillbillies,* and Jeremiah ripping off his own brother, Jed Clampett, this is a story we can all relate to. Have you ever come across an item at Best Buy that is accidentally marked down way too low? Man, it's gotta be a mistake. But *shhhhhh.* If you don't have your credit card right on you that very moment, you hide that Blu-ray DVD player in the back, under some boxes, run home, get your Visa card, come back, and stake your claim to the gold.

There's one thing we have to bear in mind in studying a parable like this one. And I kind of broke that rule in telling you about Mr. Clampett. Here's the principle: when we're studying parables in the Bible, we need to focus on the one key point the parable is trying to make, and not get sidetracked on the peripheral details that the storyteller—in this case, Jesus—is *not* trying to make.

Here's one particular example. In Matthew 13, we could immediately become bogged down in the morality, or lack of morality, involved in finding treasure in a field, and then covering it up and swindling the rightful owner of that field. And under normal circumstances, that would be an important point of discussion. Is it right for a Christian—or any person, really—to find hidden treasure in someone else's field, say nothing, cover the treasure back up, buy the field with a straight face, and then cash in? The old expression *caveat emptor,* "let the buyer beware," or in this case, the seller, comes to mind. In our revamped story, the brother who suckered Jed Clampett out of his twenty-five million dollar oil well felt guilty and gave him back half of the black gold. But I want to make clear that the morality of this man's decision is *not* the point! Jesus isn't talking about that! I remember a preacher once putting it this way: "You can't get these Bible stories to 'stand on all fours.' " So we have to ask, Well, what *is* Jesus talking about here?

In the Tyndale New Testament Commentaries, Dr. Richard T. France makes this assertion about Jesus' Matthew 13 tale: "The legal and moral justification of [the day-laborer] towards his employer . . . is not the point of the parable. It lies rather in both the *joy* which a disciple experiences in 'finding' the kingdom of heaven (i.e. in a relationship with Jesus who brings it), and in his willingness to give up everything else for this."[4]

Various Bible versions and commentators conjecture on just who this kind of person might be who is even in that field in the first place. And it has been suggested that perhaps he was a common laborer who had been hired to work in that field and accidentally finds the treasure. In the nineteenth-century book *Christ's Object Lessons,* author Ellen White suggests that perhaps this man is like a sharecropper who has rented a little plot of land from a wealthy owner.

"A man hires land to cultivate, and as the oxen plow the soil, buried treasure is unearthed. As the man discovers this treasure, he sees that a fortune is within his reach. Restoring the gold to its hiding place, he returns to his home and sells all that he has, in order to purchase the field containing the treasure. His family and his neighbors think that he is acting like a madman. Looking on the field, they see no value in the neglected soil. But the man knows what he is doing; and when he has a title to the field, he searches every part of it to find the treasure that he has secured."[5]

Now even if *Raiders of the Lost Ark* and *Romancing the Stone* and *The Adventures of Tom Sawyer* sound like far-fetched adventure stories, bear in mind that in the time of Jesus not everyone in the world had a safety deposit box or the opportunity to invest all their money using online brokerage services. Thieves were everywhere, one biblical scholar points out. And every time there was a change of administrations in Jerusalem or Rome, anyone with money was afraid that their "tribute"—meaning their taxes—would go up. (That hasn't changed a whole lot, has it?) And so it was common in the first century A.D. for people to bury their money in the ground. They really did. And then, sometimes they died and it was still there. Or they were tossed in prison, or were forced into exile, and all they had was a map hidden in their sandal with an *X* marking the spot. So when Jesus told stories about finding buried treasure, people sat up straight, because they probably had dreams of doing the very same thing.

One lesson very clearly articulated is this. When you find something truly valuable—like twelve grand in a cave or eternal life in the Bible—*you do whatever it takes.* You leave your girlfriend, Becky Thatcher, back home, and you crawl on your belly through the darkest bowels of a cave if you have to, in order to get to the gold. You sell what you have to, you sacrifice what you need to, you shed whatever is required. "This one thing I do," the apostle Paul tells us, and he was talking about a jackpot worth a whole lot more than twelve thousand dollars.

Of course, that kind of sacrifice doesn't come easy to most of us! Selling furniture to raise money is just plain no fun. Yard sales—no fun. Hocking the TV—no fun.

Rejoicing at your own rummage sale

I spotted this terrific story from a Wanda Vallasso contribution to *Leadership* magazine about a decade ago. "A gem dealer was strolling the aisles at the Tucson Gem and Mineral Show when he noticed a blue-violet stone the size and shape of a potato. He looked it over, then, as calmly as possible, asked the vendor, 'You want fifteen dollars for *this*?' The seller, realizing the rock wasn't as pretty as others in the bin, lowered the price to $10."

Well, can you tell where this is going? This is like the man in this Bible story who can hardly keep the excitement out of his voice. He goes to the owner, and trying not to let the thumping of his heart in his chest get too audible, says, "Uh, how much for that old field over yonder? I have this very casual, laid-back, ho-hum, no-big-deal interest in maybe kind of buying it. If it's all right with you." And every cell in his body is silently screaming, *Ohpleaseohpleaseohpleaseohplease!*

So here's part two, courtesy of Wanda Vallasso. What happens with the ten-dollar potato rock? "The stone has since been certified as a 1,905-carat natural star sapphire, about 800 carats larger than the largest stone of its kind. It was appraised at $2.28 million."

OK, but now let's approach the story this way instead. Suppose that the gem collector, seeing this hidden natural star sapphire, marked at fifteen dollars, hadn't been able to get the seller down to ten bucks. Would he have gone off in a huff, squealing his tires and saying to his wife, "That idiot! Wouldn't even bargain with me"? And abandoned this priceless opportunity?

Or put it this way. Suppose the price is ten bucks, and this buyer hasn't got the money on him. So he goes out to his car, and he looks for loose change in the glove box. He has to scrounge around in the backseat, trying to find a dollar bill or two. What a pain! Maybe he even has to drive eight miles back home and get cash. He grumbles the entire trip. "What an inconvenience! What a waste of three-dollars-a-gallon gas! Just to score a two-million-dollar natural star sapphire.

Maybe it isn't worth it. Maybe I'll just stay home and watch TV."

Does that kind of pouting sound realistic?

Or let's up the ante this way. Let's say you can get the two-million-dollar natural star sapphire, but it's going to cost you one million to get it. You've got to borrow major bucks. You've got to refinance your house, maybe even sell it. You've got to invade your IRAs and hit up your relatives. All of that is unpleasant, stomach-tightening work. Is it worth it? Do you complain as you work to raise one million in order to have two million?

Well, the Bible talks explicitly about the happiness this man experienced *as he raised the money* he needed to buy that field. The *Clear Word* paraphrase describes his emotions this way: "The kingdom of God can also be compared to treasure buried in a field. When a man finds it, he covers it up, goes home and *joyfully* sells everything he has to buy that field."[6]

The Message paraphrase attaches the joy to the finding, not the fund-raising, but says much the same thing: "God's kingdom is like a treasure hidden in a field for years and then accidentally found by a trespasser. The finder is ecstatic—what a find!—and proceeds to sell everything he owns to raise money and buy that field."[7]

When Jeremiah Clampett wants to buy the two acres with the hidden oil reserves on them, he has to sell his two cows, his four goats, and his one Studebaker. He slices his own financial portfolio down to nothing but a few pats of butter in the icebox and one featherless chicken. And he's happy to do so! He's happy to sacrifice. He rejoices in his temporary poverty, because he knows he's about to sell his oil rights to the O.K. Oil Company of Tulsa, Oklahoma, for a cool twenty-five million.

Years ago I pulled an Internet sermon off the Web, appropriately titled "The Kingdom of God Is Like . . ." Father Thomas Keating, in chapter 14 of "The Parable of the Hidden Treasure," makes a point about the arduous process of raising the ten dollars or mortgaging the house, or whatever, in order to get to the pot of gold. "In the mythologies of the various world cultures, the hero is always put to a test before he gets the treasure, the beautiful girl, the Holy Grail, or whatever the reward of the heavy trial. The hero has to slay the dragon to get into the cave or wherever the treasure is sequestered. All of these myths suggest that we do not access the greatest treasures of life without seeking for them ardently and passing through enormous tests. Having been through the appropriate test, we can then handle the treasure."

Admittedly, we find ourselves treading on the dangerous ground where Christians always get blurry vision. Isn't salvation free? Isn't grace simply credited to us? What's this about slaying dragons and buying expensive fields and cashing in our stock portfolios in order to obtain salvation?

Well, the answer is what the answer has always been, and the Lord has plainly told His would-be followers, "You will seek me and find me *when* you seek me with all your heart" (Jeremiah 29:13; emphasis added).

All the way through the Word of God, we find this reality. Salvation is free, but to know the Jesus who provides it involves sacrifice and work. Making friends *is* work. Calvary is an unlimited, no-strings-attached gift, but you have to prayerfully study the science of Calvary. Grace is offered to all, but it involves having a daily relationship with the generous Provider of that gift. The treasure is in the field, but you have to take possession of the field. The apostle Paul puts an almost sell-the-house spin on it in Philippians 2, when he exhorts his Christian friends: "Continue to work out your salvation with fear and trembling." Now, that sounds terrible! But he quickly adds the good news: "for it is *God* who works in you to will and to act according to His good purpose" (verses 12, 13; emphasis added).

So the buried treasure of salvation is free, but you do have to "scrounge up the ten dollars in loose change." You have to go to the rock and gem show where the sapphire is on display. You have to buy a parking permit and take the time to go through the exhibits. No one is going to just drive to your house—especially if you're a person who despises and disdains precious gems and jewels—and say out of the clear blue sky, "Here. I want you to just have this 2.28 million dollars." It doesn't work that way.

Even the brilliant King Solomon concedes that spiritual insight doesn't just fly in the window of your house. He says as much in Proverbs 2:3–5: "Cry out for insight and plead for understanding. You need to search for this wisdom"—now notice the metaphor he chooses—"search for this wisdom as if you were hunting for silver or some other hidden treasure. In the process you will learn what it means to reverence the Lord and will find the wisdom which comes from God" (*Clear Word*).

So is our search for salvation, for "free" grace, a journey of joy, or is it a fretful fiasco of fear and trembling, as Paul puts it? The Christian church says, "Read your Bible every day." Oh dear. "Go to church each weekend and be a part of a Christian fellowship." Oh dear. The preacher says, "Please put some of your money in this offering plate, so that you can learn to depend on God's mercies, and share this good news with others." Oh dear. Where's the joy in that? Are we mortgaging our house happily, or grudgingly? Do we wince when we hold a spiritual yard sale and get rid of the things that are keeping us from fully trusting in Jesus?

Well, if you lose sight of the treasure, you may struggle to be happy about it. Spending ten dollars to get a natural star sapphire is great; spending it to get nothing isn't so good. I can tell you, though, that there are a lot of Christian "rock hounds"—count me as one of them—who have found that Jesus Christ, the Cornerstone, is well worth seeking, "with all of your heart, and all of your might, and with all of your mind, and with all of your money." And please keep in mind as you make up the fliers for your own e-Bay auction, that Jesus Himself *is* the treasure! We are "laying aside the weight that so easily besets" in order to get with Him. And when we're searching for Jesus, not only is getting Him pure joy, but the searching is pure joy too.

A shovel and a concordance

It's vital for us to understand, then, where exactly the Christian ought to dig for treasure! It's been amusing, in recent years, to read the breathless accounts of scholars claiming to have unearthed hidden "codes" in the Bible. Starting with a certain verse 17, they suggest, and counting every forty-fourth letter backward—why, it spells out "Obama." Or, "Giants win WS." Which may be no big deal. But, all such schemes laid aside, God's Word itself *is* the field in which the priceless treasure is buried.

We've all heard stories about people who had a very ordinary painting hanging on the wall of their house. And then one magical day, someone discovers that inside the frame, pasted against the back of the picture, is fifty thousand dollars. Or underneath the ordinary painting, once you scrape away the three dollars' worth of cheap pigment, is an original Picasso or Rembrandt. And the poignant reality is that the hidden treasure has been there all along. "I walked right by that hidden safe a thousand times," the owner of the house says in awe. "And I never knew."

Our Adventist Church family did not endorse the elaborate rapture theologies spun out in the hugely popular *Left Behind* series of recent years. But one thing that I did appreciate about the books—and I didn't get very far into the saga—is this. These two gifted writers did urge their readers to get right with God, to make a commitment *now,* today, this very moment, to Jesus Christ, our Savior and Lord. Believe me, that part I do like . . . very much indeed. I endorse it wholeheartedly. And there's a scene from book 1, the original bestseller by Tim LaHaye and Jerry B. Jenkins, in which the airline pilot Rayford Steele is talking to Bruce Barnes, the associate pastor of New Hope Village Church. Bruce was "left behind" when Pastor Vernon Billings and millions of others were suddenly gone, raptured. And he talks with this confused, lonely pilot and his teenage daughter, Chloe, about how he had simply not read and studied God's Word for himself.

"I hardly ever read my Bible," he confesses, "except when preparing a talk or lesson. I didn't have the 'mind of Christ.' "[8]

And then, for the rest of the book, this Pastor Barnes and Rayford Steele and Chloe and the hero of the story, reporter Buck Williams, determine that they're not going to make the same mistake again. The treasure of truth, of a real—not superficial, not fake—relationship with Jesus, was hidden in the pages of this ancient Book, and they were going to commit themselves fully to finding that treasure.

So as we continue to dig here in Matthew 13, we unearth an important truth about Jesus' parable of hidden treasure. Of course, as we hear these old tales from the Master Storyteller Himself, we always want to know: What does the field stand for? What does the treasure stand for? Who is this guy digging in the field that doesn't belong to him? and so on. In the Tyndale New Testament Commentaries, Dr. France additionally informs us that people in Jesus' day loved these stories because they were so real in that culture. "Valuables such as coins or jewels were often hidden in a jar in the earth, and discoveries of such treasure trove were a favorite theme of popular stories."[9]

Most Christians would read this brief parable about the hidden treasure, and rightly conclude: "Well, eternal life is the treasure. That's the gift, the jackpot. So I should be willing to do anything, sell any possession, move any mountain, in order to be saved and have eternal life." True enough. And these heroes and heroines in *Left Behind* come, rightly, to that conclusion too. But let's look at a second application, and see whether you and I, along with Rayford and Chloe, have been sitting on a gold mine *we* didn't know we had either.

In *Christ's Object Lessons,* Ellen White takes many of Jesus' parables and suggests new meanings. Here's what she says about the hidden treasure in the field: "This parable illustrates the value of the heavenly treasure, and the effort that should be made to secure it. The finder of the treasure in the field was ready to part with all that he had, ready to put forth untiring labor, in order to secure the hidden riches. So the finder of heavenly treasure will count no labor too great and no sacrifice too dear, in order to gain the treasures of truth."

Now mark this down: "In the parable the field containing the treasure represents the Holy Scriptures. And the gospel is the treasure. The earth itself is not so interlaced with golden veins and filled with precious things as is the word of God."[10]

Frankly, this isn't one of the parables in which Jesus does the disciples and us the favor of coming back and saying, "OK, here's what it all means. The field is this; the gold is that," and so on. But certainly the gospel being the treasure, in other words, the plan of salvation, how we can have eternal life—that nugget of truth is priceless to anyone who finds it. But what do you think about this idea that the field is the Bible, the Word of God? Does that make sense?

It certainly worked out that way for the people in the fictional story *Left Behind*. Even though I don't personally agree with all the prophetic scenarios in that book, we can all assent to the obvious reality that God's plan for each of us *is* found in the Bible. And now, today, is when we should be getting out shovels and pickaxes and studying those pages.

Ellen White then suggests that the religious leaders in the time of Christ were like people who had treasure right in their own backyards, but didn't know it. "A man might pass over the place where treasure had been concealed. In dire necessity he might sit down to rest at the foot of a tree, not knowing of the riches hidden at its roots. So it was with the [leaders in Israel.]"[11]

Father Thomas Keating's classic Internet sermon adds this bit of insight about the fact that the treasure is right there under our noses: "In Christianity the risk is that the treasure of eternal life is given without our seeking it. It is already there. The kingdom is among us and within us. It is a treasure that involves our participation in the divine life, to which no other conceivable god can compare." Then these telling words: "And for all practical purposes, *most people are not interested.*"

I have to say, based on my thirteen years of living as a missionary kid in Chiang Mai and Bangkok, that if you are a poor farm laborer in a rice paddy, or if you are a thief hanging on a cross, John 3:16 is all you really need. "For God so loved the world . . ." Agreed? Or, if you could memorize only one Bible verse, you could hardly do better than Acts 16:31: "Believe on the Lord Jesus Christ, and thou shalt be saved" (KJV).

That's eleven words, and when it comes down to crunch time, eleven words are enough. But what a treasure we miss, what riches, what abundance, if we don't then dig deep and find *all* that God wants for us to discover in *all* of His Word! There's treasure there to save our lives, to make us whole, to bring us to Jesus, to teach us about the kingdom. Just here in these parables—some long, some cryptic, some complicated, some simple—we unearth marvelous insights. New ideas that change how we live, how we order our lives. We'd be so impoverished if we didn't read them and study them and embrace them.

And we need to do like the man in this story: get rid of whatever in life is keeping us from owning and plowing this field. If you have other books that keep you from this Book, sell them! Have a garage sale. If your cable TV or your DVR or your collection of Blu-ray discs keeps you from digging in the Word of God, then you better pull the plug. Or get up earlier in the morning. Or *something*. But Jesus is telling us that there's gold in these sixty-six books. There's eternal life there. There's Jesus Christ Himself there. And it's as near as your bookshelf.

Many Adventist readers know so well the story of Joy Swift, a young "mountain mama" whose four kids were shot to death by a teenage intruder, Billy Dyer. Three weeks later, her own teenage stepdaughter died of leukemia. And Joy was devastated. Being a mom had been her whole life. Now her family was gone, and she was consumed with grief and a blinding desire for revenge.

Then, in an achingly lonely motel room, she had an encounter with God. His Spirit seemed to envelop her, promise her hope, guarantee a reunion someday. And as the soft light faded away, she picked up the motel room's Gideon Bible and began to read. She read straight through. She read page after page, promise after promise. And it stunned her that there was so much in this old Book! Why hadn't she read it before? It was a blueprint for living. It told her how to forgive. It held out the promise that one day she would be with Stephanie, Steve, Greg, Stacy, and Tonya again. And she freely confesses in her incredible bestseller *They're All Dead, Aren't They?* that she absolutely would not have ever found wholeness without the Bible. And in her raw experience of healing, it meant digging *deep* into it, wielding the shovel of desperate study, until she came to the treasure of Jesus Christ.[12]

Why is it always *buried* treasure?

It seems that most good things, treasures of lasting value, don't come easy. I wear out my math students at San Bernardino Valley College with the oft-repeated bromide that getting good grades requires study! *A*s come to those who bring me a completed assignment every single day. Raises are offered when we work hard. And treasure, for some reason, *is always buried*. Why is that? And why did Jesus, in teaching important truths, so often hide them in these very stories?

One of the delightful treasure sagas of all time comes from the Klondike River and the huge mother lode of gold found on Eldorado Creek, also known as Bonanza Creek or Rabbit Creek. Just those names conjure up mental images of the wild and woolly west in Alaska. There's an old Indian legend from the Tagish Athabascan people about how one of their own, named Skookum Jim, found all the gold. According to the story, he met an apparition called "Wealth Woman," but at first she was just a frog in a deep pit.

An Internet site relates the tale. "Jim rescues the frog, takes her to a place where she can clean herself, talks to the frog, and then gives her a gift tied around her head. Later Jim dreams of a beautiful woman who has shiny things on her body that sparkle like gold. The woman introduces herself as his aunty, the head of the Frog nation, and she thanks him for saving her life. Gifts will be given to you, she says, if you don't tell anyone.

"Frog woman comes to him again and tells him to go to the creek that runs out of the mountain and look for a reddish streak under the water. Take a drink. You'll find something there, but don't tell anyone."

Well, it sounds like one of the urban legends that flit furiously around on the World Wide Web, but what Skookum Jim, and his Indian sister, Kate, who married a prospector named George Carmack, found in actuality in Bonanza Creek, was thirty million dollars' worth of gold. That's right. Miners who used to nearly starve to death to get four or five cents' worth of gold in a pan suddenly had four or five hundred dollars' worth of gold dust in each one. In today's currency, it would be close to a billion dollars.

Well, as the disciple Matthew has been trying to tell us, if you have a shot at a mother lode like that, you do just about anything you need to do. If it's cold in Alaska, you bundle up and go anyway. Back in 1896, the laws at that time didn't allow Indians—or women either—to register a claim. So these prospectors got around that law by having George Carmack stake claims and then assign shares or part interests to the others in their party of five. And there were many, many men and women with gold fever who were willing to do what the Word of God advises—"Joyfully sell everything you have"—in order to get the rich reward of eternal life.

Notice that in these stories, the gold is always hidden. It's not just "treasure"; it's "buried treasure." Indiana Jones never finds the jewels just lying on a table in his own backyard. They're always in a snake-infested cave, or in the deepest bowels of an archeological dig somewhere, or in the booby-trapped dark recesses of an Amazon jungle.

Now, if it's true that the field where the treasure is buried is actually the Bible itself, we have to ask this question: Why is the good news of eternal life often a *hidden* treasure? Why is it tucked away where we have to dig?

Interestingly, Jesus Christ Himself, in telling these Matthew 13 stories, addresses that exact question right here in this very chapter. After hearing one of His stories, the disciples flat-out asked Him, "Why speakest thou unto them in parables?" (verse 10, KJV).

The King James English makes it sound even harder, doesn't it? "But, Jesus, why do You use these opaque stories about farmers sowing seeds among the thorns and stony places? And that story about the wheat and the tares? We don't get that one. And the one about buried treasure. Jesus, the *point* of Your story is buried treasure itself . . . and our shovels are dull! We're not tracking with You, Lord! Why do You cloak Your vital truths in these strange little anecdotes?"

In recent years, as, one by one, the celebrated fantasy trilogy *The Lord of the Rings* hit theaters, I'm sure moviegoers were asking, "What was old J. R. R. Tolkien trying to tell us? He was a religious man. Does Sauron represent the devil? What does the magic ring represent? Is Frodo Baggins a type of Jesus figure?" The same phenomenon is recurring now as C. S. Lewis's Narnia stories are making their way through the Hollywood process. And the crowds listening to Jesus were much the same. "Jesus, just tell us what You're trying to say! Stop hiding it in a story! Is Aslan really *You* . . . or just a nice lion?"

At the very end of the book of Romans, which is itself a tough piece of study, the apostle Paul describes the story of God's kingdom this way: "Now to him who is able to establish you by my gospel and the proclamation of Jesus Christ, according to the revelation of the *mystery* hidden for long ages past, but now revealed and made known" (16:25, 26; emphasis added).

And the NIV scholars make this comment about the "hiddenness" of the gospel: "The so-called mystery religions of Paul's day used the Greek word *mysterion* in the sense of something that was to be revealed only to the initiated" (note from 11:25).

Sometimes this or that religion—even, I confess, Christianity—comes across this way. There's a secret handshake. Mysterious Bible codes. Brochures and PowerPoint programs portraying strange beasts in Daniel and Revelation and preachers who claim they've deciphered the symbols. People dunking each other in pools of water, or having bread and wine with their church service. It all looks very strange indeed, like a mysterious organization just for the select few.

However, the NIV students have a part two to their comment about *mysterion:* "Paul himself, however, used [this word] to refer to something formerly hidden or obscure but now revealed by God for all to know and understand."

One thing is sure as we study the parables of Christ. Jesus wanted *everyone* to understand His kingdom and to join His kingdom! "I'm not willing that any should perish," He declared. "Whosoever will, may partake of the water of life." The Bible is crystal clear about that. Why, then, did Jesus use these hidden stories? "[Jesus] said to [the disciples], 'You don't need my help to understand what I'm trying to say because you really want to know what it means. It's only those who don't really want to know who can't understand. The person who is guided by the Holy Spirit will receive all the insight he needs to understand what I'm saying, but anyone who doesn't depend on the Holy Spirit to help him understand will soon lose the little insight he does have. The reason I use everyday illustrations is to give the Holy Spirit room to work on people's hearts and minds. I can tell who really wants to understand and who does not' " (Matthew 13:11–13, *Clear Word*).

Jesus might well have been thinking of the religious leaders—the hypocrites and the Pharisees—as well as the Roman soldiers, perhaps. "They don't see, and they don't want to see," He concluded sadly. "But if I proclaim the full message straight out, it will just bring opposition, and cut My work short." So He wisely used these quiet little stories, these hidden treasures, and then, with a knowing glance or a nod, waited to see the gleam of understanding in the eyes of those who really wanted to know, really wanted to understand and to find the hidden treasure.

Ellen White suggests that the gospel is really there to be found, but that the shovel and pickax are necessary. Frankly, John 3:16 is right in front of our eyes; it's even on our television sets during the Stanley Cup playoffs. But you still have to get out a Bible and look it up. "God does not conceal His truth from men. By their own course of action they make it obscure to themselves."[13]

Either by sheer laziness or by living disobedient lives, we can make the Bible impossible to comprehend. Later in the same chapter, Ellen White adds: "[The Bible] is an inexhaustible treasure; but men fail to find this treasure because they do not search until it is within their possession."[14]

Here's one last point. Treasure is often buried so that only those who value it *will* find it. But it also follows that you have to understand what is treasure! When is the substance in your pan pure gold as opposed to fool's gold? In fact, in the very next story Jesus told, a man who knew pearls and shopped for pearls found a rare beauty. Knowing it was rare, knowing it was worth a fortune, that's exactly what he spent for it. And so it is here. You have to know that eternal life is worth something, and that a friendship with Jesus Christ is worth something, or you won't dig and you won't spend. The Internet stories about the Eldorado Gold Rush tell us that this Skookum Jim was given paper money by the people who bought out his stake. Paper money? What was that? He didn't know any better, so he tacked these strange pieces of paper up all over his cabin as wallpaper there in the Klondike. He was surrounded by a mind-boggling fortune *and didn't know it.*

Friend, may that never be said of us.

Chapter 3

SAINTS TO MY RIGHT

Sinners to My Left

It was a wet, rainy day in Los Angeles, and Dillon was in a blue funk. He hadn't had a callback in three weeks, and the rent was due. He and Grady lived on the fringe of the Hollywood scene, the epitome of the expression "starving actors." Grady had gotten a bit piece in a TV commercial for some dot-com venture, but Dillon's most recent work had been just as a walk-through-the-set extra on an episode of *Everybody Loves Raymond*. A few bucks and a free trip through their buffet line before the Tuesday evening shoot. It was a daily grind: hustle, hustle, pass out cards, call your agent, scour the Internet, read *Variety* and *The Hollywood Reporter*.

And it was in one of the industry job sheets that Dillon saw the ad: "Thirty actors needed, age 25–35, medium build, all ethnicities. White pants, black T-shirt, bring head shot, résumé." There was a phone number to call and also the time and place. Lot B, S&G Associates, which Dillon recognized as a film company in the Warner Brothers family. They had a reputation around town for being a bit quirky, but very solid. Good pay. Getting your foot in the door at S&G was rumored to be a quick ticket to HBO or Showtime movies and even feature films. So Dillon circled the ad and looked with a bemused grimace in his Palm Pilot. Yes, of course, next Tuesday was open. It was wide open. The whole week was wide open. And he said to himself, "If I don't get something, I swear, by the end of the month, I'm going back to Kansas, Dorothy."

Grady dragged himself in around eight, toting a half a carton of pizza he'd scored at the restaurant he was part-timing at. "A guy at Touchstone told me there was a Lifetime pilot we might get on," he announced. "He was going to put in a good word for us with the A.D."

"That'd be good." Dillon took a piece of the pizza and showed his roommate the ad in *Variety*. "Huh," Grady said, scanning it. "White pants, black T-shirt. Bring your own wardrobe, looks like."

"Yeah, well . . . beggars can't be choosers. And S&G is right up there with the big boys."

Grady nodded. "Can't hurt to try. It beats getting evicted from this Beverly Hills mansion."

Next Tuesday afternoon the two guys drove down to Burbank and gave the security guy at the gate their names. They parked the car and got out with their résumés and head shots in a folder. "Well, wish us luck," Grady said, looking up at the sky. Dillon scanned the lot. "Looks like it's clear over there. Studio seven."

As they made their way across the parking lot, they spotted a black Camry with its hood up. A large woman wearing the ill-fitting uniform of a Warner "gofer," a studio flunkee, was peering in frustration at the engine.

"What's up, sister?" Dillon, always the type A extrovert, walked over to her.

She sighed. "I think I left the lights on."

"All day?" he asked.

"Yes, sir. I was running late 'cause there was a shoot starting at seven, and they needed me to help with the studio audience. And I guess I just ran in and didn't think."

"Well, I've got jumper cables," Dillon offered.

Grady glanced at his watch. "You sure we got time, man? The call's in, like, ten minutes."

Dillon gave a shrug. "Well, we can't just leave her. Come on, only take a sec." He sprinted back to his own car and quickly drove up, parking next to the Toyota, hood to hood. Efficiently doing the attachments, he directed the studio lady: "OK, fire her up." The Toyota engine sputtered to life, and she gave it a grateful burst of throttle.

"Sounds like it's OK."

"All right," Grady said. "Be sure to keep it running for twenty minutes or so."

"That's no problem," she said. "My sister and I live clear out in Pasadena."

"That'll do it," the taller actor said. "But now we better hustle."

The two young men gunned back to their original parking spot, then jogged anxiously to the studio. Scattered around the lobby were a good fifty guys—all

44

wearing the white pants, the black T-shirt, the tense look, the head shot.

Right at four o'clock a nervous-looking man wearing the same Warner Brothers company jacket came into the room with a clipboard. "Excuse me," he said to the black-and-white crowd. "S&G's running a bit behind. I was told to shoo you all over to the cafeteria, and you can grab a quick snack. They'll page us when they're ready."

"Free food!" someone in the back shouted, and the men all laughed. Starving artists took that bonus every chance they could.

Dillon and Grady each piled a plate high with sandwiches, gourmet chips, and all the macadamia nut cookies their pride would permit.

Right then a waitress for the cafeteria, carrying a big bowl of spaghetti, tripped on somebody's backpack. There was a huge, sloppy *crash!* as the marinara sauce splashed all over, making a slippery red puddle on the floor. The actors gave the typical mock cheer. "Good shot!" "Splish splash, time to take a bath!" The girl, a thin woman with stringy hair, choked back a sob of embarrassment and began to dab at the mess with a towel.

Grady hesitated. "White pants, black T-shirt," the ad had said. Fifty other actors were impeccably attired, ready to wow the studio executives with their acting, their singing, their dancing, their spiked hair and Ben Affleck–chiseled looks. And on the sticky floor, this young girl was trying to mop up the marinara. A moment later, he and Dillon came over to her. "Need a hand?" Dillon asked gently.

She looked up in surprise. "Sure. That'd be great. But . . ." The woman looked around at the crowd. "You'll mess up your clothes and all."

"Doesn't matter," Grady responded. "Is there a mop any place?"

She pointed to a small closet next to the buffet line. "In there, I think." Moments later, the two artists were helping corral the tomato sauce and pasta into a plastic Glad bag. Even though they were careful, both men soon had little scarlet flecks all over their white pants. In the men's room, they washed their hands and tried to scrub out the worst of the stains, but it was a losing cause.

"Oh well," Dillon muttered. "Kansas is pretty this time of year."

The balding guy with the clipboard herded the fifty actors into a room with a large stage and a bank of lights. "OK," he announced. "I want you to meet Elaine Townsend, executive producer in charge of *Standing on My Right,* the new S&G film for CBS."

Grady squinted in confusion as a woman wearing a six-hundred-dollar business suit strode to the microphone. Without hesitation she scanned the crowd and then pointed right at him. "You," she said. "And you." She gestured at Dillon.

"What in the world . . ."

Dillon gave a sudden start. "This is wild," he said. "Grady, that's the lady in the parking lot. The one with the dead battery."

The taller actor suddenly couldn't get his feet to move. "You're right," he whispered. "What's going on?" Fifty pairs of eyes followed the two men with the stained white pants as they went up onto the platform.

Ms. Townsend shook Dillon's hand, then Grady's. "Gentlemen, *Standing on My Right* is a very special movie, a spiritual story. We wanted a certain kind of person. And I regret to tell you that there are really just two openings for this film. These actors have filled the slots, and the audition is closed." She gestured to the side of the stage where a second woman was walking toward the mike. "And here's our director for *Standing on My Right,* Shelly Black." The slender executive, also immaculately dressed, and with her hair now styled, nodded to the disappointed actors in their seats who were gathering up their things. It was the waitress who had spilled the sauce, of course, and she cleared her throat before beginning to explain.

"Earlier today, out in the parking lot, a tired gofer from Warner Brothers had a dead battery. A good number of you just trotted on by, because you were busy. You had an interview to get to, and that's all right. But these two men right here—and I still don't know their names—stopped to help Elaine get her car going. She wasn't really going anywhere, of course—it was just an act because she lives in Beverly Hills, not Pasadena—but you two men passed the test. Then when I had my little spaghetti spill, the rest of you wannabe actors cheered and laughed and enjoyed the moment, but these same two actors here, with marinara sauce still on their white pants, stopped to help a minimum-wage waitress. Or at least that's what they thought I was. Now they're going to have the costarring lead roles in a six-million-dollar TV film for CBS."

"But we didn't know!" An angry actor with a goatee stepped out from the crowd. "I'd have helped if I'd known it was you."

"These two actors didn't know us either," the powerful Hollywood director chided. "They just thought I was a dumb Warner Brothers chick who spilled the spaghetti. Well, let me tell you something. If an actor in white pants helps a waitress here at Warner Brothers, he's really helping me. That's how I look at it." She smiled. "And the whole country's going to be looking at"—she glanced at their résumés—"Dillon and Grady this coming Thanksgiving weekend as the starring lead actors in *Standing on My Right.*"

The fifty other actors slowly filed out of Warner Brothers and into the evening traffic of downtown Burbank, where there was weeping and gnashing of teeth.

Hell for the unhelpful

Timothy McVeigh forfeited his life because he killed 168 people and injured 500 others. Well, he deserves to be lost, we say. But in Jesus' classic parable, He suggests that careless, thoughtless people who simply neglect to feed the hungry around them will also share McVeigh's fate. What kind of a Christian "gospel of grace" is this?

For most Adventists who weren't born in this twenty-first century, two great storytelling names are forever fixed in your mind: the incomparable Arthur S. Maxwell—"Uncle Arthur"— and the late, great Eric B. Hare. Both of these men were classic creators of value-based stories for kids, and you can still buy Uncle Arthur storybooks all around the world.

The one that has its roots here in Matthew 25 is of the little girl who had a dual personality: nice and sweet and winsome at school, and then mean and growly and pouty at home. She idolized her sweet and beautiful teacher, but grumbled and complained to her own mom. And the cure came one day when Mother asked her to set the table for dinner. "Don't want to!" she snapped. And back and forth they went, until this bratty kid angrily threw two plates and two cups and two sets of silverware on the table, scattering things every which way and muttering to herself how she was surely the most abused child in the land.

And then right at the end—some of you remember, I'm sure—Mother asked her to set a third place setting because there was company for dinner. "Oh, but Mother, the table's not set nice enough for company! Let me do it over again." But there's no time, because Teacher has been in the next room all along, hearing every crabby complaint and taking note of the distinction between the School Susie and the Home Susie. Of course, when the girl is confronted with her dear, precious teacher, she bursts into tears and repents, while the storyteller intones at the end of the little 45 rpm record: "And she NEVER was naughty again!"

Which is what the rebels in Jesus' Matthew 25 parable say when they're assigned to the goat pen on His left: "Lord, we didn't know it was You! We didn't realize that You were in the next room listening! We weren't aware that the orphan child we didn't help was You, that it was You who was so hungry, that it was You languishing in a prison with no one coming to visit."

One man who spent many years never seeing the hurting and the lonely all around him would have to have been Chuck Colson. Keeping in mind that he was a big shot working with the president in the White House, you'd think that Chuck Colson's favorite memory would have to be some moment of triumph sitting in the Oval Office right across from President Richard Nixon, just the two of them. Or, considering that he later was a convicted Watergate conspirator, perhaps that Friday afternoon, January 31, 1975, when Judge Gerhard Gesell decided to let him out of Alabama's Maxwell Correctional Facility before his sentence was finished.

But no. Those don't seem to be his favorite memories at all. Instead, he now remembers, with tears in his eyes, a very ordinary evening when a bunch of no talent prison convicts put on a vocal recital.

Let me permit Chuck Colson to tell his own story, but keep in mind that this is a lead-in to the Matthew 25 usually called "The Sheep and the Goats." The Son of man, the King, the Judge of all the universe, lines up all the kind people on His right, and all the mean, selfish people on His left. The "sheep," the generous people, had fed the hungry, clothed the naked, given out cups of cold water. And yes, they had visited the prisoners in their jail cells. The "goats" standing on the left had done none of these things. And then the great classic line: "Inasmuch as ye have done it unto one of the least of these my brethren, ye have done it unto me" (verse 40, KJV).

Now to Colson's story: "In Manila, the capital of the Philippines, one section of the city houses more than 65,000 people in shacks that are nothing more than wood and corrugated metal lean-tos. With no sewers, no plumbing, and no city water, the stench is sickening. Children run naked in the streets while adults sit on the sidewalk, staring vacantly."

That's an accurate description, and I've been there to see some of that very heartache. But what have God's people done about it? Ever since born-again Christian Chuck Colson got out of jail himself, he's directed a worldwide organization called Prison Fellowship. Here's what they are doing: "In the midst of these desperate conditions, Prison Fellowship International has started a microenterprise project that takes people out of the nearby Mantalupa Prison, mentors them in a church, and then loans them $120 to buy a pedicab (a bicycle with a cab on the side, used for ferrying passengers and packages through crowded streets). The loan program has become a stunning success: 95 percent of those who receive loans repay them within nine months. I visited the program and saw the parking lot where thirty brightly painted pedicabs, all bearing the Prison Fellowship logo on the front, were lined up like automobiles in a showroom, polished and gleaming in the sun. Greeting us were the proud pedicab owners (all former inmates) and their families, along with the pastors who mentored them."

Then comes the moment that trumps getting out of jail, trumps sitting across from President Nixon, trumps flying around and eating strawberries on Air Force One with the leader of the free world. Colson finishes up his story: "The former inmates had put together a concert, and as they stood on the stage singing, one little girl, perhaps four years old, with brown button eyes, pulled herself up onto the platform and walked toward her father, who was standing in the front row. She clutched his legs and looked up with an adoring expression; he looked down and began to caress her hair. That picture is frozen in my mind's eye; everything I have done in the ministry over twenty-five years was worth that *one moment*—to see an ex-prisoner, ex-gang member with a loving family, a job, and hope."[1]

We can hear the Savior say, to Colson and all his fellow volunteers, and to those who contribute money to Prison Fellowship's "Angel Tree" program and other outreaches: "Chuck, I was a Prisoner without hope of parole. I didn't have any job skills. I didn't have any way to make a living and support My family once I got out onto the mean streets of Manila. But, Chuck, you and your friends gave *Me* an expression of confidence. You mentored *Me* in a church. You loaned *Me* one hundred twenty dollars so I could drive a pedicab around town and earn money and earn self-respect and earn My family's trust. Chuck, you guys did that for ME!"

Or Jesus might say to Prison Fellowship: "I was that little girl. My daddy in jail; My mom and My sisters and brothers living in poverty. But you helped Me by getting My daddy out of prison and helping him to work. You made him feel like a man again, like a worthwhile father, like a provider."

And I suppose, like in the Bible story, many of Prison Fellowship's employees would look around in amazement. "That was *You*? Jesus, that was *You*? We didn't see You in the Philippines; we just saw convicts at Mantalupa Prison. We saw orphans. We saw young wives with no income trying to stay away from the horrors of prostitution and AIDS. But we didn't see You on the streets, Lord. We didn't know it was You!" It's quite a story, isn't it—Chuck Colson's favorite moment?

On the other hand, some of us might not be convinced that this is our favorite Bible story. There are some places in the four Gospels where the born-again Christian can joyfully feed like a hungry lamb and contentedly journey like a well-protected traveler, but not here in Matthew 25. If you're one who has taken refuge in John 3:16: "For God so loved the world," or in Ephesians 2:8, 9: "It is by *grace* you have been saved, through faith . . . *not* by works" (emphasis added), then this hard-hitting little story by Jesus, about cups of cold water and prison visits, is going to shake your mountain of assurance. Because Jesus doesn't just say that nice people feed the hungry and mean people don't. He also says that our eternal reward is to be found *in this story*! Eternal judgment happens on the basis *of this story*! In other words, even if you say you accept the Cross, and you say that Jesus is your Savior, and you say that your home in the kingdom is based on grace . . . if you don't help Chuck Colson buy a Filipino prisoner a 120-dollar pedicab, you might not be *in* the kingdom. You might be standing on Jesus' left side instead, where it's uncomfortably warm.

What do you think about that? Matthew 25:45, 46, even softened up, as many verses are in the gentle *Clear Word* paraphrase, reads like this—and remember, this is Jesus talking face-to-face with the "goats": "Then the Son of God will say, 'Because you didn't care about others, I know you don't care about me.' " Now listen to this chilling indictment coming from gentle Jesus, meek and mild: "I have no choice but to end your lives forever because in my Father's kingdom everyone cares about everyone else."

I was writing parts of this book's chapter on the very day that Timothy McVeigh was executed in Terre Haute, Indiana. What a terrible reminder that there is a finality to the decisions we make in life! But can it be that not only do mad bombers meet eternal destruction, but also those who carelessly ignore the hurting and the fragile among us? This is what the Bible says, and it seems many universes away from "Amazing Grace, how sweet the sound."

Dr. Richard T. France asserts that, yes, the end-time judgment scene is found right here. "In particular," he writes, "the call to be ready for the *parousia* [or Second Coming] of the Son of man has increasingly raised the question of what constitutes readiness, of how one may be prepared."

And he goes right to Matthew 25. How does one get ready for Jesus to come in the clouds of heaven with His reward? You read this parable right here. However, France almost suggests that we shouldn't even have this story in a book on "parables." "This powerful description of the final judgment is sometimes *misleadingly* described as a 'parable.' In fact, while [verses] 32–33 do contain the simile of a shepherd, *otherwise this is a straightforward judgment scene.*"[2]

He's absolutely right. Read this parable—excuse me, this sermon—for yourself; it's right here in Matthew 25, verses 31–46. And Jesus doesn't begin, as He often does, by saying, "The kingdom of heaven is *like* such-and-such." No, He launches right into a factual narrative: "When the Son of Man comes in his glory, and all the angels with him. . . . He will separate the people one from another." Then He adds, "As a shepherd separates the sheep from the goats."

Grace or goodwill donations?

So this story is real. Each of us is going to be standing right there. Did we feed the hungry? Clothe the naked? Buy a 120-dollar pedicab for a prisoner? For the moment, at least, God's free offer of salvation seems a long way off. And we also begin to wonder, "OK, how many pedicabs? How many cups of cold water? One a day? Fifty a week? Or do I have to become heaven's permanent, full-time water-boy in order to qualify for a mansion? How much charity must I demonstrate before I can get a place in heaven? What in the world has happened to amazing grace?" Let's explore this a bit more.

In recent years, I made an art form out of purchasing "loss leader" Toyota Camrys early on a Friday morning. With a copy of the *Los Angeles Times* in my hand, I'd arrive at a dealership still in my pajamas, right when they opened, and point to the ad that promises a new car for "only $16,999!!! (2 at this exact price.)." Some of my Christian friends are an extremely nosy bunch of people, and they just about had a coronary when they found out that I had gotten a brand-new car off the showroom floor for such a low price. Their heart fibrillations come, of course, because your standard MSRP runs at about twenty-one grand, and some had recently paid even more than that. Identical Camrys, identical packages, right down to the floor mats, and one lucky person pays four thousand less for his. Go figure. (Their animosity subsided a bit when Toyota had its recent mechanical problems, and we began accidentally driving our cars into trees and accelerating into lakes.)

In that same vein, many of you, I'm sure, have sat on an airplane and found out that the person sitting right next to you, eating the exact same size bag of peanuts you're getting, and with exactly the same lack of legroom, got his ticket for a third of the amount you paid. Don't we hate to be on the sucker end of such sagas?

But we seem to find in the New Testament parables Jesus told, and the preaching He did, that He must have, at one point, had a job working for United Airlines. Because Jesus—and I say this carefully and reverently—seemed to give out various ticket prices to different people. Never mind the story in which various workers in the vineyard put in hugely varying hours, and yet all got paid the same wages. (We'll get to that in chapter 10.) But Jesus routinely gave different salvation offers to various people. Have you ever focused on that? He told a rich young ruler, "Go home and sell *everything you have*! That's the price of admission for you." But to the thief hanging next to Him on a cross, a man who, by the way, hadn't fed the hungry or clothed the naked but had spent a lifetime doing the exact opposite, Jesus said very generously, "Hey, you don't have to do *anything*. (Not that he could, nailed down as he was.) I accept you just as you are; I'm telling you right now that you're going to have a really nice mansion in My kingdom. Just because. Just because you say you believe in Me."

The reason I'm a bit flummoxed by our full-price coach fare is that my three brothers and I have spent cumulatively 120 years preaching the good news that salvation is free. Our homes in heaven are based on the free gift of Jesus' death on the cross. We preach justification, which means that Jesus' own perfection is instantaneously credited to our accounts. We preach grace, which is the "unmerited favor" of God giving eternal life to us when we don't deserve it.

Then, all at once, here in Matthew 25, Jesus upsets the applecart big time. In fact, He turns the cart over and almost throws the apples at us. First of all, we read here in this story of the sheep and goats that God's people are expected to constantly do five hard things. Feed the hungry. Give drinks to the thirsty. Be hospitable to the stranger. Clothe the poor and naked. And visit the prisoner. Now that is a legalism list if there ever was one! That is salvation by works!

And get this. He goes on and tells us right here that these deeds of charity are the *basis* of the judgment! Those who do these five things . . . are in. They're saved. They stand on Jesus' right, and on His right are mansions and harps and crowns. "Come," He says in verse 34, "you who are blessed by my Father; take your inheritance, the kingdom prepared for you since the creation of the world."

The NIV scholars jump right in and put a surcharge on this high-priced airline ticket we have to buy here in chapter 25, when they add this: "The *basis* for judgment will be whether love is shown to God's people."

In his book *Living Faith* (and that title says a lot about this topic!), former president Jimmy Carter relates a little anecdote in which a guy comes up to the pearly gates. And when Saint Peter asks him, "What have you done that you should deserve to get in here?" the man hems and haws and can't think of very much. But finally he manages, "Well, during the Depression I saw a starving family out on the streets, and I think I gave them half a buck."

"OK," Peter says. "What else?" And after about ten more minutes of straining to remember, he brightens. Oh yeah, when a neighbor's house burned down, he'd donated a table to them that had cost him fifty cents. "Any more?" Peter wants to know. And the man confesses that no, that was it. "What should I do?" the angel asks Saint Peter. And the guard to the gates of heaven says in disgust, "Give him his dollar back and tell him to go to hell."[3]

Well, we tend to laugh off such stories and decide they're not very mature, but all at once, here in Matthew 25, we discover that this story is hugely mature. It's the entire gospel truth! Help your neighbor out, or you don't get into heaven, period. And the question is this—which, by the way, is even more important than whether or not you and I personally make it through those pearly gates—What *is* the Christian gospel? What does it take to be saved? What's the plan? Are we saved by grace or by cups of cold water? And if it takes cups of cold water to get heaven and avoid hell, shouldn't we go out on the streets and alleyways with a bottled water truck and do nothing else but endless good deeds? How many good deeds would be enough to be a sheep and not a goat? You can see how salvation assurance goes right out the window with a story like this one.

The Seventh-day Adventist Bible Commentary puts all the chips on the table when it observes, "This, the last of Jesus' parables, appropriately presents the great final assize [or judicial inquiry] and reduces to the most simple and practical terms the *basis* on which judgment is to be meted out."[4]

Dr. Richard T. France comments that this story is "a guide to practical discipleship. It is by such acts that one prepares for the judgment."[5]

There's a great Adventist book that contains a beautiful answer to this apparent dilemma of different prices for Camrys and heavenly mansions. In *How Long, O Lord?* Dr. Ralph Neall, longtime missionary to Vietnam and professor of religion at Union College in Lincoln, Nebraska, puts today's parable in with two others, and makes this comment: "The three parables of chapter 25—the 10 virgins, the talents, and the sheep and goats—teach us how to prepare for the return of Christ. A number of interesting similarities exist between the three parables. Each depicts two classes of people. In the parable of the virgins, we see the wise and foolish; while in the parable of the talents, we encounter those who improve their talents and those who do not. The sheep and the goats represent those who are kind to others and those who are not. Another parallel is that each parable points to the great reckoning day, and in each case Jesus brings joy to one class and destruction to the other."

So these three crucial stories are here to teach us what we need to do to get ready for Jesus' coming. In other words, on what basis will we be judged? Neall continues, "These parables reveal what our *relationship* should be precisely *in* our daily lives." This is Christianity where the rubber meets the road. Then he adds, "The parable of the sheep and goats reminds us to employ our gifts for others. Whatever I have that I can use to help them makes me a debtor to Christ. When I relate to the poor and oppressed, I am relating to Him—this is what it means to have a 'relationship with Jesus.' "[6]

Perhaps it could be stated this way. *The* basis of judgment, of salvation, of mansions . . . is always and only and forever one thing: Do you have a trust relationship with Jesus Christ? It will never be anything else. And Matthew chapter 25 doesn't contradict that, because Jesus tells these kind and generous people: "You did these things for *Me*. Unwittingly, to be sure, but they were for *Me*. You loved Me enough to follow My example, to obey My commands, to live as kingdom people." And He tells the thief on the cross: "Yes, I give you eternal life. Why? Because you believe in Me. And I know that if you got a reprieve, you'd show the world you believe in Me by how you lived. You'd stop being a thief. You'd make restitution. You'd start feeding the hungry." To the rich young ruler, He says, "I'll give you eternal life, too, if you place your trust in Me . . . and not in your riches. Which, by the way—because I can read hearts and minds—I can see you will have to sell them off, or you never will fully believe in Me."

In the *Clear Word* paraphrase, Jesus says to the obedient people, the "sheep": "You have cared about others, which shows that you care about me." That's relationship for sure! "And the Son of God will say, 'I know you didn't realize this because a change took place in your life, and kindness and compassion became a part of your nature. What you did by caring for those [who are] thought of as insignificant was just as if you had done it for me' " (verses 35, 40).

So, if we want to be a sheep and have a home in God's kingdom, then we get with His Son. We have a relationship with His Son. And also, by the way—we won't be able to help ourselves—we'll get out there in the street and simply do what we can for Him. And for the least of His brothers. Those who truly are living in relationships with Jesus will gladly and inevitably be living by His example. Healing. Loving. Caring. Feeding. The cups of cold water will be a courtroom Exhibit B, to show that we ourselves have been drinking from the Living Water, which is the trust relationship with Jesus our Savior. That's Exhibit A. Always Exhibit A.

There's solid Bible ground for taking this gospel view, and NIV scholars point us to the fact that people in this story who are the "sheep," who are invited to stand at the King's right hand and share in His glorious kingdom, are surprised and happily sputtering at the invitation. "Who, us?" they ask in astonishment. "Jesus, we fed You? We visited You? We gave You clothes when You were destitute? We weren't aware!" And the scholars write, "Rewards in the kingdom of heaven are given to those who serve without thought of reward. There is no hint of merit here, for God gives out of grace, not debt."

So there's no trace in the story of "I must do good deeds to earn a heavenly mansion." Those who stand on Jesus' right don't have that mentality; they aren't legalists in any sense of the word whatever. But they're in such a relationship with this wonderful Savior that generous deeds of kindness are instinctive to them. Second nature. And when they hear that they were actually serving Jesus in their consistent acts of goodness, they're flabbergasted but joyful. Their happiness is even greater now!

President Jimmy Carter tells about a great old Cuban-American preacher named Eloy Cruz, who knew no other life but to witness and share Jesus and give away blankets and cups of water and stay at the local YMCA while doing his acts of charity. And this quiet giant for the Lord summed up the Christian gospel succinctly in this way: "You only have to have two loves in your life—for God, and for the person in front of you at any particular time."[7]

And really, Love one is proved or validated by Love two. This is why, on the great Judgment Day, Jesus can say to a watching universe: "These people, who demonstrated Love two—with the cups of cold water and the care packages for the prisoners—had Love one for sure. They were in relationship with Me all along, and their lifestyle of unselfish service, of *unaware* unselfish service, proves it!"

Showing mercy to the missionary

In the Tyndale New Testament Commentaries, Dr. France shares an interesting twist on this story. He contends that this "sheep and goats" story isn't really addressing charity to all and every needy person, a "humanitarian ethic, with no specifically Christian content," as he puts it. Which, of course, is why grace-oriented believers tend to fear that this story is teaching a low-end "social gospel"—getting into heaven just by running soup kitchens. He suggests and cites other Bible scholars as also suggesting that Jesus is especially talking here in Matthew 25 about how people respond to *disciples* in need.[8] When Christian ambassadors come to your town, when door-to-door lay workers for the Lord knock on your front gate, are you hospitable to them? Do you give them a bed for the night and a bowl of Cheerios in the morning? If your nephew is raising money to go to Guatemala on a mission trip, do you contribute money? If a Christian bookseller comes to your door, are you open to his invitation?

To strengthen this view, we notice that Jesus clearly says, "Whatever you did for one of the least of these brothers of Mine . . ."

Back in chapter 10, there's a similar passage of Scripture where Jesus plainly describes how people treat His emissaries: "He who receives you receives me," He says. "Anyone who receives a prophet because he is a prophet will receive a prophet's reward, and anyone who receives a righteous man because he is a righteous man will receive a righteous man's reward." And notice this, along the same vein: "And if anyone gives even a cup of cold water to one of these little ones because he is my disciple"—that sounds like Jesus is talking about His witnesses, His missionaries perhaps—"I tell you the truth, he will certainly not lose his reward" (verses 40–42).

After considering Dr. France's comments, I would be wrong to conclude that I don't need to unselfishly serve all needy people around me, but only the missionaries who come to my neighborhood. But this point of view obviously strengthens the Bible argument that this kind of service, and the salvation that comes when we obey Jesus by being generous and kind, is rooted, first and foremost and forever, in that saving relationship with Him. That's so important to keep in our minds at all times. If we're born-again Christians, if we're abiding in the shadow of the Cross, then we will treat people as Jesus did. Especially His workers! Especially His emissaries! And He says to us: "When you treat them well, you're treating Me well. If you enable someone, with your hospitality and your generous funds, to travel to distant lands and share the gospel, share My story, friend, you're doing Me the hugest favor you can imagine! You're doing it for Me! You're living out your relationship with Me!"

One theologian pointed out that this "sheep and goats" story is "the parable of unknown goodness and unconscious badness." Have you ever thought about that? The kind people look up, wide-eyed, at Jesus and say, "That was You? We didn't know!" The bad people say exactly the same thing. But you have, on Jesus' right, people whose relationship with Christ is so real, so instinctive, so consistently alive, that their very life patterns are a natural outworking of His Spirit. They don't constantly think, *Good deeds, good deeds, good deeds . . . that's Jesus standing in that bread line . . . good deeds, good deeds.* They just *do*—because Christ is their natural Example.

Unfortunately, the thoughtless rebels standing on the left are following natural impulses too. But they don't see Jesus standing in the bread line because they wouldn't know Jesus if they saw Him anywhere. The only "good deeds" they do, ever, are for self-serving reasons, not because the Savior is standing nearby as the least of these.

Shalom is easy to say and hard to do

So following impulses is great, but only if Jesus is daily embedded in them.

For some six thousand years, God has been waiting for His people, His church, to simply demonstrate Heaven's plan. Food for the hungry. Water for the thirsty. Clothes for the naked, homes for the homeless, visits for the prisoner.

One last question. Does He delay His coming until we finally get it right?

We all look forward to the day when this grand pronouncement of verse 34 is made to the joyful band who are on their way to heavenly mansions. "Come, you who are blessed by my Father," says Jesus, the righteous Judge. "Take your inheritance, the kingdom prepared for you since the creation of the world."

In *Living Faith,* former president Jimmy Carter relates one more wonderful experience during which he and others helped touch literally millions of lives for some of the truly "least of these My brethren."

The story involves guinea worms, nasty parasites which, at that time, infected people in India, Pakistan, Yemen, and about nineteen countries in Africa. When people in poverty-stricken villages drink from infested water, the eggs incubate, and within a year produce two-foot-long worms! Can you imagine that? These parasites sting their victim from the inside and then ooze their way out through the sores they create.

So, of course, when the suffering person wades into a cool stream to get some relief, the worm immediately lays more eggs, and the cycle continues.

President Carter and others began to look around for some good neighbors. What could be done? One plan of attack is to drill what they call "borehole" wells, which are free of the infestation. There's also a chemical called Abate, which kills off the eggs. In addition, a fine-mesh fabric, a filter cloth—unfortunately quite expensive—can strain out the eggs to give potable water.

So Carter approached Edgar Bronfman, a major owner of the DuPont Corporation. His board of directors convened and decided to develop a fiber and donate all the cloth that would be needed. All for free. Then Carter got together with an executive named Lanty Smith; his company, Precision Fabrics, agreed to do the weaving of the fabric, also gratis. A corporation named American Cyanamid said, "As long as everyone's in the charity business, we'll throw in a worldwide supply of this Abate chemical."

What was the bottom line? All these projects kicked in back in 1988; within seven years, cases of guinea worm had dropped from 3.5 million to fewer than 130,000. "I went to DuPont headquarters," Carter writes in his book, "to report on our progress, where President Ed Woolard and about 600 top managers, scientists, and salesmen were assembled under a large tent. When I thanked them for their gift and showed a brief film demonstrating its almost miraculous results, most of them were weeping—and so was I."[9]

What do you make of that? It's a great story, but is this how we get Jesus to come back? By fighting guinea worm?

In *How Now Shall We Live?* Colson's and Pearcey's entire thrust is that Christianity is a "worldview." The Christian faith, they write, is *not* simply a plan to get you and me to heaven. To be sure, it *is* that . . . but it's so much more. The Calvary message saves; it promises eternal life. But the Christian message is also a blueprint for the six thousand years we've spent on this rotten old planet. And for however many years there are left before Jesus comes to bring it all to an end.

And as we read these stories by Jesus, we discover that God's people aren't simply looking for the first spaceship out of here. We're here also to bring healing to the sick and food to the hungry and hope to the discouraged. We're here to be involved in politics, making bad governments better and totalitarian regimes into peace-loving, people-valuing kingdoms. We're here to demonstrate to the entire world that the Sermon on the Mount is a formula that works, that the golden rule is valid, that "turn the other cheek" isn't just a bit of poetry for patsies.

"*Shalom* refers to peace in a positive sense, the result of a rightly ordered community," Colson writes. "The Bible teaches that we are not autonomous individuals. Instead, we are created in the image of the One who in His very essence is a community of being—that is, the Trinity. God's very nature is reciprocal love and communication among the persons of the Trinity." And notice this concluding line, with its shades of cups of water and prison visits: "We were created as inherently communal beings, and the God-ordained institutions of society make rightful, normative demands that we are morally obligated to fulfill."[10]

Hiding in the core of this sheep-and-goats story is the powerful reality that the entire history of this planet is simply God's cosmic experiment, or demonstration, to a watching universe regarding this blueprint. God is saying, "Here's the formula. Loving. Caring. Unselfishness. Generosity. Putting others first." All through the Old Testament, that was actually the mandated plan. There were rules—you can read them for yourself—about how to treat the poor. How to care for the widows. The great hero Job had it down pat. In chapter 31 of his long lament, he is able to say this: "No stranger had to spend the night in the street, for my door was always open to the traveler" (verse 32).

In the New Testament, Jesus preached the same plan over and over. The early Christian church demonstrated it. Paul, often a lonely prisoner, wrote in his second letter to Timothy: "May the Lord show mercy to the household of Onesiphorus, because he often refreshed me and was not ashamed of my chains" (2 Timothy 1:16).

And for two thousand years, with many ups and downs, with many successes and many failures, the church has continued to struggle and stumble its way through this matter of caring for others. Sometimes we've done it; sometimes we've failed. Sometimes we roll up our sleeves and help solve the guinea worm challenge and donate to Teen Challenge and help fight global warming; sometimes we look the other way and do our own selfish thing. Sheep and goats.

When you get right down to it and ask the question, "What is Jesus waiting for? Why doesn't He come?" you have to point to this story. If it were just a case of Christ deciding who should be saved or lost, that would take Him very little time. He knows who are His; He knows whether you're on His side, whether you're loyal. But is it possible that He's waiting, waiting, holding out a bit longer so that the body of Christ, the community of believers, can still more fully answer this question, "How now shall we live?"

Let's briefly consider the reward phase of this story. Dr. Richard T. France points to the tragic end of these who are lost. They enter into a fire that isn't even intended for them! "The cursed are going to a fate that was not meant to be theirs!"[11]

This is a compelling doctrine: hellfire was never meant to be a destination for human beings. From the very beginning, God intended that His children would live by this golden rule of generosity, of caring for one another. That was the hallmark of Eden, where a man *was* his brother's keeper. You have to deliberately step outside God's plan before you end up sharing in Lucifer's retirement plan.

Notice how God's faithful "sheep" are rewarded. "Come," says this proud

King to His good subjects. "Come, you who are blessed by My Father; take your inheritance." Now notice this: "the kingdom prepared for you *since the creation of this world*!" (Matthew 25:34; emphasis added).

Isn't this an exciting truth? God has had this plan in place since before He made this world! He planned the reward for the sheep of this story before He ever created a single sheep! He began preparing mansions, heavenly homes, for those who would unselfishly share their earthly homes before Adam and Eve even had a home. He created the river of life for you and me to drink from centuries before the first Christian ever offered his neighbor a drink. This plan of "love your neighbor" was carved in the halls of heaven when planet Earth was just a twinkle in the Creator's eye.

So we can say in closing this chapter: *Shalom*. Get out there and make some *Shalom* happen.

Chapter 4

BEDROCK OR JELL-O
for the Foundation

It was a hot, humid August night when Justin Thompson and his wife, Tracy, made the big decision. She'd been lounging on the bed, trying to stay in range of the slow-moving fan while she watched the latest *Survivor* program on CBS. With energy costs soaring all over California, they were trying to not run the air conditioning unless the house became unbearably warm. But that didn't stop Justin from jumping his way from one Web site to another one just to see what kinds of bargains were out there. After just six years of marriage and some lucky guesses on E*Trade, the young couple had an impressive portfolio to play with; in fact, Justin sometimes bragged to his friends that they should really bow low before him and call him "Justin Time" because he'd bailed out of Cisco when the stock had peaked at around eighty dollars.

Anyway, right when all the survivors took a commercial break from their coconut-tree-climbing contests, he suddenly clicked on the printer and began to spin out a gorgeous four-color brochure.

"Whatcha got?" Tracy asked him, as she mopped her damp forehead with the corner of the sheet.

"You gotta look at these houses," he told her, tossing the first sheet of paper in her direction. "Actually, those are models; you just buy the lots."

"Whereabouts?"

"Right where we want one," he said, looking at the final sheet as it slid out of the color printer. "Malibu Shores, right on the beach. This builder has a partnership program where you pick the lot, and then if you have any skill at contracting—"

"Which you do," Tracy said, saluting him.

"Which I do." He gave her a little mock bow. "Then you actually work with Simonson and West Builders to design and build the place you want. They give you a lot of help, plus all their connections, subcontractors, their getting stuff at cost, and all that. But you get the house you want, where you want, the kind you want, the whole nine yards."

Tracy turned off the TV and fanned herself with the pieces of paper from the laser printer. "Well, baby doll," she told him, "I don't care what kind of house you build me, or what lot you build it on. Just please, whatever you do, get one where the ocean breezes come gusting through the master bedroom. That's all I ask, and I'll love you till I die."

The very next weekend Justin and Tracy Thompson drove down the Pacific Coast Highway and soon found themselves standing literally on the beach, checking out the available lots. And these were huge: great big oceanfront pieces of prime California property, with the roar of the surf right below where the dream houses were going to go up. Mindy, the real estate broker, *ooh*ed and *aah*ed when Justin told her he already had a contractor's license, and that he'd built several houses with his dad and his brother while he was still in high school. "That's fabulous," she told him. "You guys are going to get such a bargain here; I can't believe it."

"Which lots are still available?" Tracy wanted to know.

"You're standing on the best piece," the lady told her, glancing down at her buzzing cell phone before switching it off to keep the lookie loos from fouling up a potential sale. "We have the ten parcels here that come right out to the edge of the shoreline, and then around the corner, there are two odd-sized lots that run a little more."

"Why are they higher?" Justin asked her.

And she gave a little impatient shake of her head. "Oh, the developer who owns the entire project just assigned all the prices, and he wants more for them. See, right here, where you're standing right now, we're essentially on the beach. It's sand here and some good solid topsoil . . . but basically . . . beach. This is beach; that's why people want to live here. Around the bend there you are getting some property that is set on granite—but between you and me and the property stake markers, I wouldn't pay the extra money. Why bother?"

"Well, why does the builder want more then?" Tracy asked, wrinkling her forehead. A little gust of breeze came spinning across the sand, bathing the trio in ocean fragrance, and she sucked in her breath. "*Mmmm!* It's so nice and cool out here!"

"It really is," Mindy agreed. "But back to—you were asking about the builder?"

"Yeah."

She gave a little dismissive wave of her hand. "I guess you could always say that a rock foundation for your property is better. I mean, true, if the killer tidal wave of all time came along, the terrain right here is obviously more vulnerable. And if a 9.0 Richter-scale rock-and-roll-show earthquake hit this part of town, sure, those two houses are going to be in the best shape. But look. There are no fault lines anywhere near here. And I can show you weather patterns and how high the waves ever come along this stretch of real estate; and S&W Builders has all the satellite charts going back to when Richard Nixon was sunning himself just down the beach at San Clemente. Oh, sure, you do get storms, but not the kinds of storms that are ever going to blow windows in on this stretch of real estate. It's just not something to worry about. So I always say, why pay the extra seventy-five thousand dollars? Of course, if you want to, that's a bonus check of forty-five hundred for *moi*, but I just don't think it pays to spend money on that kind of what-if that ain't going to happen."

"Still," Justin said slowly, "someone's going to buy those two best pieces. If we're thinking long term, maybe we should at least look."

"No problem," the lady wearing the company coat told them. "Glad to take you over there. But obviously, the majority of buyers are taking these lots right on the beach. The best view is right here; over around the bend, the peninsula here sticking out knocks off almost a good forty percent of your ocean view. And you're definitely off in the corner there; just two families all by themselves versus being right here on Lover's Lane Malibu."

Justin kind of went *hmmmm*, trying to figure all the angles and how much of a mortgage it was going to take if he upgraded to the lots where all the rocks and stones were. But Mindy, the lady with the coat and calculator, had one more teaser sales bulletin to share. "Don't forget," she said, "that it's going to be a whole lot tougher building on those two lots out back. That's pure rock over there, and it's a bear to drill into for your pilings and all that. I don't know the construction jargon and all the words you boys throw around when you're drilling—and believe me, I don't want to know—but you can essentially count on adding at least six months to the project. Right here you can move the dirt and sand out of the way, and be framing in less than a week."

Well, that last piece of news cinched the deal. Together with Mindy, the real estate lady, Justin and Tracy went back to the sales office, filled out the paperwork for the oceanfront parcel they'd been standing on, got their financing set the very next Monday afternoon, and within six weeks of time Mr. Justin "Time" Thompson was out on his own property, driving the heavy caterpillar equipment, moving sand and soil, and building his little bride a dream house right on the beach. The week before Thanksgiving they were able to move in, and on Turkey Day itself they had fifteen friends over to watch the Cowboys play the Vikings on their big-screen hi-def TV in the living room, with the huge glass panels that looked right out on the gray Pacific Ocean. It was a view to die for, and Justin spent the entire Thursday afternoon hearing his high school buddies tell him how lucky he was. A house on the sandy beach of Malibu. Sweet!

The pigskin contest on FOX had almost gotten down to the two-minute warning when a reporter for channel 11 cut into the game with a breathless announcement. Swirling satellite photos showed a nasty hurricane front moving in from six hundred miles off shore, and people all up and down the California coastline were being warned to evacuate their property. "And this is no joke," the anchorman panted, adjusting his earpiece. "Our Doppler storm sensors are telling us that this front could be packing some power unlike anything that's come along since the upheaval in '71. If you're on the shoreline between Point Mugu and Long Beach, the CHP is saying to get out right now. Don't wait for the end of the Dallas game; you just get in your car and get yourself inland. Go and watch the rest of this game at a Pizza Hut in Pasadena."

Tracy turned to her husband, her face white with terror. "Honey, what should we do? It's coming right at us."

Justin was about to answer, when one of his racquetball friends, Steve, pointed out the picture window. "Whoa!" he said, fear thick in his throat. A huge tidal wave was rising up out of the gray currents, building higher and higher as it thundered its relentless way directly toward Malibu Shores and the fragile mansion built so precariously on the shifting sand.

* * * * *

There was a story in the *Los Angeles Times* some years ago that made me want to weep . . . for *joy* because the story wasn't about me. That sounds kind of mean, but let me tell you about it.

It did seem smart at the time

Before the dot-com crash of 2000, it had been a hot bonus for workers in the field of technology to be able to buy, for just pennies, stock in the company that employed them. An engineer named Jeffrey was permitted, through a plan at Cisco, to snap up corporate stock for just five or ten cents a share. So he did the smart thing: he bought a hundred thousand shares, which made sense. Any time you can buy something that lists at sixty-three dollars on the NASDAQ ticker, and pay just a nickel for it . . . well, you grab all you can. Everybody was doing it.

And there was something else all the financial advisors were saying in their newsletters: "Buy it and hold it. Hold it for the long term." So this Jeffrey, who was suddenly walking around Silicon Valley with something like seven million dollars he'd paid twenty thousand dollars for, put the stocks in his sock drawer and said, "Thank you very much, Cisco. I'm set for life."

Well, hold on. This particular *Los Angeles Times* story was dated April 13, the Friday before income taxes come due. And all at once, Jeffrey the engineer, and literally thousands of other instant millionaires like him, began to hear of a time bomb out there called the AMT. Not the ATM, which can rob you of your fortune twenty dollars at a time, but the AMT, the alternative minimum tax. Uncle Sam considered Jeffrey to have received income from Cisco Incorporated to the tune of seven million dollars minus the twenty thousand dollars he'd actually paid. The difference between the pennies-per-share price he'd paid, and the official Wall Street valuation of that same stock—on the day you bought it—is a profit subject to the AMT tax, which runs between 26 and 28 percent.

But hold on to your big board bandanna. After Jeffrey bought the stock, which was once worth sixty-three dollars, the NASDAQ took a nosedive, and all of a sudden, Cisco was selling at $17.98 a share. And the bottom line was this: Jeffrey owed the IRS two-and-a-half-million dollars in taxes, and now had stock worth only one-and-a-half-million bucks. So this thirty-two-year-old engineer with a wife, eight-month-old daughter, and a three-bedroom townhouse didn't have seven million bucks in his sock drawer; instead, he was *in hock* to the government to the tune of a crippling one million dollars.

Isn't that a tough story? And it's so reminiscent of this parable told by Jesus two thousand years before the short-lived dot-com phenomenon began turning computer whiz kids into rich young rulers. "There was a man who built his house on the sand," the Savior told His audience. "And it worked out fine until an unexpected storm came along. But when the rains came down and the floods came up, the house on the sand went *splat!*"

For just a season, everything this Jeffrey did made sense. If you can buy a sixty-three dollar Cisco share for ten cents, obviously, you do it. And if the market's been going up and up and up, with no end in sight, with more pots of gold out there at the end of every Internet rainbow, then you buy and hold. You put that seven-million dollar bonus into the safest thing you can think of, like a great big mansion on the sandy beaches of Malibu. Put it into appreciable real estate, which everybody knows goes steadily up forever until the end of time. That's the conventional wisdom. And the only thing that can go wrong is if a killer storm comes along, in the form of an unanticipated visit from the tax man on the fifteenth day of the fourth month.

Now, I'm not making any particular observations—except sympathetic ones—for this man Jeffrey, and the thousands of others just like him. There wasn't anything unethical or wrong or malicious about the moves he made, and really, there but for the grace of God, go all the rest of us. But from a spiritual point of view, this parable by Jesus tells us that we can live our lives according to certain principles and have surprises that wipe us out completely.

Let's go to the Bible and pore through this fascinating story. It's recorded in both Matthew and Luke, and speaking of the IRS, why not read it from the version written by the tax man himself? "Everyone who hears these words of mine," Jesus said, "and puts them into practice is like a wise man who built his house on the rock. The rain came down, the streams rose, and the winds blew and beat against that house; yet it did not fall, because it had its foundation on the rock. But everyone who hears these words of mine and does not put them into practice is like a foolish man who built his house on sand. The rain came down, the streams rose, and the winds blew and beat against that house, and it fell with a great crash" (Matthew 7:24–27).

It's one thing to be entertained by stories—and no doubt the crowd standing around Jesus day by day at the beach or in the temple enjoyed His marvelous talks—but Christ certainly wanted His listeners to get beneath the surface, to get past the sand and the wind, and understand what He was saying. And God's followers in this twenty-first century need to do that as well. What does it mean to build your house on the rock? In one sense, Christ comes right out and tells us: it's to hear Jesus' words and to do them.

The house is your life, of course, and you want to base your life *on* something. And that something has to be the words, the teachings, the examples, the principles of Jesus' kingdom. To *do* the agenda of the Christian faith. To do that is wise, because a life based on the rock of the Christian faith is not going to crash down when the inevitable storms come, whether on April 15 or any of the other 364 windy days out there where an enemy named Lucifer is stirring up strife.

In the marvelous book *Descending Into Greatness,* Pastor Bill Hybels tells about a man who had enough money to buy that mansion on the beach, so to speak. Actually, a mansion enters into it; here's how he relates the story.

"Each year, I talk with hundreds of people who have chased the American Dream. More often than not, they are broken people shattered by the hidden costs of 'success.' One man recently had to choke back tears while he talked to me. All his life he had tried to make it to 'Easy Street.' Every waking moment of his days was spent trying to achieve his dream. It's not that he didn't love his wife and children; on the contrary, he wanted to provide what was best for them. They could wait awhile until he achieved all those wonderful things they deserved. He should have been happy as he spoke with me. He was just a deal away from the big time, a breath away from a vice presidency, one client away from Easy Street. And he had just taken possession of his dream house."[1]

So far so good, right? Work hard. Make money. Pile it away. Buy a big house right on the edge of the Pacific Ocean. A dream house and a dream ending. Correct? But here is the rest of Hybels's story.

"The only problem was that it was an empty home. His wife and children had left him, and he was alone with the echoes of his footsteps. The price tag of his dream had cost him everything of value. He found himself spiritually alienated, relationally isolated, emotionally drained, and physically broken. All that was left was a pile of things that mocked him."

And so Jesus says to him, and to the people standing around Him there in a grassy meadow, and to you and me today: "Friend, build your house, your life, on Me. I am the Rock. A life based on My teachings and, even more, on a personal relationship, a saving relationship, with Me, is going to last throughout eternity. It's going to survive any storm, because I've already been through the cemetery, and that's the worst storm there is."

Ellen White encourages us with these words: "It is necessary that every individual member build upon the Rock, Christ Jesus. A storm is arising that will wrench and test the spiritual foundation of every one to the utmost. Therefore avoid the sand bed; hunt for the rock. Dig deep; lay your foundation sure. Build, oh, build for eternity!"[2]

There's a verse in Proverbs that our friend Justin should have read before building his beautiful mansion at the edge of the beach. Constructing his dream home right on the sparkling sand seemed so smart; everyone else was building there too. It was cheaper there; it was easier there; it was the expected thing to build there. But Proverbs 14:12 tells us, "There is a way that seems right to a man, but in the end it leads to death."

So *seeming* right is not the same as actually being right. And it's tragically true that many of us construct a life that, to outside appearances, is solid and righteous. But deep inside, we know there is a problem with the foundation we've chosen.

Hearing but not doing

It pains me to time travel back two tumultuous presidencies ago, to some Monica memories most of us Christians would just as soon forget, but you might remember back a few years when a certain United States president went to church one morning. In fact, it was Easter Sunday. Any time a chief executive attends services, it's always a well-publicized media event, and the network cameras duly noted the occasion. And then, after all the hymn singing and the sermon and the prayers, the nation's leader went back to the White House on April 7, 1996, and had a romantic dalliance that same day with a young intern. That was a typical pattern for the forty-second president: church in the morning and adultery in the afternoon. And yes, that deeply offended many, many Christians who had put their faith in the man from Hope, Arkansas.

Well, I have to daily remind myself of how often I get home from looking pious at church on Sabbath morning and then commit sins of pride or selfishness even before I pull into the garage. But Jesus' parable about solid foundations contains a key point right in the middle of this fascinating parable.

The *Clear Word* paraphrase describes the second building contractor in Matthew 7:26: "The ones who make a show of respect for me but don't really follow me are like the man who built his house on the sand."

It's clear from this story that Jesus Christ is describing the importance of basing our lives on the best *Foundation*—which is Him! "The wise man hears My words and puts them into practice," He tells us.

Apparently, it's possible to hear the words of Christ, actually to be sitting in the church where the Christian words are being proclaimed, and also to go through the motions of building a good house. To all outward appearances, the genuine Christian and the hypocrite Christian look as if they're living identical lives. Both are in church. Both are clutching hymnals. Both are hearing the words. Both are "building houses." And they both look like good houses. But the difference is that one person is actually living by the words, while the second guy is only hearing them. The house on the rock is built upon actually *doing* what the Lord says, actually following the commands you heard in church when you get back to 1600 Pennsylvania Avenue Sunday afternoon.

There was a story in the winter 2001 issue of *Leadership* magazine, submitted by Ron Koustas, who directs an AIDS outreach ministry called the Isaiah 58 Project at the Village Church in New York City. A man named Riley began to attend the prayer meetings they ran there, and eventually Ron heard his life story. "In a soft voice he told us about 36 years of living a triple life. He taught Sunday school and played the organ for morning worship, and then he would leave to rob the houses of his fellow parishioners, returning in time for the closing hymn. After church he was off to the West Village gay leather scene."

Isn't that a story? This Riley, organist of the church, was taking note that the Jones family was there in their appointed pew, and the Smiths, and the Browns. And then during the sermon, he would drive over—no doubt using the church directory to look up addresses—and burglarize their homes, and get back to the church in time to slide, perspiring, into his place on the organ bench, and play for the congregation, "I Will Follow Thee, My Savior." What a way to make a living! That might be, right there, where we got the expression "living the life of Riley." And we're reminded of those words of Jesus: "The ones who make a show of respect for Me but don't really follow Me are like the man who built his house on sand."

Well, perhaps we aren't in as desperate a condition as this Sunday-morning thief. But isn't the same pattern true for us? To sit in a pew, to keep up appearances. To have a Sabbath School quarterly and carry it prominently under our arm. But then to simply hear the words without doing them. It's not enough to stand on the sand and admire the solid rock in the lot next door. You have to actually roll up your sleeves and begin to build your house on that rock.

I've always appreciated a book written by Pastor Tony Evans, who leads a growing body of believers at the Oak Cliff Bible Fellowship in Dallas. The book is titled *The Victorious Christian Life,* and just that title implies that victory is more than simply cheering in the stands. Evans defines *meditation,* one step toward victory, like this: "Meditation is a round-the-clock awareness of God's principles and His presence *in our lives.*"[3]

Not "out there" somewhere, but in our lives. Instilled in our minds and also in our behavior patterns. Just four pages later, Evans adds something we all should reflect on. "As we learn [Bible lessons from God], *our next goal should be to consider what we should do differently.*"

Going back to the story of the chief executive who heard a good Easter morning sermon and then went back to the White House to sin, we have to all see ourselves in that up-and-down challenge. The president really did wrestle, trying to take biblical truth and bring it right into his own life. The biography *Monica's Story* includes scenes in which the president sat down with this young woman and confessed, I want to stop doing this. I'm a Christian. I want to live by what I know is right. I want to be faithful to my wife. I want to obey the Lord. But, of course, as is true of so many of us, his resolutions were made of sand, and every time the storms of seduction blew into the White House, the house on the sand went *splat*.

Tony Evans describes how we need to take the teachings of Jesus and ask, "What does this mean I should really do differently?" then takes us to a powerful passage found in James 1:22–24: "Don't deceive yourselves into thinking that all you have to do is to listen to God's Word. You have to put it into practice. Whoever listens to God's Word and doesn't do what it says is like a man who takes a good look in a mirror, sees himself as he really is, and then goes away and ignores everything he just saw." That is the very epitome of a house built on sand.

I recall a terrific chapter in a book called *How To Be Filled With the Holy Spirit—And Know It* by Adventist pastor Garrie Williams. And this great gospel preacher, who knows all about the doctrine of grace, actually invites his readers to delve into the Ten Commandments. Go right there to Exodus 20 and read down them: One . . . two . . . three . . . four . . . And then ask yourself, with a prayer in your heart, "Am I *doing* this one? Lord, I look at this first commandment, and I look into my life right now, today. Lord, am I truly keeping this first commandment—Thou shalt have no other gods before Me? Jesus, I want to honor You by making You my first priority. Am I following Your Word as found here in commandment one?" And then two and three, and right down the line.[4]

That's a terrific way to ask ourselves each day: "Sand . . . or Rock?" The shifting sand of Satan's kingdom, where we hear but don't do? Or the everlasting Rock of Jesus, where we hear His words and then gratefully follow them? How long has it been since you actually had your life pattern collide head-on with what you knew Jesus wanted you to do? That's a chilling moment, and it comes to all of us courtesy of our Friend, the Holy Spirit, who points out, "This is the way; walk ye in it" (Isaiah 30:21, KJV). But do we actually walk in that path, or do we just gaze at it, winding up a lonely mountainside, while we stay in the guilty green pastures below?

The good news is that God is in the moving business. Perhaps you've constructed a house on the sandy beaches of compromise. I know I've hammered a few nails myself over on Malibu Shores. But God is in the moving business. He is able to take houses that were built on sand, and personally move them over to the rock-solid foundation of His own Son. Let me go back to that *Leadership* magazine story from New York City. Because here's the end of Ron Koustas's story about Riley, the organist who was robbing his fellow parishioners during the sermon.

"Today he lives as a Christian with AIDS but considers it a blessing, 'I would never be this close to the Lord if I was healthy.' "

Does that sound like a storm? Here's a man who has full-blown AIDS. He used to be the worst of hypocrites. But now he's built his house on the solid Rock, and no storm in the world can blow away his abiding friendship with Jesus.

Having said that, we have to concede this difficult reality: sand is not only the easier and cheaper and more convenient option. It's also the *default* option.

Sand is the default option

If you're like me, and you have eight weekend projects piled on your desk, or there on your kitchen table at home, there's probably one that's harder than the others. One assignment you dread. One term paper you can't seem to get started on writing. And so you dribble around with the other seven, doing the easy stuff, shuffling the easy papers . . . and allowing the difficult chore to just sit and develop its own compound interest of grief. One university's academic advisor once observed with a sad smile: "College really isn't that hard. Most freshmen do an entire semester's worth of work in the final week!"

Have you ever noticed, though, that so often the hard thing to do is also the right thing? Isn't that depressing? It's easy to gossip and hard to stop. Easy to be selfish and difficult to share. Hard to get to church; easy to get to the movies and the mall. Hard to pray; easy to watch TV. Inconvenient to live for Christ; wonderfully easy to live for yourself. It's a spiritual fact of life: the right thing is the hard thing. The moral gravity of sin pulls everything in our lives down . . . and us with it.

C. S. Lewis remarks in *Mere Christianity* that we often face two competing impulses. And the right one is usually the more difficult! If a man is drowning and you come upon the scene, there are two choices. You can wade into the current yourself, risking current and cold and inconvenience and even your own possible demise. Or you can continue blithely on your merry way. Which is easier? But which is right?[5]

You've heard the old story, I'm sure, of the kid who was watching a caterpillar turned butterfly trying to emerge from its cocoon after the long slumber of metamorphosis. And it was struggling to get out. That little hole at the bottom of the cocoon was just too tiny. Obviously, God had made a mistake in design. So the kid, with a pair of scissors, cut a larger hole so the butterfly could get out. Well, it slithered out in a slippery heap, all right . . . and then just lay there on the ceramic floor. And continued to lie there. Because the exercise and work and struggle of coming out, of doing the right thing, the appropriate butterfly thing, was going to give it strength for the journey. Having slid down the greased chute of convenience, it was now doomed.

In the cradle roll song my granddaughter Kira sings in Sabbath School, "The Wise Man Built His House Upon the Rock," why is there even a second stanza where foolish people get out their bulldozers and knowingly build on the flimsy foundation of sand instead?

Our fictional couple, Justin and Tracy, made their decision based on several variables. It was easier to build on the sand; building on rock was difficult. Most of the people around them were building on sand too; there were attractive young couples all over the place, marking out their lots, planning their futures. Lots on the sand were what the crowd was opting for that particular year. And in all the catalogs and over at the home improvement center, houses built on sand were the popular choice.

Here's another point. If no killer storm ever blows in, a house built on the sand is enough. If things are calm, sand will do. If the ocean stays flat, sand is sufficient. If there's no earthquake, then paying extra for rocks and granite and cement pilings is just money out the window. Who wants to fork out extra for a tragedy that isn't ever going to come along?

And one more thought as we continue to link physical sand to spiritual sand. But is it possible, out there at Malibu Shores, that building on sand was the default mode? If you didn't specifically ask for an upgrade, then sand would be what you got. If you just went to Simonson and West Builders and said, "Gimme a lot. Any lot" . . . you got sand. If you put in no extra effort, you got sand. You had to step outside your comfort zone, buck the crowd, do the hard thing, the unpopular thing, in order to get a house built on the rock. Sand was the default purchase, the easy thing.

This story is in Matthew 7, but let's recall an earlier verse from chapter 6, where Jesus tells people, "No one can serve two masters. . . . You cannot serve both God and Money" (verse 24).

And all through the teachings of Jesus, there's this sense that serving Jesus is the hard thing, and serving self, or money, or the world isn't just the easy thing but the default thing. If we just get out of bed in the morning and do our own thing, that's exactly what it is—our own thing. It's not God's thing. If you go about your life and just live, that's a house built on sand. You have to choose God, choose Christianity, choose the rock foundation of a life of faith, or you'll get sand without even asking for it.

But let's take a brief detour in Matthew 7 and find out just what Jesus was talking about before He got to this story about sandy beaches and storms and smashed-up skyscrapers. This is called "getting the context of the story," always a good idea for any Bible student. And there are essentially six threads of thought to the sermon of Jesus before He tells the beach story. First of all, "Judge not, that ye be not judged" (Matthew 7:1, KJV). Meaning, leave God's business with God. Number two, "Ask and it will be given to you; seek and you will find" (verse 7). That's obviously also about trusting God. Number three, the golden rule, which, as we've already observed, would fall into the category of "hard things"! Doing what doesn't come naturally, being good to your enemies.

"Beware of following the crowd," Jesus says, as number four. "Because *down* is the default mode. Destruction is where most people will automatically go without thinking. The road to lostness is a broad, smooth, comfortable one; the path to the kingdom is hard and winding and lonely." Then comes point five: "Beware of nice-sounding, charismatic leaders who suck you into their false theology," He tells us. "Don't go after a false prophet whose own life doesn't bear good fruit." And then this companion piece of advice: "Watch out for miracle workers, or people who use My name, or who talk a seductive spiritual line, but who don't obey My Father's will. Beware of people who fill their conversations with Christian platitudes, but who aren't doing what I invite them to do, who aren't living sanctified lives of obedience to My Word, My commandments."

In this sermon outline of six things, the lessons from Malibu Shores are so very clear. The easy thing is to judge others. The easy thing is to seek our own way, rather than to seek divine answers to prayer. The easy thing is to treat our neighbors and coworkers, and especially our enemies, with spite, and to disregard the golden rule. We have to step outside of ourselves, force our way out of our comfort zones, in order to do what Jesus is describing here. And that's precisely what this parable is about—the difficulty of an obedient life.

I'm thankful when other voices outside our own Adventist communion give a stalwart endorsement to the idea of obedience. The president of the Southern Baptist Convention, the late Pastor Adrian Rogers, in *Believe in Miracles but Trust in Jesus,* hits this very point: "True faith, strong faith, is always linked to obedience. In Romans 16:26 Paul speaks of 'the obedience of faith.' And the apostle James writes, 'As the body without the spirit is dead, so faith without works is dead also' (2:26). Sitting in church and taking notes is not faith. You must obey the Word. 'Well,' you say, 'are you telling me that I'm saved by faith and works?' No, I'm saying that you are saved by faith *that* works. If it doesn't work, it is not faith. Simply saying that you believe but not obeying is not faith. There's no substitute for obedience."[6]

That's a sober thought and a sober reality as well. Obedience to God is not default; if we don't stop and think and pray and wrestle, "[resisting] unto blood, [and] striving against sin," as Hebrews 12:4 colorfully puts it, then we're going to automatically live an autopilot life of comfortable, easy, natural, "sandy" disobedience.

The great news is this: your house and mine is being built right now, today, at this very moment in time. It's still going up, still being constructed. Are you on the sand? Well, move! Better yet, let Jesus help you move. Get on the Rock today, and then daily choose to stay there. The Master Mover, and also the Master Architect, is ready and waiting for you.

Has it taken you some time, though, to finally realize that this Master Architect can be trusted in the matter of selecting home sites? We almost have to drag the phrase "Your will be done" out of our reluctant lips when the lot we've picked out looks so much easier to build on and even more attractive.

Why should I listen to you, Dad?

A fall-down-funny article by Dave Barry in a long-ago edition of the *Reader's Digest,* lamented the timeless reality that teenagers are always and forever ashamed of their parents. In his own childhood, Dave's dad had a hat he liked to wear, which was the most hideous thing ever made. It was the kind of Russian hat the poorest Russian in Moscow wouldn't dream of putting on. Dave was embarrassed to tears to be seen anywhere near him, or to have Dad pick him up after school. But now that he has a kid of his own, the same phenomenon is equally true. If he even approaches his son in public with the possibility of bringing massive doses of geekiness anywhere near his teenager, the boy miraculously vaporizes himself like in an episode of *Star Trek,* and then rematerializes several football fields away. This kid can just *think* and will himself to disappear from his father's embarrassing presence.

Of course, this actually gives parents a secret weapon, according to Mr. Barry. If you want to get your kid to do what you want, he suggests, simply threaten to sing in public. Just clearing your throat and getting out some sheet music is probably enough to get your child whipped back into shape. In fact, Dave takes us to a courtroom where a frustrated judge is lecturing a juvenile delinquent. "Young man, we've tried detention, we've tried probation, and community service, and jail. There's really only one thing left for this court to consider. I'm going to have your mother come up here on the stand with our karaoke machine and belt out all four verses of 'Copacabana.' " And the manacled kid shudders in horror. "No, Your Honor! No! Anything but that! I'll be good! Please!"

Another great humorist from a bygone era suggests that this is how it has always been and always will be. "When I was a boy of fourteen," he writes, "my father was so ignorant I could hardly stand to have the old man around. But when I got to be twenty-one, I was astonished at how much he had learned in seven years!"

Well, it's a far piece down the road from Malibu, where we were about to build our houses on the sand, to suddenly finding ourselves talking about Dave Barry's dad's hat and the humorist's idiot father. But here's the point: Sooner or later, most of us realize that Father knows best. That Dad actually has a few smarts in his head and might be worth listening to. And from a biblical perspective, we finally come to understand that our heavenly Father is indeed a wise Builder. So if He tells us, "Build the house over here; build your house on the Rock, on the solid foundation, on *Me,*" well, we bow at His feet and agree to do what He suggests.

There's a fishing story in Luke 5, and this is very early in the relationship between Jesus and His disciples; in fact, they hadn't really gotten to the point yet of leaving everything in order to serve and follow Him. But after fishing all night and catching not a single fish—zero, zip, *nada*—Jesus tells Peter: "Go out again and put out your nets."

And Peter, experienced fisherman that he is, doesn't get into a big dialogue with Jesus, who is a Preacher, not a fisherman. He just gives this classic answer:

"Because you say so, I will let down the nets" (verse 5).

And that's really where we need to get to in our decision about where to build our house, this structure called our life. Will we build it on the Rock called Jesus because He says so? Will we obey Him because He says so? Will we seek to not only discover His will, but to do it . . . because He says so?

I confess with some crimson in my cheeks that I recently read a Christian bestseller written just for women. I cheated a bit and took a peek when my wife, Lisa, wasn't looking, but Donna Partow's recent book, *Walking in Total God-Confidence,* describes this very decision to just do what Jesus asks us to do. "If we can come to the place where we *rely on God's discretion* rather than our own— when we can say from our hearts, 'Lord, You know best. You decide'—we'll truly be walking in Total God-Confidence."

Then she takes readers right to the point of conflict, where we want to do *X* and God tells us to do *Y*. We want to build on the sand of selfishness, to build our home on the foundation called ego or money or position or revenge. And God explicitly says to us, "No, build your home over here instead. Put your fishing net down over here, not over there where you think there are a lot of fish. Trust Me on this." And Donna observes about these day-to-day building decisions we face constantly. "If God doesn't want me to go somewhere, then why on earth would I want to go? If God doesn't want me to have something, then why on earth would I want to have it? If God doesn't want a certain person to be part of my life, why cling to that person?" Then she adds her personal confession: "What a liberating moment it was when I finally said, 'Lord, I only want whatever you want me to want!' "[7]

Really, if you are calling Jesus "Lord" in these prayers, that means you're going to be willing to let Him be Lord, allow Him to be the Leader and Director and Boss in your life. You'll be willing to build where He says to build.

John Stott, author of *The Contemporary Christian,* who passed away in 2011, quietly suggests that to even call Jesus "Lord" implies a willingness on our part for this to happen. "The early Christians gave Jesus a God-title ('Lord'), transferred to him God-texts (regarding the salvation he bestows and the homage he deserves) and offered him God-worship (the bowed knee)."[8]

Back in the book of Isaiah, Stott points out, God the Father is described by verses like this one from chapter 45: "By myself I have sworn, my mouth has uttered in all integrity a word that will not be revoked: Before me every knee will bow; by me every tongue will swear" (verse 23).

New Testament champions like Paul came along, centuries later, and told followers, "Hey, that verse now belongs to Jesus! By virtue of the Cross, and by virtue that Jesus Christ *is* God, too, that 'God-text' is now His!"

Then Stott adds this compelling argument for all would-be builders who are looking enviously at the sandy lots their neighbors are enjoying, "The tradition in some evangelical circles is to distinguish sharply between Jesus the Saviour and Jesus the Lord, and even to suggest that conversion involves trusting Him as Saviour, without necessarily surrendering to him as Lord. The motive behind this teaching is good, namely to safeguard the truth of justification by faith alone and not introduce works-righteousness (obeying Christ as Lord) by the back door." That's true, isn't it? But he hastens to add this: "Nevertheless this position is biblically indefensible. Not only is Jesus 'our Lord and Saviour', one and indivisible, but his lordship implies his salvation and actually announces it. That is, his title 'Lord' is a symbol of his victory over all the forces of evil, which have been put under His feet. The very possibility of our salvation is due to this victory. It is precisely because he is Lord that he is able also to be a Saviour. There can be no salvation without lordship. The two affirmations 'Jesus is Lord' and 'Jesus saves' are virtually synonymous."[9]

Isn't that a great challenge to consider? Jesus is our Savior today only because He *is* Lord, because He is the Son of God, divine, victorious over Satan, eternally preexistent with the Father. And when He invites us to build our lives on Him, the solid Rock, the Cornerstone, He does so because He is both of these things: Savior and Lord.

Stott concludes by reminding us of Peter on that Thursday night before the Crucifixion. "Lord, I'll do anything!" he boasted. "Fight any foe, swing any sword, turn away from any temptation." Half an hour later, he was a defeated, broken man. This great evangelical writer observes, "The way to prove our love for Christ is neither by loud protestations of loyalty like Peter, nor by singing sentimental ditties in church, *but by obeying his commandments.* The test of love is obedience, [Jesus Himself] said."[10]

This is the invitation that comes to us. A loving Friend, with nail prints in His hands, tells us that He knows best. He knows where the fish are biting. He knows where the building of houses is good. He knows where the roots of your vine ought to be planted. And the reality is that all of us are building this structure called "one human life" every day of our lives. Brick by brick, tile by tile. Decisions yesterday, today, tomorrow, and right up to our own finish line, when escrow closes. Chuck Colson, in *How Now Shall We Live?* observes, "Everything we do now has eternal significance, because one day there will be a judgment, and then it will become evident that our choices in this life have consequences that last into eternity."[11]

Chapter 5

WHEN TO PULL
the Weeds

"Is This Any Way to Run an Airline?" was the headline in a major U.S. news magazine. An upstart billionaire named Danny had gotten himself into the aviation business after riding the NASDAQ roller coaster right to its peak and then climbing out with his winnings. Securing just four planes at first, and beginning with only three puddle jumper routes on the West Coast, he had astonished the industry by expanding to thirty states in just over three years. With Danny—and by the way, that's what he had every single one of his nine thousand employees call him—service was key. You served your people, you served your travelers, you served the people standing in line, you served the people who logged onto your Web site to make reservations, you served the people with complaints on the rare occasion when one of Sky High's planes left the gate more than three minutes behind schedule.

And you just never knew when you would actually see the big guy himself: checking luggage in at Portland; giving you an upgrade in Albuquerque; going up and down the aisles of the plane between Sacramento and Colorado Springs, pouring out cans of soda and giving his customers the promised cookies. "Don't tell the boss," he'd say, slipping extra ones to the kids. "I don't want to get fired."

"You *are* the boss!" they would squeal with laughter.

"I am?" He looked pleased with himself. "Cool!" They loved it.

Well, the general public ate it up too—not just the cookies, but the whole concept Sky High was promoting. No more Saturday night stayover rules; no more crazy patchwork fares; no extra fees if your meetings in Dallas got done half a day early and you wanted to get home ahead of schedule. "Sure," Danny would say, writing you up a new boarding pass himself. "Let's get you home, mister, and free up a seat on that later flight. Maybe I'll meet a pretty girl on that airplane, marry her, and let her fly for half price after that." Then he'd laugh, and everyone standing in line would laugh too. "Isn't this fun?" He would grin. "Man, we're building us a kingdom of joy here. We're Sky High and happy."

Danny's number two at the airline was a guy named Pete, who was in charge of keeping the whole operation running smoothly. There was hardly ever even a ripple of employee discontent, but if someone had a question or suggestion about morale, Pete would zip off an e-mail and fix it. He did a corporate newsletter each month, and there was always a Q&A section in which people who worked at Sky High, from the glass-tower offices to the men and women out on the tarmac putting suitcases on the planes, could have their say. It was Pete's job to make sure that Danny's slogan, "We're Sky High and Happy," always stayed true.

Then one day Pete came into his boss's office and shut the door. "We got ourselves a situation," he said without fanfare.

"What's up?" Danny asked him.

Pete shook his head. "Don't know how to tell you this," he said, "but Sky High's got itself a small bunch of subversives. Working undercover."

Danny took his cowboy boots off the mahogany desk and sat up straight. "No way," he said. "What are you talking about, Pete?"

The shorter man took out a folder and ran his finger down a list. "The way I've been counting on my fingers," he said, "between our operation in Tucson and a little group of people in Oakland, there are just about twenty people on the payroll this very minute who are trying to do us in from the inside."

"How come?" The CEO couldn't believe it. "We're going so well. What are they grumping about?"

"They're not grumping out loud," Pete corrected him. "If they had complaints, they know they could come to you or me, or use the newsletter to sound off, or just come to the next roundtable meeting, or whatever. And we'd do our best to fix it. It's nothing like that. It's just that these employees have decided to poison the well from inside the well, hoping to send us down the tubes. Whether they have underground connections to some other airline and are helping to sabotage us on their behalf, I don't know. Doesn't matter, though. I've got confidential memos from supervisors, I've got backups of certain e-mails that have been sent around, I have friends who have tipped me off to some real monkeying around with reservations . . . and I can just tell you, big guy, these people are costing us a severe amount of income. And it's only going to get worse."

A stab of pain showed on the owner's face as he digested the news. "Man, that hurts," he said at last. "We tried to make something unique happen here, create a family for these folks."

"It still is," Pete said hastily. "Look, boss, Sky High is still *the* airline to work for. Wall Street says so; I mean, our stock is just two points off our all-time high of eighty-two. We're still OK that way. But in the long run, there's no doubt about it—this little bunch of malcontents is cyanide. And what's penny ante now might get bigger if they recruit others."

Danny got up from the desk and walked over to the big picture window looking out over the huge multimillion dollar slab of concrete where Sky High jets took off and landed every day. "So our investors and the crowd at CNBC don't really know this is brewing."

"Nope. From all outward appearances we're still one big cookie-eating happy family. The way these twenty bad apples are operating, they still look as good as the other apples in the barrel. You'd never know by looking." The diminutive vice president walked over and stood next to his mentor. "So what are we going to do, Danny?"

The older man turned to face him. "What do you think? You've been with me ever since the start-up. I mean, we built this puppy from the ground up, you and me. It's your family, too, bro. What's your call?"

Pete scratched at his goatee. "You got no choice, man. Pink slips. You gotta fire 'em. Like, right now. Get the pus out of the wound before an infection sets in. I call them, I tell them they get two weeks severance, and *sayonara*."

A 747 jet thundered past, on its way to a distant paradise, and Danny watched as it rose into the air heading west. Very slowly he came back to his desk, sat down, poured himself a drink of water, and sipped at it, his face expressionless. A minute passed in silence.

"Well?" Pete prompted him. "So I can them? Or what?"

"No." Danny shook his head. "This is Sky High, Pete. Don't fire them."

"But I'm telling you, these people are bad news," Pete protested. "The competition slid them onto our game board when we weren't looking, and they're going to wipe us out."

"No, they're not," the CEO said calmly. "We're still Sky High. We're not going to get beat by twenty renegade workers in Tucson and Oakland."

"But what are you going to do?"

Danny looked right at him. "I'm going to wait," he told him. "Let some time go by."

"How come?"

The airline's owner pointed at the wall where there was a huge photo showing about 350 smiling employees standing around one of the company's brand-new Airbus jets. "Look," he said. "We're a young company. Wall Street still calls us an upstart. And now, out of nine thousand employees, we've got twenty or so who got planted in our yard by some enemy."

"So we pull 'em out right now." Pete was still determined to have a showdown. "Get them by the roots and yank."

"No," Danny said firmly. "Not yet. If we fire twenty people now, right in the middle of the peak summer season, we'll lose others for sure. It'll dominate the headlines. When we ax the bad workers, we'll uproot some of the good employees at the same time. Plus," he said, "how can you know for sure, Pete, that you've got a handle on exactly who the renegades are? What if there are others, and because we didn't know, they stay on? Then we look unfair."

Pete shook his head in frustration. "This is nuts," he said. "These guys are going to contaminate everything. You can't just let them sit in front of our computer terminals, infecting our whole corporation like a virus."

Danny came over and put an arm around his friend. "Pete," he said quietly, "I'll handle it. When the time comes, I promise you, I'll take care of it. There's going to be a huge shake-up anyway, in this crazy flying business. And we're going to end up on top. I know that, and you know that. That's why we've stuck together. And I promise you, in the end, we're going to have our family whole again. The enemy troops are going to be gone."

"Are you sure?"

The president of Sky High Airlines nodded. "Yeah," he said. "I'm sure."

* * * * *

In the world of politics, it's become a cardinal rule: you get rid of your problems quickly. If you have to fire someone, you fire them the same day, go through the flames, and get it over with. If someone on your staff has to walk the plank, you give them five minutes to get out of there and start walking.

"It's time to go, John!"

Back during the presidency of George H. W. Bush, the White House chief of staff was an abrasive man named John H. Sununu. If you watched CNN's old *Crossfire* program back in the very early 2000s, you saw him "on the right," still duking it out with the pinkos and liberals on the other side of the aisle. But in dealings with Congress, Mr. John H. Sununu was just a wipeout. He was turning people off, even loyalists and friends. He made enemies unnecessarily. There was a mini-scandal in which Sununu was enjoying the perk of having Air Force planes take him all around the country on personal jaunts. The media had a field day with that one, of course, and a cartoonist captured the moment with a picture of Sununu in the cockpit of a huge B-1 bomber. "There! Right there's Disney World! Set 'er down!" And the pilot says with resignation, "Yes, sir, Mr. Sununu."

Well, that kind of headline wasn't helping the Republican Party one little bit. And finally somebody had to go in to see the chief of staff and suggest that he shouldn't be chief of staff any longer. Interestingly, as the story has it, it was young George W. Bush, the president's son who had to bear the tough news. Robert Bryce, a reporter for the *Austin Chronicle,* described the younger Bush as a "loyalty Doberman" whose role it was to make sure staff members were fully on board. "The abrasive Sununu, George W. believed, simply didn't have his father's best interests at heart." And so, with a little help from Boyden Gray, Bush Jr. told Sununu: "John, it's time to go."

We find in God's Word another very intriguing political story that only predates our fictional Wall Street imbroglio by about two thousand years. But in Matthew chapter 13, Jesus was telling the crowd a whole string of parables, and after telling one about a man who planted seed in four kinds of soil, with varying results, did a part two with His "sowing of seed" motif and got to this one, which revolves around the question of "when should the bad guys be fired."

"The kingdom of heaven is like a man who sowed good seed in his field. But while everyone was sleeping, his enemy came and sowed weeds among the wheat, and went away. When the wheat sprouted and formed heads, then the weeds also appeared" (verses 24–26).

So here's the scenario. There's a field full of wheat—that would be nice people, good people, loyal members of the cabinet. And then, all at once, the hired farmhands begin to spot weeds here and there—imposters and enemies and bad people. In the high-tech world of aviation and Internet computer viruses, the owner of Sky High Airlines came to realize that there were some disaffected workers on his team. People who were right there in his company, getting a paycheck and wearing Santa Claus hats to the office Christmas party, but devoted to destroying everything from within.

Jesus continues with His story in verse 27: "The owner's servants came to him and said, 'Sir, didn't you sow good seed in your field? Where then did the weeds come from?' 'An enemy did this,' he replied. The servants asked him, 'Do you want us to go and pull them up?' "

So that's the question the boss is wrestling with in the corporate penthouse. What do we do with the bad people? Should Sununu be fired? Should the rebels in God's world be gathered up in a bundle and burned?

The NIV text notes make this observation about the "weeds" or tares Jesus was describing. "Probably darnel, which looks very much like wheat while it is young, but can later be distinguished."

So there was an element of reality to this story. In fact, Dr. Richard T. France, in the Matthew portion of the Tyndale New Testament Commentaries, tells readers that this kind of thing—a bad guy sneaking in at midnight to plant weeds in with the wheat and soybeans—was actually quite common in Israel. "To sow darnel among wheat as an act of revenge was punishable in Roman law, which suggests that the parable depicts a real-life situation. . . . A light infestation of darnel could be tackled by careful weeding, but mistakes would easily be made. In the case of a heavy infestation the stronger roots of the darnel would be tangled with those of the wheat, making selective weeding impossible."[1]

So any time we're tempted to say about the Bible, "Oh, man, it's just a bunch of dusty old stories about cows and fish and coveting your neighbor's donkey; it's not relevant here in the twenty-first century," remember that people who were listening there in person could relate. They probably were saying, "Hey, I just read a story like that in the *Jerusalem Post*! A guy was arrested by three Roman soldiers for doing that exact thing—planting weeds in somebody's wheat field." It's good news to realize that these really were marvelous sermon illustrations in Jesus' day, and we need to be smart enough to sift away the chaff, so to speak, and still find the powerful truths Jesus has for us here in our supposedly high-tech world.

As Dr. France points out, though, in this early stage of growth, the darnel and the wheat are indistinguishable from each other. And with their roots so impossibly intertwined, how does Christ finish up His story? In verses 28 and following, the servants ask the master, " 'Do you want us to go and pull them up?' 'No,' [the owner] answered, 'because while you are pulling the weeds, you may root up the wheat with them. Let both grow together until the harvest. At that time I will tell the harvesters: First collect the weeds and tie them in bundles to be burned; then gather the wheat and bring it into my barn.' "

There are several interesting lessons we can learn from this short story told by Jesus. As we warm up our own rototillers and Weed-eaters, let's first notice this important point: there's an enemy in this tale. When everyone notices the weeds in the garden and the servants complain, "Hey, who did this?" the owner gives them a poignant answer. "An enemy hath done this" (verse 28, KJV).

I can tell you, there have been times when I stood at funerals, and we all had tears in our eyes and grief in our heart. And I said to those seated there with me, "An enemy hath done this. A villain named Lucifer came in here at midnight, and sowed these seeds of sorrow. Look at the cemeteries dotting the landscape; see all the sickness and death and destruction everywhere you point your camera. Without any doubt, an enemy hath done this."

There's another thing Jesus tells us the enemy has done. He's caused the hearts of men and women to rebel against heaven. There are people out there in the field who are opposed to heaven's government; their hearts have turned against God—and it's the enemy of this world who came in at midnight and did that. I like how *The Message* paraphrase puts it: "That night, while his hired men were asleep, his enemy sowed thistles all through the wheat and slipped away before dawn" (verse 25).

Of course, we have to sleep sometimes, but I want to stay awake all I can—spiritually awake, that is—and not let Lucifer do his midnight work. Sometimes we don't pay attention, and Satan comes in and poisons the minds of our young people with drugs and discouragement. He hardens fragile new Christians' hearts because of the hypocrisy they see in the church.

But the most important lesson is this: The Owner of the field isn't going to lose. No, He doesn't uproot the weeds just yet. The time isn't right just yet. At this fragile moment, when people are still deciding, still thinking, still choosing their side in the cosmic war, and while all the roots are so tangled up, the Owner patiently waits. But in the end of the story, the good harvest comes in, and the Owner triumphs over Lucifer and his stealth campaign. If you're discouraged because the world seems to be going to hell, and all the bad people are living in lazy luxury, be patient. Because the Good Owner, the loving and strong Master of the manor, is about to make His move.

In the meantime, though, we do want to study the *why*s and *how*s of Jesus' method of dealing with insurrection within the church. Because there's often a hue and cry from the laity for the offender to be quickly bounced out of office.

People doing the job of angels

Have you ever been personally eager for an evil person to get his punishment? When a United States president was impeached back in 1998 and the Senate had to vote whether or not to convict him, did you tend toward acquittal or removal? Were you leaning up against your TV set, shouting, "Get rid of that guy"? When Timothy McVeigh was condemned to die, did you quietly rejoice? When Saddam Hussein was hanged, what were your emotions that day?

This is not to say that there's anything wrong with wanting good to triumph and for wickedness to be punished, even extinguished. The Bible is full of such sentiments, and this parable of the wheat and the tares is a classic case. When the hired hands discover that an enemy had climbed over the fence at midnight and planted weeds all among the wheat, the zealous employees of the owner get red in the face and say to him, "What shall we do? Do you want us to go out there and pull them up?" There are other places in the Gospels where Jesus' disciples say to Him: "Lord, these are bad people! They don't love You! They make fun of You! And what's even worse, they make fun of *me* for being Your friend. Lord, is it OK with You if I smite them? Please, oh please, oh please?"

In verse 29, the owner of the field is very calm. "No, that's all right," he says. "Leave everything just as it is."

"But, Lord, these weeds are nasty! You leave them there, and they'll wipe out the crop! They're dangerous!"

All of that was assuredly true. The Greek word for *tares* is *zizania,* which likely referred to a plant known as *Lolium temulentum* or "bearded darnel." One Bible commentary makes this point: "This common Palestinian plant grows about two feet tall. In its earlier stages it is indistinguishable from wheat. Only when the plant matures and the seeds of the darnel turn black is it easy to tell the difference. These seeds are poisonous, and if eaten, produce violent nausea, diarrhea, convulsions, and sometimes death."

But even with all of that, the owner tells the servants to back off. "At these early stages," he explains, "if you pull out the weeds, you'll uproot a lot of the wheat at the same time." Also, as these Bible scholars point out, when they're just planted, the wheat and the darnel, the weeds, look alike. You can't tell the difference. An untrained field hand could easily pull out wheat instead of tares and cause some real damage.

What does all of this mean? Our American judicial system decided, after the Oklahoma City tragedy, that Mr. Timothy McVeigh was a poisonous weed, and really, who could disagree? So we destroyed him. And again, not too many of us would disagree. What is this old Bible story from two thousand years ago really telling us?

Interestingly, a bit later in this same chapter, when the crowds had gone home, the twelve disciples came to Jesus and said, "Lord, we don't get it. That story about the weeds . . . none of us know what in the world You're talking about. Explain, please." And Jesus gives this answer: "The man who sowed good seed in the field is the Son of God." In other words, Himself. He goes on, "The field is the world and the good seed are the people who love God. The weeds are the people who do not love Him. The enemy who sowed weeds is the devil. The harvest is the end of probation for the world, and the sorters are the angels. Just as the weeds are sorted out from the wheat during harvest time and later burned, so it will be at the end of the world. The Son of God will send His angels to weed out of His kingdom everything that causes sin and all who do evil. The angels will throw them into a fiery furnace where they will weep and gnash their teeth. But those who love God will radiate a joy that cannot be imagined and will live in their Father's house forever" (verses 37–43, *Clear Word*). The End.

It's ironic that Jesus shared this insider's peek, this explanation, with just the twelve disciples. Because sitting right there among them was a perfect illustration of the entire story.

Have you ever heard of a man named Judas? Mr. Iscariot was right there in the inner circle with Jesus and the other eleven. Now, was he a "wheat" or a "weed"? Looking back now, the answer is obvious. The Bible plainly says that Satan worked on his heart; Satan "entered into him" on the night he betrayed Jesus to His death (John 13:27, KJV). This guy was a weed with a capital *W*.

But there in the early going, did Judas appear to be a weed, to be poison? Not at all. He looked like the other eleven. He walked with Christ; he talked with Him; he even healed people in the name of Jesus. If you had a police lineup at the beginning of Jesus' ministry, and asked someone, "OK, pick out the guy who is going to sell out the cause," Judas might have been the last person you'd choose. And if even Jesus, there in the first year or two, had said to Judas: "You're a sinner! You're a hypocrite! You're not really one of us! I'm going to zap you out of My kingdom!" the other disciples would have been hugely confused. Jesus might have lost half His entourage right there. *The Seventh-day Adventist Bible Commentary* for Matthew 13 has this to say, "Christ permitted Judas to become a disciple because otherwise the other disciples, not recognizing his true character, would have questioned the wisdom of their Master. . . . Until the very close of His ministry Christ never openly rebuked Judas, because the disciples, who looked upon him with favor and admiration, would have been inclined to sympathize with him. . . . Furthermore, he would have considered such a rebuke as justifying revenge."[2]

In *Christ's Object Lessons,* Ellen White reinforces this same idea. "There is in the Saviour's words another lesson, a lesson of wonderful forbearance and tender love. As the tares have their roots closely intertwined with those of the good grain, so false brethren in the church may be closely linked with true disciples. The real character of these pretended believers is not fully manifested. Were they to be separated from the church, others might be caused to stumble, who but for this would have remained steadfast."

A bit later, the same author then adds, speaking specifically of Judas: "Judas Iscariot was numbered with the apostles. The Redeemer does not want to lose one soul; His experience with Judas is recorded to show His long patience with perverse human nature; and He bids us bear with it as He has borne."[3]

So we learn several things from this old story of wheat and weeds, especially as we look at the saga through Jesus' eyes as He personally had to deal with Judas. First of all, the task of pulling out the weeds isn't man's job. Christ specifically says that the angels of heaven will do that sad task, and, of course, they will do it under God's omniscient guidance. Rebels will be lost and destroyed only because God in His wisdom gives that directive.

But the second point is this. Notice Jesus' reluctance to lose these rebels. God puts it off as long as possible. He delays to the very end. Partly because by then the results of "weed-ness" will be evident; the dark seeds of the mature "darnel" make it plain that they're poison. And in the last days, the Bible is clear in telling us that God's righteous saints will be easy to spot, and Satan's rebellious hosts will be equally identifiable. There won't be confusion then; the angel reapers won't have any difficulty following the instructions of heaven about who should be saved or lost.

But even then, as the Owner of the field goes about the business of judging between wheat and tares, let's appreciate His reluctance. That "wonderful forbearance and tender love" mentioned by Ellen White. What a tragedy it will be when people created in God's image end up dying.

Let's never forget that when the weeds are bundled and burned, this is God's "strange act." He puts it off. He keeps Judas right there in the inner circle right up until the last Thursday evening. Hoping even against His own divine foreknowledge that somehow this thistle, this confused, rebellious man, could be redeemed.

So when the loving Owner, the gracious God, tells us to back off, and says, "I'll handle it," that's exactly what we should let Him do.

Punishing the pastor

The unavoidable flip side of this issue, then, is why the church so often seems to be forced to burn up weeds right now, today. If judgment is God's affair, how are we to understand when pastors are fired and when dissident groups are defrocked and disfellowshiped?

That's the word we use when someone is voted out of church membership and their name is taken off the books. They've been "disfellowshiped." "Booted out." You've probably read stories where somebody sued the local church because it had publicly removed him from the group. Sometimes pastors—this is certainly true in our Adventist denomination, and I think it runs pretty much across the board— have their "credentials" taken away. "Turn in your papers; you're through" is something no preacher never wants to hear from the local conference office or the presbytery or diocese. But it happens.

And here in this Matthew 13 story, in which the Owner of the field, Jesus Himself, says to the workers, "No, *don't* pull out the weeds; no, *don't* gather them up and burn them. Just leave them right where they are," we honestly have to wonder, Is the Christian church obeying this parable of the wheat and the tares? Why do Christians sometimes throw their own people under the bus, as the current expression says? Why, when a pastor has what we call a "moral fall," which is usually a euphemism for a problem with the seventh commandment, is he or she quickly let go?

Just in recent years, I've heard close-to-home stories of men who stood in the pulpit Sabbath by Sabbath. Leading the flock. Preaching good sermons. And later it came out that they were regularly visiting prostitutes. They were addicted to Internet porn. Sometimes it's revealed that a minister is also a pedophile. They embezzle church funds in order to enrich themselves. And listen, those people are gone! They're history. They're stripped of their credentials.

So one issue we have to grapple with is the question, To whom does the story apply?

"The kingdom of God is like a man," He said, "who sowed his whole field with good seed" (verse 24, *Clear Word*).

All right, so what is that field? Does it refer to the church? Is this a story dealing with internal church discipline, when a congregation has to fire its pastor, or remove the membership of a person who is indicted for tax fraud, or say "Let her be anathema!" to a woman who is brazenly living with her lover out of wedlock?

Dr. France correctly points us to verse 38, where Jesus runs through the entire story and says, "The good seed is this. The bad seed is that. The harvesters are the angels. Etc." And Christ plainly says, "The field is the world." Not specifically the church, but the world. And Dr. France comments, "The canvas is broader than the specific issue of church discipline. Jesus announced God's kingdom, and this would lead many of his hearers to expect a cataclysmic disruption of society, an immediate and absolute division between the 'sons of light' and the 'sons of darkness,' as the men of Qumran put it."

The children of Israel were eager for the Messiah to come sweeping in and split the world's population right down the middle. "The chosen people" and the "eternally lost." But that didn't happen. Dr. France finishes his thought: "Yet things went on apparently as before. It was to this impatience that the parable was primarily directed. God's kingdom does bring division, and that division is final, but while it is already present in principle, its full outworking is for God to bring about in the final judgment, not for man to anticipate by human segregation."[4]

So as we look out over the seven billion people living all around us, it's God's place to divide things up and say, "Saved . . . lost. You stand over here on My right; you, on My left." The church isn't supposed to segregate itself, go off into its own little corner, and be exclusive.

However, is it possible that this parable still has a secondary application to the church? As we read this story, are there lessons for us to learn within the body of Christ? Many Bible students think so, and again, the example of how Jesus treated Judas, the betrayer, is worth considering. Judas was in the infant "church" of Jesus; in fact, he was a charter member. And Jesus Himself followed the principle of this parable, leaving Judas in, bearing long with him, tolerating his mistakes and even his disloyalty. Keeping Judas in, instead of throwing him out, was very much a church issue. And the Adventist commentators remark about all of these parables by Jesus: "Taken as a whole, the parables as recorded by Matthew present a composite picture of the essential facts concerning the kingdom of heaven."[5]

Most of these stories start, in fact, with the same six words: "The kingdom of heaven is like . . ." So how Christians in the church should deal with fellow Chris-

WHEN TO PULL THE WEEDS

tians in the church is very much part of this discussion. The author of *Christ's Object Lessons* brings this parable right into the church sanctuary, as well: " 'The field,' Christ said, 'is the world.' But we must understand this as signifying the church of Christ *in* the world. The parable is a description of that which pertains to the kingdom of God, His work of salvation of men; and this work is accomplished through the church. True, the Holy Spirit has gone out into all the world; everywhere it is moving upon the hearts of men; but it is in the church that we are to grow and ripen for the garner of God. . . . By bringing into the church those who bear Christ's name while they deny His character, the wicked one causes that God shall be dishonored, the work of salvation misrepresented, and souls imperiled."[6]

So the enemy, Lucifer, wants to put weeds right into the church. He worked to poison the heart of Judas. He works to bring about those "moral falls" and financial scandals that so pain a local congregation. It works to his advantage when a person sits in the pew as a believer, and yet is an unbeliever. In fact, Satan himself was the first "weed" in the heavenly church above, and look how patient God has been with him, allowing the devil these many centuries to work out his failed, fallen plan and demonstrate it to any who will watch and show sympathy.

So if this story has application to the church, then what is the church to do? The parable seems to say, "Hang in there. Be patient with the wicked. Don't kick them out." And yet we do kick them out. Frankly speaking, we don't want pedophiles running our Sabbath Schools. We don't want brazen liars and adulterers to be standing in the pulpit, or thieves to be managing the books. And there are other places in the Bible where God's people are told very clearly that some kinds of sin have to be dealt with.

Here is a hard and inescapable fact. There are times when the church must say to someone: "Friend, brother, sister . . . you are sinning. And it's a kind of sin that can't be in this fellowship." But there's a difference between saying, "You are sinning; you must leave," and saying, "You are lost; you must be destroyed."

Notice in the parable that when the weeds were gathered up and burned, God did that. He and His angels. Not the workers. Not the diocese or the presbytery or the Southern California Conference of Seventh-day Adventists. When people are declared lost, and when rebellious sinners finally meet their end and are no more, that grieving moment belongs to the Lord and not to fallible men.

Years ago I found on the Internet an actual sermon by one Pastor Martin Luther on this exact topic: "The Wheat & The Tares." He observes that there will always

91

be, along with true Christians and pure doctrines, "false Christians and heretics." He should certainly know, having himself been violently accused of being one. But the parable, he says, teaches patience and forbearance toward even heretics and false teachers.

"We are not to uproot nor destroy them," he writes. "Here [Jesus] says publicly let both grow together. We have to do here with God's Word alone; for in this matter he who errs today may find the truth tomorrow. Who knows when the Word of God may touch his heart? But if he be burned at the stake, or otherwise destroyed, it is thereby assured that he can never find the truth; and thus the Word of God is snatched from him, and he must be lost, who otherwise might have been saved."

Then he adds, again from agonizing personal experience: "What raging and furious people we have been these many years, in that we desired to force others to believe; the Turks with the sword, heretics with fire, the Jews with death, and thus outroot the tares by our own power, as if we were the ones who could reign over hearts and spirits, and make them pious and right, which God's Word alone must do."

Some thistles do need pulling

It's hard to stand back, isn't it, and let God be God? But this quiet countryside story by Jesus reminds us to do just that. And when it does painfully fall to us to do some necessary weeding even now, let's do it in the spirit of this following true story.

Pastor Richard Dortch was not as infamous as his former boss: Jim Bakker, fallen leader in the PTL scandal. After also spending time in jail for his part in the sordid church quagmire, he emerged from the pain and the punishment to write a couple of excellent redemptive books. In *Fatal Conceit,* he describes an experience he once had as the executive presbyter of the Assemblies of God denomination for a Midwest region. A church in his territory was experiencing political turmoil, and the pastor asked Dortch to come and attend a board meeting and see if he could help.

That wasn't his favorite thing, but Pastor Dortch agreed to drive down and sit in on the meeting. And as they got started that night, he could just sense an attitude of division, of unrest, in the room. *This church doesn't have things together,* he thought to himself. And sure enough. Not too far into the agenda, the group voted to spend a certain amount of money for some project in the church.

However, as people were lowering their hands, Dortch heard a large man sitting at the end of the table say right out loud: "I won't write the check."

Dortch had already figured out that this guy was the treasurer of the church, so this was a rather interesting statement to make. And after an awkward silence that hung right there in the room, the visiting Christian leader turned to him and said, "Excuse me. I thought I heard you say that you wouldn't write the check."

"Yes, I said it," the treasurer said. "I won't write the check to give that money they just voted on." And he stared insolently at both Dortch and the pastor.

Wow! It was a heavy moment, and the other board members held their breath. Maybe they were thinking back to this Matthew 13 parable by Jesus. Sitting right there in the board room, or "field," as the Savior put it, there was a poisonous weed or thistle among the wheat. Many good members and one rebel. So maybe the board members were thinking with a sigh, *This man's a stinker. He's always been a stinker. He disrupts everything. He ruins our harmony. He's holding us hostage to his every whim. But we just have to live with it until the end of time.*

So what happened? Dortch paused for just a moment as this man's rebellious statement hovered over the group like a cancerous cloud. "I won't write the check . . . and what are you gonna do about it, big shot?"

Finally Pastor Dortch spoke. There was no anger in his voice, no screaming, no tantrum. But this is what he said. "Well, sir, if that's the case, then we would be willing to accept your resignation. Your unwillingness to follow what the board has decided makes you unqualified for the office."

The man at the end of the table heard these strong words. They hit him in the face. They stung his pride. And after flushing red in anger, he stood up, pushed in his chair, and exited the room. He was gone. The weed was gone. The problem was gone. The division was gone. And the pastor said after the meeting, "Thank you, Pastor Dortch. That man had been bullying everyone on the board long before I became the pastor."[7]

Well, the human side of us says, "Right on! Go, Pastor Dortch!" to that story. We relate to that kind of good power, that quiet strength that pushes the bully to the side of the playing field.

But the Christian side of us, the Bible-reading side, the side that listens to the parables of Jesus, still says, "Uh, wait a minute! Why didn't that weed just get left where he was? Aren't we supposed to be patient with sinners, including the big, overbearing, check-writing kind?"

Again, we must concede this stark truth that, parables or no parables, no

Christian church is going to install a pedophile as a Sabbath School teacher. A pastor who has rampant, promiscuous affairs shouldn't be kept on as a marital counselor or as a man assigned to tutor young girls. There are some things that wisdom and common sense dictate. But in the ranks of every church in the world today are believers who struggle with lust, with alcohol, with pride, with tax improprieties, with chronic lying, with bossiness. How does the body of Christ know when to pull up a weed, and when to leave the weed right there in the field where it can do some lasting damage?

If you think this is a tough call, let me make it even more difficult. In 1 Corinthians 5, the apostle Paul writes to scold the young, fragile church there. Why? There's a man in the church, holding office in the church, sitting there in the church Sabbath after Sabbath. And this man is having an ongoing affair with his own mother-in-law. "That's a kind of sexual immorality that doesn't even occur among pagans," Paul writes in plain anger. And what does he say about letting this poisonous weed stay in the field? No way! "Get him out of there!" Paul writes, almost shouting with his pen.

Here's his response, as modernized in *The Message* paraphrase by Eugene Peterson. And consider this in light of the wheat and the tares. "I'm telling you that this is wrong," Paul advises. "You must not simply look the other way and hope it goes away on its own. Bring it out in the open and deal with it in the authority of Jesus our Master. Assemble the community—I'll be present in spirit with you and our Master Jesus will be present in power. Hold this man's conduct up to public scrutiny. Let him defend it if he can!" And take note of this next line: "But if he can't, then out with him! It will be totally devastating to him, of course, and embarrassing to you. But better devastation and embarrassment than damnation. You want him on his feet and forgiven before the Master on the Day of Judgment" (verses 3–6).

At the very end of the chapter, Paul quotes from Deuteronomy 17, where the children of Israel are told, "Expel the wicked man from among you" (1 Corinthians 5:12).

So what do we conclude here? Kick 'em out. Don't kick 'em out. Get rid of the weeds. Don't get rid of the weeds. What's going on here?

We have to be wise in reading stories, and here are two careful conclusions we can make. First of all, when a church kicks out an adulterer or a cheater or a rebellious treasurer, that action is not on a par with bundling up a pile of weeds to be burned. When the weeds are burned—an act reserved for God alone—that refers to eternal lostness. A weed that is burned up is a soul that is damned to be lost. You and I couldn't do that if we wanted to, although there have been tragic periods in the history of the Christian church when it tried to take on that role. In contrast, here Paul says explicitly that a man who sins in this flagrant, defiant way needs to be sent away from the church in the hope that he can eventually be redeemed. Verse 5: "You need to condemn this man's actions because, in so doing, you may be able to wake him up, turn his life around, and save his soul."

So the Bible teaches us that a Christian isn't to be permitted to coast along in a precarious way where his or her soul is in jeopardy. A person can't flagrantly live in adultery, for example, with the church, by its silent assent, saying to him, "You're all right, man. Grace is cheap; obedience isn't required; witnessing to others through our holy living isn't important. Sin away. We've got your back." The church cannot send that kind of message, either to its own people or to the watching community.

It's also true that the fragile flock in the church, the helpless lambs, do need to be protected. As much concern as we might have for a particular "weed" in the church, if it really is already to the point of poisoning others, through pornography or abuse or even just wrongful use of power like that treasurer was doing, then this principle of 1 Corinthians needs to be invoked. All through the New Testament, the church is warned that false teachers will come along. Jesus Himself, in Matthew 7:15, called such people "ferocious wolves" "in sheep's clothing" and said to watch out for them. We have a responsibility to make sure the lambs in our care are taught the truth and protected from lies.

Well, as we shut the barn door here and move to other stories, we still aren't always sure what to do with the weeds. We need an extra measure of wisdom; that's for sure. Just as farmers in their blue denim overalls are often out in the field on their knees, those of us working in the spiritual garden need to be on ours a lot too.

Chapter 6

THE LADY WHO WON
a Million Bucks

Hi, everyone. This is Connie Vandeman Jeffery, doing a guest editorial here!

I guess it's common knowledge that I'm the biggest *Who Wants to Be a Millionaire* fan here at the Adventist Media Center. Me and Donna Webb. We watch it every night. And then the next day at lunch, or during break, we're always going, "Did you see that guy who called his *mother* for a lifeline?" "Did you see that moron miss the two hundred dollar question? Unbelievable!" And at least three times a week we call the toll-free number to see who's going to get on the show first.

And then finally, about two months ago, I got on! They called me back after I qualified, gave me the next round of fastest-finger questions over the phone, and it was all stuff I totally knew. I mean, easy! And when one of the producers told me, "Connie, you're on!" I freaked out. Donna Webb and I were both dancing around the office. "We're going on the show! We're going on the show!"

Right before we headed to the airport, my son Craig said to me, kind of teasing, "If you see my friend Seth, who works at ABC in New York now, be sure to get that twenty bucks back from him." And I said, "What are you talking about?" And he got real—you know how teenage kids are with their moms, like we're idiots—"Seth. You remember, with the spiked hair." Then I remembered right away. We drove this high school senior clear from Camarillo down to the airport, three and a half hours round trip, stop and go all the way, and when we get to curbside, he just says, "Oh yeah, I forgot to get the gas money for you from my mom. But I'll try to give it to you later." And I said, yeah, right. No big deal, but it did kind of grind our gears the whole way home how he stiffed us.

Anyway, Donna and I had a marvelous flight to New York, flew right over the Statue of Liberty, went out to eat at La Bernardin, had a wonderful time. And when we got to the studios, it was just so much fun to be around all that showbiz stuff.

We were riding up in the elevator to where they do makeup, and there was the nicest lady in there with us. About my age, forty-five, Asian, and she had on a silk scarf that looked like it was maybe Chinese or Vietnamese or something. So I asked her, "Where are you from?" And she said, "Bangkok." She and her husband both worked in some kind of import-export business, came to New York about once a year. I asked her if they had a version of *Millionaire* in Thailand and she said yes, but she wanted to see the Regis variety. And as we got off she told me, *"Kor hai chok dee,"* which she said meant "good luck." Really sweet.

So I got my makeup on. Donna had a wireless mike, I had a wireless mike, and I was ready to go. They were finishing up with some contestant from the night before, he quit with $64,000, and we did a fastest finger. "Put these TV dramas in order, starting with the earliest." And I just hit them perfect: *"Bonanza, Lou Grant, Law and Order, West Wing."* Boom, boom, boom, boom. Three point four one seconds, my screen lit up, people were clapping, and I was on the hot seat three feet away from Mr. Regis Philbin himself. Behind me Donna was already smarting off, and kidding back and forth with Regis as only she can.

And we got started. First five questions, no problem. I was really sailing. Two thousand, four thousand, eight thousand, still all my lifelines. I finally polled the audience to get the $32,000 answer, and about 84 percent of them picked *D,* and I got it right.

After the commercial break, the $64,000 question was something I'd heard my older brother George talk about, so I got that correct. I got the next one myself, phoned my friend Ruth on the $250,000 one, and all of a sudden was down to two questions left, one lifeline remaining. Regis was really rooting for me to get it, Donna was going nuts behind me, like, "I get half!" and my heart was really pounding. Then, on the question for half a million, it was something about the Hunza people who lived in what is now Pakistan. Which my dad had talked about on the *It Is Written* program a hundred times. And before I could even think, we were up to the fifteenth question. One million bucks. My one million bucks . . . and I lose $468,000 if I miss.

And here it came. Something about the longest-reigning current monarch from Thailand. What's his name? And I didn't know. I had no clue. But I knew that Thai people always have really long names, and one name was short. So I didn't think that was it. And the *D* answer sounded more like Korean, and I didn't think that was it either. It had to be either *B* or *C*. So I used my last lifeline, the fifty-fifty, and, of course, it still left *B* and *C*. But I was thinking back, racking my brain, praying, everything I could think of, and it seemed like on a *Voice of Prophecy* program, the host had mentioned the king of Thailand. And maybe his name started with a *B*. I couldn't remember for sure, but the *C* answer was "Bhumibol." The *B* name, still up there, was something like "Vitiamyalaksana." Which was Thai-sounding too. But this was for a million bucks, and I was totally freaking out.

And then, all of a sudden—I don't know why—I remembered that Thai lady from the elevator. And just instinctively—I swear, I wasn't meaning to cheat or anything—but I looked over there. I could see her in the audience, out of the corner of my eye, giving a little motion to the right. She was just sort of giving a little point, to the right. Which would be *B*. And you know what? Even though I'd been leaning toward *C*, when I saw her point to the right, I said to Regis, "*B*. Final answer. *B*."

And there was this long pause. Like he always does . . . waiting . . . waiting. And just as he started to speak, something in my brain screamed, *NO! That lady was pointing to* her *left, which looked like right to me. So she meant* C! And Regis, his face kind of white, said to me: "No . . . Connie . . . I'm sorry. It was *C*. But you leave . . . with thirty-two thousand dollars."

And right at that moment—I was just dying, of course—a TV producer came charging out. "Hold it! Stop tape!" And right in front of everybody, with the cameras stopped, he told Regis: "There was a lady signaling. We got it all on camera three." And the place freaked out. They saw her signaling, and saw *me* seeing it.

So they took me in a back room—Regis Philbin and me and the producers—and began going over it. Did I know that lady? No, I just saw her on the elevator. Had we set up to signal each other? Obviously not, because I got it wrong. And that really had Regis bothered. He asked me, "Did you *intended* to get an answer from her?" And I didn't know what to say. No, not really. It didn't go through my brain, *She's from Thailand, she might know. Take a peek over there.* But maybe in my subconscious . . . I just don't know.

And finally, after about twenty minutes, Regis said, "Look, it's not her fault. And that lady in the audience obviously threw her off, maybe made her miss."

Which—I don't know if that's true or not—I probably would have just walked with $500,000. But he wanted to give me another shot at a million.

And you know what? That's what they did. They told the studio audience there had been an "irregularity." They set up another question, rolled the cameras again. And I couldn't believe it! We just did a radio program on *Voice of Prophecy* about the Julius and Ethel Rosenberg spy case, and here was the question: "Who was the prosecuting attorney?" The same guy who prosecuted Alger Hiss. And there was the answer: "A: Irving Saypol." I didn't even wait, I didn't use my lifeline, I didn't go into histrionics: I just said, "A, Regis. Final answer. A." One million bucks. Confetti, music, Donna was crying, everything. One million dollars. And as Regis hugged me, he whispered, "You lucked out, sweetheart. Don't forget that." And I told him: "I know." I was shaking so hard, I could barely breathe.

And now, get this. We get out to valet parking, where our Dollar Rent a Car is, and lo and behold, that kid Seth is the attendant! Sure enough. From Camarillo, California, with my twenty dollars, and he's getting the cars at the ABC network. And as he gives us our keys, I remind him of it. "Oh, hey. By the way, do you have that twenty dollars gas money you owe Craig and me?" And he kind of winces. "No, ma'am, not on me. I just started working here a week ago Tuesday and had to pay first and last month's rent." He looked in his pocket and said, "I've got, like, five. You can have it if you want." And I said, "No, come on. Twenty. Twenty bucks. We choked our way through the smog to LAX for you, and the agreed upon price was twenty bucks. Not five. Now have you got it or what?" And Donna kept saying, "Connie, forget it. Just forget it." But I didn't want to forget it. It had been a long, tense night, this dumb kid was still stiffing me, and I wanted my twenty bucks.

And then—we were in the exit for gate one—a limo pulled through gate two. And lo and behold, who gets out but Mr. Philbin. He says to the kid, Seth, "What's the problem here?" And he tells him: "This lady says I owe her twenty bucks. And I haven't got it. What shall I do, Reege?" He called him "Reege" like he's his uncle or something.

And Regis Philbin just gives me the longest hard look; I'll never forget it. He reaches in his pocket and pulls out a twenty-dollar bill and walks over and hands it to me. "You want twenty bucks?" he asks, his voice ice. "Here. Twenty bucks." And he pulls a cell phone out of his pocket and hits speed dial. As he climbs back into his limo I hear him say, real cold: "Get me the producer. *Now.*"

An earned-run average of infinity

If you owe your college roommate fifty bucks, you can probably scrape that together somehow and get even. If you've run up a debt of six million dollars, it might be a bit tougher. What recourse do you have, besides filing Chapter 11, if it turns out you're up to infinity in the red?

It's one of my favorite topics in college algebra. What happens when you divide by zero? The answer's not zero, by the way, and most calculators just flash up an LED "Error" message. Sometimes a teacher will say that "undefined" is the proper answer.

Actually, if you stop and dissect the situation, the correct reply is that you get "infinity" with a zero in the denominator. As the bottom number in your fraction gets smaller and smaller and smaller, the entire number, of course, gets larger and larger . . . and finally, just as your denominator gets to zero, it explodes into infinity. In theory.

In higher-level classes, such as calculus, where "limits" are a much bemoaned topic, students are always warned to not allow a denominator to even approach zero, and to label a solution as extraneous if it creates such a dilemma.

It was fun to notice, many years ago, that in a World Series game between the Dodgers and the Yankees, a Los Angeles pitcher named Bob Welch started Game 4 at Dodger Stadium, but didn't get a single batter out. Technically, then, his earned-run-average for that game, because he gave up four runs but didn't officially pitch even one-third of one inning—according to the formula his ERA was infinity. Not a good bargaining position for next year's contract!

Here's one more high-end math concept . . . and then we'll quickly flee to the relative simplicity of God's Word! If you had the numbers 2, 4, 6, and so on, going forever and forever—in other words, all the even integers clear out to the end of the number line—how many would you have? Well, infinity, of course. Wouldn't it be nice if they were dollars? But suppose your next-door neighbor has all the positive integers 1, 2, 3, 4, et cetera—not just the even ones, but all of them, going clear out to the end of the rainbow too—then does he have twice as much infinity as you do? Is there such a thing as infinity and double infinity, or infinity plus fifty? My daughter, Karli, who has a sheepskin proclaiming her a "doctor of philosophy" in these matters, tells me that there's actually an entire branch of higher mathematics, called *set theory,* developed by a German named Georg Ferdinand Ludwig Philipp Cantor, where these kinds of questions are kicked around by people wearing powdered wigs.

Well, what does this have to do with this very colorful Bible parable? A million dollars isn't infinity, although it's certainly close enough to satisfy most of us. And in this teaching story by Jesus, we find a lucky man who is essentially handed a monetary gift so huge that it's clear out there off the mathematical charts.

Here's the verbatim court transcript as told by the tax man Matthew himself: "The kingdom of heaven"—this is Jesus talking—"is like a king who wanted to settle accounts with his servants. As he began the settlement, a man who owed him ten thousand talents was brought to him" (18:23, 24).

Right away we have to call for a Brink's truck. *The Seventh-day Adventist Bible Commentary* ran the math on this, converting from talents and denarii into dollars, and suggested this number: $6,221,880.[1] However, that was in 1956, so those would be Eisenhower dollars. We're quite a ways down the inflation superhighway since then, and the NIV Bible text notes put this cryptic P.S. on the story: "Millions of dollars." This guy didn't just forget his lunch money three days in a row; he owes a whole bunch. He's seriously underwater, and the loan sharks are coming to get him.

By the way, he lived in a culture where you weren't allowed to file Chapter 11. Notice what he faces. "Since he was not able to pay, the master ordered that he and his wife and his children and all that he had be sold to repay the debt" (verse 25).

There's quite a bit in the Bible about the fact that this is frankly how things were. In 2 Kings 4, there's a similar scenario: "The wife of a man from the company of the prophets cried out to Elisha, 'Your servant my husband is dead, and you know that he revered the LORD. But now his creditor is coming to take my two boys as his slaves' " (verse 1).

In actual fact, Exodus 21 and also Leviticus 25 and elsewhere describe some of the rules God put in place while these wayward, spiritually childlike people worked their way through issues like divorce and slavery. Bond servants were to be treated kindly and fairly, and, in the seventh year, they were always given their freedom, regardless. But Jesus often told stories that reflected the political and social realities of the day—for good or for ill. We need to understand that as we read these stories. So here's a man who owes six million or so dollars, and, of course, he can't pay. As a result, he and his wife and his kids and his pet dog are all going to debtor's prison; in fact, they're sold into slavery as a means of at least paying down a few dollars on the debt.

Richard T. France, whose *Matthew* commentary in the Tyndale series is a magnificent resource when studying the parables, quotes from Dr. J. D. M.

Derrett's volume *Law in the New Testament,* which suggests that a man like this might have been the chief minister for a large province in charge of tax returns for an Asian emperor. In that case, being in arrears to the tune of six million bucks, or ten thousand talents, is an understandable dilemma.[2] In such a situation, being permitted to carry over the year's assessment into the next year might be a realistic plea bargain. In any case, here's what this man does when threatened with jail: "The servant fell on his knees before [the king]. 'Be patient with me,' he begged, 'and I will pay back everything.' " And here's the kicker to the story: "The servant's master took pity on him, canceled the debt and let him go" (Matthew 18:26, 27).

Wow! With one click of a computer key, or with one wave of the financial wand, the debt is erased. Isn't that something?

Before we continue on to part two of the story, several points should be observed. First, this man, this servant to the king, is an insider. It would be hard for a commoner, an average guy out on the streets, to run up a debt of six million bucks against his own king. There'd be no way to ever owe that much. So this person is in the inner circle, a trusted confidant. In our Adventist denomination, we might suggest—hypothetically, of course—that perhaps the General Conference president has run up some enormous debt against God, a big list of sins. Sometimes the greatest leaders have the biggest falls; have you noticed? And yet there is mercy even for the hypocrites sitting in the kitchen cabinet. Even when betrayed by a close friend, Jesus forgives. (Remember the story of Peter denying his own Lord, at the most crucial hour?)

But the second thing to take note of is this. This man essentially owes God infinity. Even if he's a delinquent tax collector, the money's gone. He's spent it, lost it . . . otherwise he'd pay up on the spot. Plus, now that he's being sold into slavery or imprisoned, how's he going to earn $6,221,880 from there? There's no way.

This is such an important lesson for us to learn, because even the most devout Christians in the world usually wake up in the morning and tell the Lord, "I'll pay up for my sins. Somehow I'll stitch together enough good deeds to earn a home in heaven. I'll set aside ten dollars worth of obedience right now, and then add to it when I can." That's the default mind-set for human beings: "I'll pay the tab myself." And we forget that the debt is infinite!

In the *Matthew* commentary, Dr. France gives us an interesting bit of insider information. In that culture, the "talent" was the highest form of currency in existence. In the Greek system, there were drachmas, staters, minas, and then talents. On top of that, ten thousand was really the biggest numeral they had. So Jesus, instead of trying to say $6,221,880, is really just saying "infinity." The biggest coin in the realm, multiplied by the biggest number on your abacus. That's how much this desperate official owes. And that's how much he's forgiven.[3]

So this is what each one of us needs to keep on our nightstand all the time. How much do I owe? Infinity. And, by the way, the biggest kind of infinity there is, superinfinity, if there are indeed gradations of that concept. I owe it all, man.

And then the good news is that *this is how much I have been forgiven*. Not ten thousand talents. Not six million bucks and change. No, infinity. What I have been forgiven cannot be calculated; it cannot be illustrated, it cannot be portrayed . . . and it most certainly cannot be paid back. Whether I'm sitting in debtor's prison or in Regis Philbin's hot seat as a permanent player who gets to hold a thesaurus in his lap, I cannot *ever* pay God back by my own efforts. No wonder my cousin Morris Venden refers to this as "super forgiveness."

The follow-up question, then, is this. Once I realize that fact, what should I do when I then meet a guy in the street who owes *me*? Every day of our lives, we forgive somebody, and then, half an hour later, we take it back. A day later, that trespass, that hurt, is still pounding in our brain and, ideally, we forgive again.

The flickering flame of forgiveness

Another question is this: according to this story, does God do that too? On-again, off-again, on-again, off-again?

I cracked up when I read this grim little story quoted out of the *Arizona Republic* magazine many years ago. A man named Terry Mikel was pulled over one bright sunny day by a highway patrolman who had a meaningful dialogue with him about the spiritual topic of velocity. How fast the man's car was going relative to the posted speed limits for that freeway. But the one-way conversation ended up in a Matthew chapter 18 kind of way; the Arizona policeman said to the naughty driver, "I'm going to let you off the hook. I am taking pity on you and canceling your debt."

Wow! Wonderful! Thank you very much! (We all know the feeling!)

"Well, that's all right," the officer said. "Now, listen, you slow down and drive safe." And, closing away his ticket book, putting his sunglasses back on, and adjusting the brim of his hat, the lawman began to walk back to his car.

Now get this. The speeder, the guy who's just been forgiven, Mr. Mikel, clears his throat and says to the cop: "Excuse me, officer, but you should say, 'Slow down and drive safe*ly*.' You said, 'Slow down and drive *safe*,' but 'safely' is really correct." *Safely* being the adverb form, modifying the verb *drive* and so forth and so on. He must have been a high school English teacher.

Well, guess what happened next? Without a break in stride, the policeman turned around, came back to the car, wrote out a seventy-two-dollar speeding ticket, handed it to Terry Mikel, and then drove off, flashing his red light authoritativeLY—speaking of adverbs. And that is a true story! You can file that little gem away under the category of "Stupid, stupid, stupid." Sometimes you just keep your big trap shut, and correct the grammar only of people who don't wear badges, carry guns, and wield ticket books.

And here in Matthew 18 we find the same thing happening again. A man is forgiven a huge debt running in the neighborhood of $6,221,880. So he drives down the highway rejoicing over his good fortune. "Thank God I am free!" he sings along with the car radio.

But exactly seven verses later we find that this same Mr. Lucky has had his own forgiveness taken away. It's gone! The debt is back on! The loan sharks and the sack-of-cement guys are on his case again with the "juice" or "vigorish" running at full tilt! And Jesus leans into us and says very firmly: "The king was furious and put the screws to the man until he paid back his entire debt. And that's exactly what my Father in heaven is going to do to each one of you who doesn't forgive unconditionally anyone who asks for mercy" (verses 34, 35, *The Message*).

Now, what's going on here? Christians everywhere cling to the belief that when a person is forgiven by heaven, the forgiveness is permanent! It's irrevocable! God never changes His mind! Or does He? Can we be happy if we're living with salvation that's on-again, off-again, on-again, off-again, like the faulty dome light in your car?

First, let's consider what this forgiven man did to lose his forgiveness. A man who owed his majesty ten thousand talents—essentially the largest monetary figure Jesus could come up with—has been forgiven the entire debt. It's wiped out! But what happens exactly seventeen seconds later in the story? "But when that servant went out, he found one of his fellow servants who owed him a hundred denarii" (verse 28).

The NIV text notes say, "A few dollars." Actually, it was a sizable amount—quite a few days' pay for a common laborer—but a mere pittance in comparison to the six million he'd just had erased on *him*. And what does he do to this nickel-and-dime friend of his? "He grabbed him and began to choke him. 'Pay back what you owe me!' he demanded. His fellow servant fell to his knees and begged him, 'Be patient with me, and I will pay you back' " (verses 28, 29).

Word for word, that's the speech this same man had just used on the king. But he doesn't see it that way *now*. The former charity is completely forgotten. Digging his thumbs into the other man's throat, he demands his money. Verse 30 tells how he responds to the man's plea for mercy: "But he refused. Instead, he went off and had the man thrown into prison until he could pay the debt."

And we see the cop getting his ticket book back out and saying to himself, "On second thought . . ." In terms of divine mercy and forgiveness, the Lord giveth and the Lord taketh away. Here's the end of the story: "When the other servants saw what had happened, they were greatly distressed and went and told their master [the king] everything that had happened. Then the master called the servant in. 'You wicked servant,' he said, 'I canceled all that debt of yours because you begged me to. Shouldn't you have had mercy on your fellow servant just as I had mercy on you?' In anger his master turned him over to the jailers to be tortured, until he should pay back all he owed" (verses 31–33).

On a human level, this story makes all the sense in the world. That's what scares us. A lot of Jesus' parables are filled with Heaven's mercy and what we sometimes call "the upside-down math of the kingdom"—but not this story. This story teaches fairness; we believe in fairness. It has a ring of "do unto others," and we nod our heads to that too. All it doesn't seem to have is the Christian gospel: forgiveness being an unconditional free gift. Because here's a huge condition. "*Forgive,* and you will be forgiven." Ephesians has it, "Be kind and compassionate to one another, forgiving each other, *just as* in Christ God forgave you" (4:32; emphasis added).

We're reminded of the fact that this little rejoinder is right in the Lord's Prayer too. Matthew 6:12: "Forgive us our debts, as we also have forgiven our debtors." Then Jesus adds a bit more tit-for-tat theology: "For if you forgive men when they sin against you, your heavenly Father will also forgive you. But if you do not forgive men their sins, your Father will *not* forgive your sins" (verse 14; emphasis added).

So how does this difficult story fit into grace and Calvary? Notice again that the man who was forgiven the large amount obviously hasn't grasped the enormity of what was given him. He was let off to the tune of *six million bucks*! How is it possible that he's choking his own underling, trying to get $11.31 from him? Richard T. France calculates the proportion between these two debts: ten thousand

PICTURES OF JESUS

talents versus one hundred pence. "Any limitation on the forgiveness [this servant] shows to his brother is unthinkable. The fact that the second servant's debt is *one six-hundred-thousandth* of the first emphasizes the ludicrous impropriety of the forgiven sinner's standing on his own 'rights.' "[4]

It was rather fun, leading into this parable, to let my old pal and broadcasting partner Connie Vandeman Jeffery pretend she had been a big winner on the now defunct *Who Wants to Be a Millionaire?* In our (unfortunately) fictional story, she wins a cool million bucks. And scores the million, by the way, with the help of some out-and-out charity, forgiveness from Regis Philbin. Then, fifteen minutes later in the parking lot, she's shaking the parking attendant by the throat and screaming, "Give me that twenty bucks you owe me!" Again I say, totally unadulterated fiction . . . and if you could meet Connie, you would instantly know it. She's a generous and unselfish sweetheart. But someone who gets out of that hot seat with a check for one million dollars, and then is obsessing about a twenty-dollar bill in the parking lot has a problem. Either he is the most stingy person in America, or it hasn't really sunk in that he is now a millionaire.

Here's the reality. We simply cannot be unforgiving if we truly grasp what God has done for *us*. It makes a mockery of Calvary if we go around trying to get twenty dollars out of each other, spiritually speaking, all the time. In fact, that mind-set almost reveals that we're still trying to pay off the original debt. In the book *Christ's Object Lessons,* Ellen White makes that very suggestion: "When the debtor pleaded with his lord for mercy, he had no true sense of the greatness of his debt. He did not realize his helplessness. He hoped to deliver himself. 'Have patience with me,' he said, 'and I will pay thee all.' So there are many who hope by their own works to merit God's favor. They do not realize their helplessness. They do not accept the grace of God as a free gift, but are trying to build themselves up in self-righteousness."

And what's the result of this delusion? "Their own hearts are not broken and humbled on account of sin, and they are exacting and unforgiving toward others. Their own sins against God, compared with their brother's sins against them, are as ten thousand talents to one hundred pence—nearly one million to one; yet they dare to be unforgiving."[5]

Getting a favor from the Don

The question remains, can Regis Philbin take back the million bucks you just won?

Have you ever found yourself adopting a "bean counting" approach toward forgiving someone in your life? "I'll forgive those jerks *one more time,* and if they mess up again beyond that, forget it! Never again!" Then we argue about how many beans. Seven? Forty-nine? Four hundred ninety?

Let's tackle this final issue by posing what is purported to be the easiest question in the Christian faith: how do you get forgiveness? That's it. How do you get God to forgive your sins? According to one of my favorite texts, 1 John 1:9, all you have to do is clear your throat and ask. "If we confess our sins, he is faithful and just and will forgive us our sins and purify us from all unrighteousness."

Well, that's wonderful. Thank You very much. But all of a sudden, here in this rough-and-tumble parable by Jesus, God does a total U-turn, and it sounds as if forgiveness is an extremely conditional thing. You have to jump through a flaming hoop called "Forgi*ving*" before you get to the reward called "Forgive*ness.*" "I won't forgive you," God says, "unless you forgive everyone around you."

That's hard to consider, isn't it? From a point of view of fairness, it makes sense. But we rather like it when the gospel doesn't make sense, when the deck is stacked our way. Like the Calvin in *Calvin and Hobbes* once asked, "Why can't things ever be unfair in my favor?"

A recent Tom Hanks film suggested that all important world questions can be answered out of the pages of the old crime story *The Godfather.* And perhaps this theological issue is important enough that we should go to the mattresses, too, so to speak, in addressing the question.

You may recall (and I salute you if you don't!) that Mario Puzo's story opens with an undertaker named Bonasera. His daughter has been assaulted by two New York City punks, and he comes to Don Corleone—on the wedding day of his daughter, when no true Sicilian can refuse a request—and asks Corleone, played by Marlon Brando, for vengeance. But the subtle thread underlying the exchange is very clear: he doesn't want a relationship with the Godfather. He just wants this disconnected favor. "I will pay you anything you ask," he pleads. But he's afraid to swear loyalty; he doesn't want to get involved in the Corleone empire's shady dealings. He doesn't want to risk friendship. In a spiritual sense, we would liken this to wanting forgiveness from God—but not a faith relationship with God.

In the story, the Godfather points this out. "If you were willing to be my friend," he says, "then this problem would be gone. The men who did this would be weeping already. Your enemies would become my enemies, and then—believe me—they would fear you."

Later in the story, the same scene plays out again. A film producer named Woltz refuses to be "in relationship" with Corleone and give the Don's godson, Johnny Fontane, a part in his new war picture. Even when the Godfather, as an incentive, offers to have some studio labor problems cleared up, he says No. No deal. But then he asks, How much would it cost me—in cash, right now—to just pay you to have my labor situation fixed? He didn't want the friendship, the relationship; he just wanted a noncommittal, no-strings-attached, transaction.[6]

I apologize for borrowing an illustration from such a dark story, except that it so explicitly portrays the attitude of this servant in Jesus' parable. Because his problem is our problem too. This man was very excited about receiving forgiveness from a good king. He was glad for the gift. But he did not want to be a part of this generous king's king*dom*—which was a kingdom of grace, of forgiveness.

Let me illustrate this concept another way, but first let's notice how the story begins. Peter asks Jesus a plain question: "Lord, how many times shall I forgive my brother when he sins against me? Up to seven times?" (Matthew 18:21).

The rabbis in Jesus' day, interestingly, taught that you had to forgive someone only three times, so Peter was very proud of himself, offering up a *seven* to Jesus. The perfect number, he might have been thinking. Double what the rabbis teach, plus one for good measure. "What a good boy am I!" And he was stunned by Jesus' answer: "I tell you, not seven times, but seventy-seven times" (verse 22).

Here's the interesting thing. Some translations put "seventy times seven" here, which, as a college math professor, I can assure you would be 490. And we seize on that as being the more impressive number. In the Tyndale New Testament Commentaries, Dr. France points out that, no, in both the Hebrew of Genesis 4:24, where Jesus gets this concept, and in the Greek right here, 77 is the correct number. But then he points out that if we get excited about 77 versus 490, we're falling into the exact trap Jesus is warning about! If we're "bean counting" at all, looking for a forgiveness discount, we're completely missing the point.[7]

"The defect in Peter's inquiry [about three versus seven] . . . was that the kind of forgiveness referred to in it was not from the heart, but rather a legal, mechanical kind of 'forgiveness' based on the concept of obtaining righteousness by works. How difficult it was for Peter to grasp the new concept of obedience from the heart, prompted by love for God and his fellow men!"[8]

In his terrific book *What's So Amazing About Grace?* Philip Yancey confesses his own bean counting tendencies. "I grew up," he writes, "with the image of a mathematical God who weighed my good and bad deeds on a set of scales and always found me wanting. Somehow I missed the God of the Gospels, a God of mercy and generosity who keeps finding ways to shatter the relentless laws of ungrace. God tears up the mathematical tables and introduces the new math of *grace*, the most surprising, twisting, unexpected-ending word in the English language."[9]

Here's the point—and it's so enormous that it's hard to articulate. Forgiveness from God isn't like a little stack of poker chips or Disneyland E-ticket coupons (back in the old days), where you have a certain number you can cash in. Forgiveness is, instead, like a kingdom, a wonderful, beautiful, new, perfect universe that you move to. God's grace is there: not like a few parceled-out drops, but like a mighty river. It washes endlessly over you. The fact that the king was willing to forgive this first man a debt of six million bucks illustrates that point. And you can only get forgiveness—*any* forgiveness, *all* forgiveness—by moving *to* this kingdom. You can't just go by a drive-through window and pay two dollars to get one sin forgiven. You can't bargain for just a bit of it from Don Corleone. You have to move to the kingdom and fully ally yourself with the Forgiver, and then allow all of Calvary to ceaselessly cover and envelop you.

And then this second point is there too. Others are also in that kingdom, in that mighty ocean of forgiveness. Not just you. God's forgiveness extends to them as well. It washes you; it washes them. And when you and I forgive others their trespasses, all we're really saying is that this is OK with us. "It's all right if God's grace extends to you too," we say to that person who hurt us, who injured us, who lied about us. "I get grace. You get grace. All God's children get grace." I don't think forgiveness is really anything more than letting other people get into the same river that we're in too. Giving their wickedness to God, allowing Him to deal with it any way He chooses to.

So Jesus tells this story. "My Father is willing to forgive you for *huge* things," He kindly says. "For your lifetime of sins." Then He adds this: "But that can happen only if you're also willing to let that get passed along to your peers, your friends, and your enemies. You are forgiven *as you forgive*."

This new kingdom, this swimming pool, or ocean, of forgiveness, is found all through the Bible. First John 4:11: "If God so loved us, we ought also to love one another" (KJV).

Matthew 10:8: "Freely ye have received, [Jesus says,] freely give" (KJV).

Maybe it sounds like rules or conditions. "God can't forgive you unless you forgive others," et cetera. But no. Really, all this story is explaining is the reality of this incredible kingdom built on relationship. And Jesus tells us: "Your only hope is to join the club, to get into the pool."

Here's a quotation from the much-loved book *Christ's Object Lessons;* notice how this reminds us of that "ocean of forgiveness" imagery. "We ourselves owe everything," Ellen White writes, "to God's free grace. Grace in the covenant ordained our adoption. Grace in the Savior effected our redemption, our regeneration, and our exaltation to heirship with Christ." Then she adds, "Let this grace be revealed to others."[10]

Just a paragraph or two later, we find the same picture again. "He who is unmerciful toward others shows that he himself is not a partaker of God's pardoning grace." He hasn't joined the club, we might say, or gotten into the swimming pool. "In God's forgiveness the heart of the erring one is drawn close to the great heart of Infinite Love. The *tide* of divine compassion flows into the sinner's soul, and from him to the souls of others. The tenderness and mercy that Christ has revealed in His own precious life will be seen in those who become sharers of His grace."[11]

Wouldn't you want to stand in the spray, the powerful current of that tide of divine compassion? And let others stand there too? I've got to tell you—it sure sounds like the kind of offer we can't refuse.

Forgetting we live in the kingdom of grace

Let me conclude with one more thought. It's a daily discipline to just *remember* that we now live in this kingdom of grace, in a place where both we and all those around us bask in the ocean of endlessly flowing forgiveness.

Picture this, though. It's a great, great morning, your first day in heaven, as you stroll down the golden avenue. And then, all of a sudden, you see Fred. Fred! That idiot! Back down on earth, his dog ran through your rosebushes. Repeatedly! Forgetting that you are now living in *heaven,* you begin screaming at him just like before. Oops!

I have an anonymous question for all of you married people. Have you ever had a midnight dream where you forgot that you were married? And in this dream you were out there in the social jungle again, trying to find a date for Saturday night? Then, all at once, it came flooding back: "Wait a minute! I'm already married! My wife is really nice, and she's sleeping here just seven inches away from me. What kind of foolish dream is this?"

Well, let's not analyze too deeply the Freudian implications of this illustration.

I have my own rather embarrassing story to tell on myself, going back about thirty-one years now. I was twenty-four when I first met Lisa, and it was a head-over-heels, foggy-night-full-moon experience. I mean, within five weeks of when I first laid eyes on her in church, we were engaged. Six months to the day, we got married, and the happy decades have just flown by.

But here's my truly dumb moment. About a week and a half after we had begun dating, I drove, alone, to my parents' place in Northern California to spend the Thanksgiving break. And already, Lisa and I were a serious item. She was The One. I had a picture of her in my wallet, there were steamy love letters in the glove compartment of the car, a box of cookies on the back seat. I thought her little girl, Kami, was the cutest thing in the whole universe. Lisa and I phoned each other every night. This was serious stuff, and even now the marriage altar was looming on the horizon. I told Mom and Dad: "I've met her. The hunt is over; she's the one. Start saving up for some really expensive wedding gifts."

Dad was pastor of the St. Helena Adventist Church at the time, so of course, we enjoyed a wonderful holiday Sabbath service there. But right after church, as we were all heading out to the parking lot, I happened to bump into an old female friend. Nothing serious had ever transpired between us, but what do you know? There was Cindy again! And *out of force of habit,* I said to her: "Well, hey, pretty lady. Nice to see you. Why don't we get together this evening, let me buy you dinner?"

"OK," she said. "It's a date."

An hour later, over Sabbath dinner, I mentioned to my mom that I was going out. And she got very perplexed. "What are you talking about?" she wanted to know. "I thought Lisa was The One. Wedding bells. Expensive presents. Commitment. Faithfulness. Love. Are you nuts?" Not those exact words, maybe, but she was genuinely confused. And I have to confess that I, too, was baffled by my own idiocy. "Oh, yeah," I groaned, smacking my own forehead with an I-coulda-had-a-V8 ferocity. "What was I thinking? Ack!" And you know, it was simply the momentum of my old dating habit. For years I'd been on the prowl. PUC coeds within a two-hundred-mile radius were always hiding and ducking my phone calls and inventing hair-washing alibis. But any girl who came along, I instinctively fished for a phone number, almost like the fictional Sam Malone, the bartender at *Cheers,* who was eternally looking for a girlfriend. It had been second nature for so long that I essentially forgot I'd now become a citizen, so to speak, of a new and better kingdom.

Well, to make a long story short, I phoned Cindy and babbled awkwardly, explaining the best I could. I extricated myself from the date, she frankly sounded relieved, and the rest is happy history. But in accepting the spiritual reality that forgiveness and grace are a brand-new kingdom we as believers must move to, often we just plain forget that we've gone there! We forget that we've moved into a house in the kingdom of grace. Even though we're "married" to this loving, forgiving Friend, we keep forgetting . . . and dialing up our old girlfriends back in the land of legalism and unforgiveness.

It's interesting that sometimes when the disciples asked Jesus a question, He would almost give a divine sigh. "Oh, come on, you guys," He would say. "Are you serious?" As if to say, "Are you still clear down *there*? We don't live there any-more!" He doesn't do that in this story, but He must have been tempted to when Peter asked Him, "Uh, Jesus, how many times should we forgive each other? Seven would be way enough. Right?" For Jesus to hear a question like that must have been like the man who went on a cruise ship, didn't understand that all the food was free, and packed along a whole stash of peanut butter sandwiches. It wasn't until the last day where a steward found this starving vagabond and said, "Are you serious? It's all free! It's all included! All these feasts, these banquets, these buffets! It's all included in the ticket price, which was already paid!"

I remember reading once how NBA players, who are all multimillionaires fly-ing first class and staying on the concierge level of five-star hotels, are tempted to take the extra bars of soap home with them. According to the gossip, Kurt Rambis, a very colorful player formerly with the Lakers, didn't just take the soap from his own room, but would mooch from next door, taking Magic Johnson's soap and Kareem Abdul-Jabbar's soap too. Because he forgot he was a millionaire! He forgot he was a Laker, living in the Laker kingdom of championship banners and generous seven-figure paychecks. Somebody once observed, "That's like a Rocke-feller clipping coupons."

And anytime we develop a hardened, unforgiving attitude toward those around us who are in the same ocean of God's grace as we are, we're just plain and simple forgetting that we are *in* that ocean. God is telling us in these verses, "You can't be in My swimming pool of forgiveness all by yourself. It's not just your pool; it's everybody's pool." And like I did on that Sabbath afternoon, when I realized that I already had a beautiful lady to love, a permanent date, we have to blush and say, "Oh, yes. I forgot. I forgot about grace. Please forgive me, Jesus, for forgetting."

And, of course, we have an enemy who wants us to forget, who wants to help us forget. Satan is always screaming in your ear: "You're poor! You're broke! You're destitute! You're not forgiven! Grab! Grab! Grab! Choke your neighbor over the five bucks he owes you! Devote your life to getting revenge!" So, every single day, we've got to just immerse ourselves in the ocean of grace, of forgiveness, and remind ourselves that this is where we live. "Forgive, and ye shall be forgiven." Or, even better put, "Forgive because you *are* forgiven."

In *What's So Amazing About Grace?* Yancey does a little bit of his own bean counting, or coupon collecting, or soap stealing for our consideration. "Hindu scholars have calculated with mathematical precision how long it may take for one person's justice to work itself out [according to *karma*]: for punishment to balance out all my wrongs in this life and future lives, 6,800,000 incarnations should suffice."

How about that for math? Would you rather struggle through 6,800,000 cold, sterile lives of self-improvement and revenge and bean counting, or simply bask in God's generous ocean of grace freely given *and* received *and* passed along to others? Yancey goes on with a cute metaphor: "Marriage gives a glimpse of the karma process at work. Two stubborn people live together, get on each other's nerves, and perpetuate the power struggle through an emotional tug-of-war. 'I can't believe you forgot your own mother's birthday,' says one. 'Wait a minute, aren't you supposed to be in charge of the calendar?' 'Don't try to pass the blame to me—she's your mother.' 'Yes, but I told you just last week to remind me. Why didn't you?' 'You're crazy—it's your own mother. Can't you keep track of your own mother's birthday?' 'Why should I? It's your job to remind me.' " Then Yancey concludes, "The inane dialogue bleats on and on through, say, 6,800,000 cycles until at last one of the partners says, 'Stop! I'll break the chain.' And the only way to do so is forgiveness: *I'm sorry. Will you forgive me?*"[12]

That brings it right down to the kitchen debate, doesn't it? Right close to home, where you're so angry with that spouse, that teenager, that coworker, that boss. Despite these stories of Jesus, it's so hard to forgive, and so sweet to hold a grudge. But it's a temporary sweetness, and we all know it. We've all proved it. Long term, an unforgiving spirit is going to destroy you. And besides, are our neighbor's trespasses really so different from our own? C. S. Lewis once advised, "To be a Christian means to forgive the inexcusable, because God has forgiven the inexcusable in you."[13]

By the way, do you know where Jesus got His famous number of seventy-seven here in this story? Back in Genesis 4, a great-great-great-grandson of Cain named Lamech was locked in bitterness. A young man had injured him, and he swore to get his revenge. But not just revenge: he was going to get even, he said, seventy-seven times over. "If Cain is avenged seven times"—remember that God promised vengeance "seven times over" to anyone who harmed this rebellious vagabond—"I'm going for seventy-seven."

And here in Matthew 18, Jesus quietly tells us a better way. It's a classic point-counterpoint spanning three thousand years. "No," He says. "Instead, *forgive* seventy-seven times." Which was His way of saying, "Don't count. Don't keep track. Get rid of your pathetic little pencil and your scorecard. Don't live down there. Move up here to My Father's kingdom instead, to this gentle ocean of grace and forgiveness. My lost, rebellious, red-in-the-face friend, please, come on home."

Chapter 7

THE COST
of Saving Private Ryan

The acrid smell of hot motor oil and Harley Davidson grease floated across the hot Mexico sky as Josh thumbed the "talk" button on his two-way radio. "Yo, Benji," he said, his voice scratchy from all the dust being kicked up by the bikes doing their wheelies and doughnuts. "You out there?"

"Right here, boss." The second in command guy for Team USA was a distant speck, about four hundred yards out, corralling some of the bikers. "We're about fifteen minutes from the green light."

"Well, I want our boys on the line in five," Josh told him. "Let's start getting in position right after I talk to them."

"Roger that." Josh could see Benji waving the American racers toward the team's designated rendezvous area. He motioned to the elite motocross participants standing next to him. "This is it, gentlemen," he told them. "Gather around."

Several bikers, fresh from topping off their tanks, rumbled to join the rest of the guys representing the United States. Josh picked up his portable megaphone and gave the team a quick pep talk. "This is a long, nasty ride," he told them. "Two hundred miles of the ugliest dirt and scrub brush I've ever seen. And even though we've got this enormous team—one hundred bikers and the best two-bangers money can buy—there's no telling how the race is gonna come out."

He could see a distant ESPN camera zooming in, trying to pick up his words. "Now, I know there's going to be some trail slicing happening out there this afternoon, but not by my guys." He resisted the temptation to glance over to where Greg, a tall, arrogant kid from Marin County, was refastening his gloves. A two-time champion, he had a reputation for cutting corners on his XK80, trying to shave twenty, thirty seconds off his score by leaving the trail and slicing through dangerous terrain. "I'm telling you, Benji and I have been over this trail ourselves, and there just ain't no way that the few extra seconds you save with a slice is worth the risks. The way bikers spread out across this piece-of-garbage two-hundred-mile track, you could wipe out. You could be injured. You could even just flat out get lost. The off-road terrain is that lousy. Just stay on the track, watch for the markers, and I hope we'll beat these other teams gold, silver, bronze. Best of luck to you, men. I mean that."

His last words were almost drowned out as a hundred motocross bikes roared to life, their high-pitched 125 cc whines a choir of angry bees. More than eight hundred cyclists, representing thirteen countries, packed into the long dirt corridor marking the start line. A local official from Monterrey, wiping his face with a little towel bearing the race logo, got ready to fire the starter's pistol.

"And they're off!" A TV camera on a minicam dolly got down low to capture the frantic scene of sixteen hundred rubber-shredding tires as they screamed out into the hot June desert. "Go USA," Josh said quietly to his lieutenant as Benji took off his sunglasses and vainly tried to dust them off. "Safely into harbor, boys." He added the last with real affection.

The team coleader grinned. "Think we'll win?"

Josh nodded. "Yeah." He relaxed a bit, now that the Kawasaki confusion had died down. "I just don't want to lose anybody out there in that lonely wilderness."

"Santana's the main one to worry about," Benji observed. "Kid's been trail slicin' for years. Everybody knows it."

"Yeah, well, I hope he ain't dumb enough to do it on this race," the captain responded. "I think these race guys imported some California rattlesnakes and stocked the desert with 'em. Just stay on the trail, I always say. Stay with the team." He glanced at his wristwatch. "Come on, let's go to the chopper."

It was a brief forty-five-minute ride by helicopter to Cabo San Lucas, where team sponsors had already begun setting up camp. Camera crews from FOX and ESPN were just starting to position themselves, even though the first finishers weren't due for a good two hours still. Remote camera feeds from along the trail showed that Team USA had two riders leading the way, with a hometown hero from Mazatlán holding a strong third position. The line of motorbikes had already spread out over more than four miles of trail, as dirtbikers carefully picked their way through the rugged Mexican terrain.

"Boy, the old hot tub is gonna feel good tonight," Benji sighed later, rubbing a sore place on his arm where the ruptured upholstery in the chopper had failed to protect him. "And the guys'll enjoy the banquet." Nike and Honda were picking up the tab for a huge fiesta party for all the motocross teams. And both team leaders had been assigned to comfortable suites in the plush resort hotel just outside town. It would be a relaxing end to a tension-filled day.

"They're comin'!" A spotter for CNN, high on his lookout tower, had his binoculars out and was motioning. "I think USA is in front. But it ain't Carmichael. Wow!" Race officials scrambled for good positions at the finish line and waited anxiously as the first distant whine of the motorbikes was heard.

In the dusty confusion, it was hard to see jersey numbers, but the American team did indeed score a photo finish. The first two bikers to cross the line had on the red, white, and blue helmets of Team USA, and the sports networks flashed the results: 29, Dicky Bennett, and 95, Jamaal Jackson, edged out a Canadian biker from British Columbia, who had to settle for the bronze medal, with Mexico coming in fourth. Over the next forty minutes, more and more bikers came into view and gunned past the camera crews and over to the huge booth where Gatorade and PowerBars were being dispensed.

"Pretty sorry finishers," a TV gofer with a headset smirked as the last few stragglers limped into town an hour later. A couple of American riders, their bikes obviously damaged and missing on one cylinder, coughed out a finish to the two-hundred-mile course, and Josh took out his team score sheet and ticked off their names.

"Are our chickens all home?" Benji wanted to know. "Gotta be. There ain't anybody else still out there; no way. Not this late. Come on, boss man, let's party."

"Hang on." The older man scanned the sheet again, concern on his face. "We're down one rider still."

"Are you sure?" Benji looked at the setting sun. "We're coming up on four hours plus. Come on, Josh, they're here."

"No." Josh showed him the sheet. "We got ninety-nine in, and still one man missing."

"Who? Or have you got that tracked?"

The tall American tried to keep his voice even. "Greg."

"What!" The assistant coach took off his hat and flung it angrily in the dirt. "Santana! I knew it! That jerky kid went out and trail sliced. I betcha fifty pesos, boss. After everything you told the guys, he went right out and cut corners."

117

Josh motioned to one of his best riders, a New York boy who had finished in the top thirty. "Guzman, did you happen to spot Santana out there?"

The rider reacted instinctively, not meaning to, then tried to hide it. "What about him?"

"Did you see him?" Josh's voice was no-nonsense. "This is serious."

The muscular athlete hesitated. "He sliced off a huge piece of dirt way back around mile eighty-five. There's this big, big loop to the right, and the terrain going straight was unbelievably torn up, but I saw him leave the trail and go right at it. There was a great big bunch of boulders, cactus, real ripped up stuff, but he was running something like fortieth at the time—just ahead of me—and I guess he figured he could make up most of it right there. Take the lead even, maybe." He looked from one team leader to the other. "Why? What's going on? I know he didn't win."

"Didn't even show," Benji informed him. "Crazy guy's still out there somewhere."

"That's a drag," the New York boy grunted. "But he'll turn up. Another guy from Bay Area said that Santana has done this before, cheatin' the course, going his own way. He either comes in first, or he doesn't hike into camp till the next day, seems like."

The American cocaptain shook his head in resentment. "You know what, boss?" he said. "Let's just forget him. There's a couple of plates full of tacos and Mexican refrieds just waitin', plus all the ice-cold soda we can chugalug. Then a hot tub with your name on it. Let Santana walk one hundred fifteen miles to camp if he's that stupid. No kidding." Benji had clearly lost all patience with the rebellious motorcycle rider.

Josh hesitated, then shook his head. "I can't do that," he replied. "Greg might be injured out there."

"No way," Benji dismissed the thought. "I don't think so, boss. This kid just does his own thing and then comes home when he feels like it. I think he's just pulling our chain, frankly." He took a few steps toward the amphitheater where a mariachi band was striking up some lively music. "Come on, Josh, let's eat. It's a hot night in México, we got ninety-nine riders safely home, and I honestly don't care about one kid, Mr. Stupid, missing the party. It's time to cha-cha-cha."

Josh didn't respond. Motorcycle riders streamed past him, carelessly heading toward the comforts of the fiesta and the fun. Soft Marriott beds, satellite movies on Showtime, and relaxing soaks in Jacuzzi tubs awaited them. Without looking back, he went over to the Team USA jeep and climbed in. The silvery moon cast its lonely shadows across the foreign landscape as he slowly drove out of town and began to retrace the route, looking for his one lost biker.

Because Mama loves her son, that's why

It does not make sense, economically, to leave ninety-nine sheep alone and go chasing over hill and dale after *one*. It equally does not make sense, in World War II, to risk the lives of eight guys, just to go fetch one lowly private from Payton, Iowa, and make his mama happy.

"Is this mission worth it?" Those five words sum up one of the most wrenching cinematic war stories of all time. A Private Richard Reiben, twenty-four years old, from Brooklyn, New York, asks the question all the men are inwardly thinking. "You know, Captain," he says, "this little expedition goes against everything the army taught me. The math of it. Maybe you could explain it to me. Strictly just talking arithmetic here, what's the sense, the strategy, in risking eight lives to save one? I mean, it's not like we're goin' in to save Eisenhower or Patton or something. The guy's a [lowly] private, sir."

Captain John Miller—if you've read the book by Max Allan Collins or seen the Spielberg film *Saving Private Ryan*—has been assigned, along with seven other soldiers, to go directly into the war zone and bring this kid, Mama's fourth and only surviving son, home from World War II. And so the private from New York asks the obvious: Why risk eight guys to possibly—and only possibly—save one? Ryan might have already been killed in action. Why hike through ambush territory, why go across enemy lines, why risk hiking directly into the gun sights of German snipers, to save a soldier you've never met? And who's probably already dead?

Early on in the expedition, when they get to Neuville-au-Plain, a German sniper named Wolfgang Gottberg picks off Caparzo, one of Miller's boys, who slowly bleeds to death in the rain. Later, as the remaining seven men encounter another sniper's nest out in a field and wipe it out, they lose another man, Wade, their medic. He dies in their arms, a wrenching, agonizing loss. And at one point, Captain Miller says to one of his fellow officers, "This Private James Francis Ryan better be pretty special. He better get home and cure cancer or invent a lightbulb that never burns out or a car that runs on water. Because the truth is, I wouldn't trade ten Ryans for one Caparzo."

And finally, in Ramelle, when they find Private Ryan and insist that he leave his post and return home with them—which he devotedly refuses to do—this Private Reiben screams at him in anger: "Hey! Two of us died buyin' you this ticket home! *Take* it! I would." And the farm boy from Payton, Iowa, is staggered by the news. "You lost two men just coming to save me?" He can hardly believe it.[1]

Well, those are the horrors of war. Eight men dying to rescue one. One man giving his life that another might live. "Greater love hath no man than this . . ." and so on. And threading its way through all such stories is an old Bible parable told by Jesus. You can find this story in both Matthew and Luke, and as we explore it together, we'll move back and forth between the two. Not just because the details are slightly different, but also because the context is different and we learn new lessons from both settings. For now, here's the way an army medic, in this case Dr. Luke, would tell the story: "If you owned a hundred sheep, wouldn't you be concerned if one of them was missing?" Jesus asks (15:4, *Clear Word*).

Remember that Jesus told stories that were beautifully designed to be received by the audience of His day. Who was out there in the crowd listening? Shepherds, of course. And it's been pointed out that the listeners that afternoon might also have included wealthier men who had financially invested in flocks and herds. So these people knew about the value of one lost sheep. *The Seventh-day Adventist Bible Commentary* makes this point about the seemingly insignificant one-out-of-a-hundred math involved here: "The loss of one might seem a comparatively small matter, but to the owner of the flock the loss of even one occasioned serious concern. . . . The Eastern shepherd commonly knew each sheep personally and cared for it not only as one of the flock but for its own sake."[2]

Now that He has their interest, Jesus asks the question: "Wouldn't you leave the ninety-nine who are peacefully grazing in someone else's care and go looking for that one lost sheep until you found it? When you found it, what would you do? You would lay it across your shoulders and come back singing. Then you would tell your friends and neighbors that you found the lost sheep, and they would celebrate with you" (verses 4–6, *Clear Word*).

And there you have it. The good shepherd in this story ignores the normal math of *our* lives: that having 99 percent of your inventory safely in the barn is typically enough. Most guys who look after flocks would be delighted to have all but one sheep safely home. Frankly, any merchant in town who opens up his shop knows that he's going to sacrifice 2.5 percent on every single sale just for letting people swipe their Visas and their Mastercards through his slot. Those losses are part of the game. Shoplifters are going to rip you off for 2 or 3 percent; you order fries at McDonalds, and a few of them always fall on the floor. Early on in *Saving Private Ryan,* as the men at Normandy are getting ready to storm Omaha Beach in their LCVPs, they're openly predicting that two-thirds of them won't come out of it alive. Those are the fixed costs of waging war. And here a shepherd is worried about one lost sheep? With all due respect to the nomadic sheepherders of Jesus' day, come on. Let's get real.

But we keep going back to that text note by the Bible commentators: "The Eastern shepherd commonly knew each sheep personally."

You see, this particular Shepherd knows this particular sheep. Knows it by name. Has taken care of it from the moment of its birth. Has had an interest in it from the very beginning. "I have called you by your name; you are Mine," He tells us in Isaiah 43:1 (NKJV). As God counts up His sheep at the close of the day, He instantly knows that this particular lamb is missing.

And then this dilemma: what to do? We've always painted a graphic picture of that decision: a delicious meal at home, a warm bath, and a comfortable bed . . . or a night of searching out in the cold, lonely hills.

Perhaps we think of this story as little more than a metaphor. Ninety-nine sheep in the fold. One missing. What to do? But this fierce dilemma was faced by Jesus Christ, up in the comfortable splendor of heaven's courts centuries before this little story in Luke ever got written. God had so many worlds . . . and then one got away from Him. One planet spun itself out of God's orbit and found itself out in the galactic wilderness of sin. Just one soiled little planet in an otherwise pristine, perfect universe. And heaven was a warm, elegant place for the Son of God to live. Why go where it was cold? And dirty? And hostile? Why go out among the briars of Lucifer's tiny domain to rescue just one insignificant world? Better to stay home where the ninety-nine billion unfallen worlds are bowing low and singing Your praises.

In *Christ's Object Lessons,* Ellen White paints the picture for us: "This world is but an atom in the vast dominions over which God presides, yet this little fallen world—the one lost sheep—is more precious in His sight than are the ninety and nine that went not astray from the fold. Christ, the loved Commander in the heavenly courts, stooped from His high estate, laid aside the glory that He had with the Father, in order to save the one lost world. For this He left the sinless worlds on high, the ninety and nine that loved Him, and came to this earth, to be 'wounded for our transgressions' and 'bruised for our iniquities.' "[3]

Jesus didn't just tell the story to describe, in theory, how much God cares. He was living right in this story *at the moment He was telling it*. He doesn't make a big deal about it in the telling, but He could so easily have said right then: "Folks, this is where we are right now! I'm clawing My way through the ravines of Satan's territory this very moment as I speak to you, trying to reclaim for My Dad this one planet that slipped away."

In *Saving Private Ryan,* this kid Reiben would be right. Do you spend eight guys to save one? Of course not. Don't be stupid. You don't win wars that way. A man is a man is a man, and you don't trade a Caparzo and a Wade for one Ryan. It'd be like sacrificing both rooks, a bishop, and a queen—all for one pawn.

The only telling factor, then, to upset the normal math of the battlefield, is this: back home in Payton, Iowa, is Mom. Mrs. Margaret Ryan loves her son. Mrs. Bixby of Boston, if you remember the letter from Abe Lincoln to a grieving mother, loved her five sons. And when a parent's love is involved, you can take all the math in the universe and just throw it out. Love beats numbers every time. There are a lot of pretty poems about man's search for God. And perhaps you have read some books or slipped into the back of a darkened chapel or scanned the radio dial to find the voice of a preacher. But the wonderful fact is that it's God who looks for us.

The mouse looking for the cat

That actually reminds me of one of the greatest chase stories ever recorded, although I don't suppose Hollywood will ever make a high-octane, tire-screeching film about it in the genre of *The Fast and the Furious* or *The French Connection*. But in his autobiography *Surprised by Joy,* C. S. Lewis tells how he was the object of an intense manhunt. He was the chased, not the chaser, and it got to where, as the quarry, he was firmly in the enemy's sights. There was no escape.

Chapter 11 is titled "Check," and then, right near the end, chapter 14, is the one-word title "Checkmate." "My Adversary began to make His final moves," he writes.

Now, young Jack Lewis was a determined atheist. He was happy as an atheist. He was devoted to being an atheist. He tried to organize his thoughts around atheistic concepts and ideals. But, in the background, in the lurking shadows of his scholarship and his reading and his midnight reflections, he began to fear that God was, after all . . . well, God. God was his Creator, his Ruler. He could close his eyes and try to block it out, but God was still out there. And God was making His move. Lewis finally came face to face with the reality that God simply *was.* "I am the Lord." Or, more simply, "I am."

And he makes this confession: "People who are naturally religious find difficulty in understanding the horror of such a revelation. Amiable agnostics will talk cheerfully about 'man's search for God.' " And what a telling metaphor Lewis uses! "To me, as I then was, they might as well have talked about the mouse's search for the cat."[4]

So, in terms of a DreamWorks movie, Lewis was roaring down the interstate, weaving in and out of traffic, going the wrong way on one-way streets, cutting corners, trying to get away . . . and God was after him. God was chasing, desperately searching for the heart and soul of this brilliant but confused atheist. And He finally rescued him. Morris Venden tells about the man who stood up in a revival meeting, and with tears in his eyes, said, "All my life God chased me and chased me . . . and He finally got me."

This points out the most important truth in Jesus' parable of the ninety-nine sheep. The Shepherd goes out looking for the one lost sheep; the lost sheep is not looking for the Shepherd. This tender Person with the rod and the staff and the oil of comfort to put on the sheep's head, this gentle Caregiver with the strong arms and the caressing hands takes the initiative by going out into the gloom to find His one lost sheep. "If a man has a hundred sheep," Jesus asks, "and just one of them gets lost, doesn't he leave the others at home and personally go out and search everywhere to find that one lost sheep?" (Matthew 18:12, *Clear Word*).

The Seventh-day Adventist Bible Commentary for Matthew makes this point so well. "God has taken the initiative in effecting man's salvation. Salvation consists, not in man's search for God, but in God's search for man. Human reasoning sees in religion nothing more than human attempts to find peace of soul and to solve the mystery of existence, to find a solution to the difficulties and uncertainties of life. It is true that deep within the human heart there is a longing for these things, but man of himself can never find God. The glory of the Christian religion is that it knows a God who cares for man so much that He left everything else in order to 'seek and to save that which was lost' (Luke 19:10)."[5]

It's true that many a person in the gutter has said to himself or herself: "I need something better. I need God." And yes, they get up and stagger to the nearest chapel. But who put that impulse in their hearts? Who directs their steps to the chapel? Who puts a loving preacher or friend in that chapel at the right moment? Let's never think that we can get from the wilderness of lostness back to the fold by ourselves. It has never worked that way, and it never will.

This isn't to say that the lost sheep isn't aware that it's lost. It knows that it's lost. Theologians sometimes point out that in this parable, the sheep represents people who are lost—and know it—and the lost-coin parable, which follows right after in the Luke 15 trilogy, is a metaphor for people who are lost and *don't* know it. In both cases, God comes looking. But most of us who find ourselves out in the weeds of iniquity, of loneliness, know full well that we're lost! We know we're a long way away from the safety of God's house. But our attempts to find our own way home are doomed to fail. The same commentary adds this thought: "The fact that the sheep became lost was evidently due to its own ignorance and folly," they point out, and we might sometimes add, rebellion. Some of us just plain stomp out into the woods. "And once lost it seemed completely helpless to find its way back. It realized that it was lost, but knew not what to do about this. The one lost sheep represents both the individual sinner and the one world that has been lost. . . . This parable teaches that Jesus would have died had there been but one sinner . . . , as He did die for the one world that had sinned." Then, just a bit later in the text, they add, "Left to ourselves we might seek for Him throughout eternity without finding Him."[6]

Some of the world's great religions mark out a map for men and women to try to find God, to make their own way home. *But the Christian story is this parable right here.* We're lost. We can't get home. And God comes to find us. Corporately, globally, that is the Calvary saga, of course. God coming to rescue this one planet through the gift of His Son. And then for each of us, for you and for me, the Father shows this same initiative.

In *Christ's Object Lessons,* Ellen White has some heart-stirring things to say about the status of this lost sheep. In the chapter " 'This Man Receiveth Sinners,' " she writes, "The soul that has wandered away from God . . . is as helpless as the lost sheep, and unless divine love had come to his rescue he could never find his way to God."[7]

And of course, the Shepherd knows our helplessness. He's not angry; He's not impatient. He knows we are but sheep. And how does He respond, knowing our situation? The same writer adds, "The darker and more tempestuous the night and the more perilous the way, the greater is the shepherd's anxiety and the more earnest his search. He makes every effort to find that one lost sheep."[8]

I've had encounters with people who describe to me horrific scenes of their own lostness. I mean, they are *miles* out there in the forest. They're in the deepest of spiritual ravines. All that means is that Jesus is even more eager to find them.

THE COST OF SAVING PRIVATE RYAN

The deeper the pit, the more desperate His search, and the more complete His dedication to the journey.

And if you and I can't find our way back home, what *can* we do? What is our role out there in the tall weeds with sin and the snakes? Ellen White shares this remedy: "Every one that will *submit* to be ransomed, Christ will rescue from the pit of corruption and from the briers of sin."⁹

It's possible that the lost little lamb was too small and too weak to protest, if it even wanted to, when the strong Shepherd scooped it up and carried it back home. But it's reality that if you and I say, "No! Go away! I *wish* to be left alone! I choose this ravine and these rags and these rocks!" the Rescuer would sadly return home empty-handed. We have to submit; we have to climb into His net and allow Him to pull us to safety.

Here's one more encouraging thought from Ellen White: "Desponding soul, take courage, even though you have done wickedly. Do not think that *perhaps* God will pardon your transgressions and permit you to come into His presence. God has made the first advance. While you were in rebellion against Him, He went forth to seek you. With the tender heart of the shepherd He left the ninety and nine and went out into the wilderness to find that which was lost. The soul, bruised and wounded and ready to perish, He encircles in His arms of love and joyfully bears it to the fold of safety."¹⁰

Wouldn't you like to find yourself in those arms right now? To know that Jesus loves you and is even now carrying you home to the Father? This is the only time I can think of where the other person says, "Checkmate" . . . and you win.

A lesson for the good sheep back home

But let's also spend some time considering the spiritual condition of the ninety-nine other sheep! What about them? We spend a lot of time wringing our hands over the "one lost sheep." But what about all the good sheep who stayed close to home, who didn't wander off? What should we be doing while the Shepherd is fifty miles away in the darkness, rescuing our naughty little brother?

Have you ever gotten really excited about a sermon that so-and-so sitting two pews back really needed to hear? *Man, I hope they're getting this!* you think to yourself, almost risking a glance behind you to make sure the preacher's fiery darts are hitting their target and that Mr. Stupid isn't dozing through the spiritual barrage. Which, of course, he always is.

My old writing pal Steven Mosley passes this story along in his book *A Tale of*

Three Virtues, and he discovered it in the great biography *Moody,* by J. C. Pollock. "During one long preaching tour [Dwight L.] Moody was traveling by train with a singer named Towner. A drunk with a badly bruised eye recognized the famous evangelist and started bawling out hymns. The weary Moody didn't want to deal with the man and suggested, 'Let's get out of here.' Towner told him all the other cars were full. When a conductor came down the aisle, Moody stopped him and pointed out the drunk. The conductor gently quieted the man, bathed and bandaged his eye, then led him back to a seat where he could fall asleep."

Most of us would label the drunk guy in this story the one lost sheep, although Moody finds himself in another of Jesus' parables instead. The story concludes, "After reflecting on all this for a while, Moody turned to his companion. 'Towner, this has been a terrible rebuke for me! I preached last night to that crowd against Pharisaism and exhorted them to imitate the Good Samaritan. Now this morning God has given me an opportunity to practice what I preached, and I find I have both feet in the shoes of the priest and Levite!' " Then Mosley adds, "Moody included this story *against himself* during the rest of the tour."

It's a terrific tale, and Mosley sums up with this great tribute about Moody: "This man who could shoot straight about sin and salvation to receptive crowds on both sides of the Atlantic could also respond humbly when God shot straight at *him.*"[11]

It's an interesting sidelight how Moody's sidekick musician, Ira Sankey, found the words to this poem "The Ninety and Nine" written six years earlier in 1868 by an Elizabeth C. Clephane. He'd spotted the poem in a British newspaper, tore it out, and stuffed it in his pocket. Later that very same day, in Edinburgh at the nightly meeting, Moody turned to him and abruptly asked for a closing song. So the story goes, the Holy Spirit reminded him of that poem in his pocket, he pulled it out, breathed a prayer, and composed the tune to "The Ninety and Nine" as he sang! It was his very first attempt at hymn writing!

We have to actually critique Mrs. Clephane for her lyrics, though, because as she puts it: "There were ninety and nine that safely lay, / In the shelter of the *fold.*" And quite frankly, the Bible doesn't say it that way. In the King James, in both Luke and Matthew, Jesus describes the ninety-nine sheep being left "in the wilderness," as the Shepherd goes to find the lost sheep. In the NIV: "Suppose one of you has a hundred sheep and loses one of them. Does he not leave the ninety-nine in the open country and go after the lost sheep until he finds it?" (Luke 15:4). The *Clear Word* paraphrase takes a bit of license by suggesting it this way: "Wouldn't you leave the ninety-nine who are peacefully grazing *in someone else's care?*" (emphasis added).

The bottom line, certainly, from a spiritual point, is this: there are times when God's faithful children have to stand by while God gives a lot of attention to lost and wandering sinners. Sometimes the most faithful saints seemingly don't have their prayers answered. Sometimes they don't seem to get the same generous blessings that degenerate rebels appear to get. And we wonder, "God, what's going on? Where are You?"

That's not to say that God can't multitask and do two things at a time. He certainly can. But is it possible that sometimes God says to His church: "Nurture each other. Care for each other. Stay together; press together; stay in unity, you ninety-nine saints. I'm going to be on a search mission, but you carry on doing the Lord's work"? And He trusts that the ninety-nine of us can hold things together while He seeks and saves the lost.

With that in mind, let's study the biblical backstory, as they say, and find out why Jesus is even talking here about leaving ninety-nine sheep stranded on a hillside while He goes into the deep weeds to find the hundredth. Here in Luke 15, Jesus has just been stung by a bit of criticism. "Now the tax collectors and 'sinners' were all gathering around to hear [Jesus]. But the Pharisees and the teachers of the law muttered, 'This man welcomes sinners and eats with them' " (verses 1, 2).

In response, Jesus immediately tells this story. It's obvious from the setting that He isn't just telling us how the Father feels about lost sinners. He's also telling us how *we,* the church, the ninety-nine good sheep that didn't stray away, should feel about the lost sheep too! We think immediately about another story Jesus told—in fact, it's also right here in Luke 15, the third parable in the trilogy—where the younger brother, the prodigal son who was lost, finally comes home. And the attitude of the older brother who faithfully stayed by is an important part of the story. So the ninety-nine sheep are very central to the lesson Jesus wishes to teach us here.

The Seventh-day Adventist Bible Commentary has this to say: "The parables of [chapter] 15 emphasize God's care for those whom men often despise, His efforts to win their confidence, and His joy when they respond to His appeals."[12]

Are there people we think aren't fit for God's kingdom? People we hope are listening to the sermon? Drunks on the train who we think are living on the very edges of God's grace? Certainly there are. And God has a few things to teach us twenty-first-century Pharisees.

The Seventh-day Adventist Bible Commentary also makes this astute observation: "The rabbis taught that the sinner must repent *before* God is willing to love him or pay any attention to him. Their concept of God was all too frequently what Satan wanted them to think about God. They conceived of Him as One who bestowed His affection and blessings upon those who obeyed Him, and who withheld these from men who did not. In the parable of the Lost Son . . . Jesus endeavors to set forth the true nature of the love of God."[13]

The Pharisees considered it the task of the sinner to come to God, to find God. "Repent, and then maybe God will forgive you" was their tight-lipped sermon every Sabbath of the year. And this story turns that teaching on its head, as Jesus says, "No! The Shepherd comes looking for the sheep! That's how My Father feels about the lost! And how I feel about the lost! And how *you* ought to feel about the lost too!" In *Christ's Object Lessons,* Ellen White concurs: "We do not repent in order that God may love us, but He reveals to us His love in order that we may repent."[14]

Now one final point. This story is also found in Matthew 18, and the minute we hear the term "Matthew 18," many Christians immediately think of one thing. You've had a fight with a fellow believer, an argument, a disagreement. And the pastor of the church immediately says, "Brother, have you followed the rules of Matthew 18?" I've said that to others and have had it rather forcefully said to me. Are we following the principles of Matthew 18?

And what does Matthew 18 teach? A method for reclaiming someone about to lose his way over sin. First, you go to him alone. You don't gossip it to the whole church; you don't put it on the Internet; you don't tweet all over town about it. You go to him alone, in an effort to rescue him. If that doesn't work, you take one or two other people with you. If that doesn't work, you involve the whole church in this reclamation project. And finally, regretfully, if even that doesn't work, you sadly permit the sheep who has determinedly walked away . . . to *stay* away.

What a huge lesson this is! And what an indictment of how we usually operate! Christians remember with reluctance the regulations of Matthew 18 and almost always forget that this precious, poignant story of the one lost sheep is right there next to it! The two are really parts of the same story! God is forever and always gently reclaiming lost sheep, and when someone sins, we should always do likewise.

We do glean one more powerful truth from the blood-soaked shores of Normandy. John Miller's small band of brothers was required to make a supreme effort to save the one missing man.

An all-out rescue attempt

Here's a parallel scenario. Your own child is dying. And only a herculean effort—all your money, all your work, all your waking hours, all your prayers and pleadings—can save her. Would you do it? Would you give the 110 percent? All three parables of Jesus in Luke 15 reveal a God who goes *all out* just to save one sinner.

A tension-packed first-person story in the July 2000 issue of *Reader's Digest* told of a man named Rick Murdock who abruptly found himself in a fight for his life. In August of 1995 he noticed an enlarged lymph node on his neck; after several months of procrastinating and putting it off and being bugged by his wife, Patty, he had it checked out. Diagnosis: mantle-cell lymphoma, a runaway type of cancer. This forty-nine-year-old man with two teenaged sons was facing an enormous battle.

The ironic thing was this: Murdock was the CEO of CellPro, a Seattle-based biotech firm that was in the business of searching for cures for lymphoma. His own company was chasing the solution to the very disease he now had in his body.

Needless to say, the race was on. Murdock describes how he became a driven man: scouring magazines, medical journals, getting on the Internet, attending seminars. And, of course, CellPro and its team was ready to go around-the-clock to save the boss. After a series of late-night sessions fueled by Cheetos, they decided to go with a transplant using Murdock's own stem cells: take out the stem cells, blast the cancer with chemo and radiation, then reinject the stem cells, and hope to rebuild his immune system. But CellPro would have to come up with a way to purify his own stem cells, which were already tainted. That was the bottom line of this race against time: the Rick Project. And the clock wasn't just ticking; it was spinning frantically around the dial.

"We weren't going to simply cut corners," Murdock writes, "we were going to slice them right off."

It's a beautifully told story, condensed from the book appropriately titled *Patient Number One*. And it illustrates a theme we often find in *Reader's Digest* articles and in our own lives. When it's life or death, especially *our* life—or the life of one of our children—we go all out. We spare no expense. We stay up night and day. We burn up the phone lines and wear out the Internet modems. Our motto becomes four words long: "Whatever it takes, baby." Whatever it takes.

In their book, *Becoming a Contagious Christian,* Bill Hybels and Mark Mittelberg adopt that same slogan as they point out that every single person on this planet is worth, to God, that kind of desperate rescue. Here in Luke 15, we find three stories about lost things: a lost sheep, a lost coin, and a lost prodigal son.

"That which was missing," they write, "was important enough to warrant an all-out search."

The point has already been made that in this story of the ninety-nine safe sheep and the one that got lost, it's God who goes searching for it. God takes the initiative. But not just initiative: *all-out* initiative. He doesn't just search; He scrambles on His hands and knees, He wades through deep currents, He fights through thorn bushes and alien, battle-scarred territory. The search is an all-consuming, complete, total effort. Heaven's best.

I love this line from the same book by Hybels and Mittelberg: "Jesus' stories in Luke 15 tell us that *you have never locked eyes with another human being who isn't valuable to God.*"[15]

Think about that the next time you want to be impatient or dismissive of that certain someone who "doesn't deserve" eternal life. Doesn't deserve Calvary or heaven. Doesn't deserve for God to make more than a casual, discounted two-dollar effort. Can you think of someone like that? Well, good for you, because Heaven can't. Every single person on our discard list, on our throwaway pile, isn't just targeted for redemption by God, but for His very best, all-out effort. The old college try.

Christ's Object Lessons has a couple of marvelous paragraphs on this very point. "These souls whom you despise, said Jesus, are the property of God. By creation and by redemption they are His, and they are of value in His sight. As the shepherd loves his sheep, and cannot rest if even one be missing, so, in an infinitely higher degree, does God love every outcast soul. Men may deny the claim of His love, they may wander from Him, they may choose another master; yet they are God's, and He longs to recover His own."[16]

Recall that Jesus shared these parables within earshot of the religious elite, the Pharisees and priests. In fact, He tells this "lost sheep" story right after the rulers grumble among themselves: "This Man eats with prostitutes and pornographers and scuzzballs and tax collectors!" This is a direct response to their criticism; He wants them to know that these lost, desperate, wandering sheep have made God desperate to win them back.

Ellen White continues her description of the value Christ places on each person: "The value of a soul, who can estimate? Would you know its worth, go to Gethsemane, and there watch with Christ through those hours of anguish, when He sweat as it were great drops of blood. Look upon the Saviour uplifted on the cross. Hear that despairing cry, 'My God, My God, why hast Thou forsaken Me?'

Mark 15:34. Look upon the wounded head, the pierced side, the marred feet. Remember that Christ risked all. For our redemption, heaven itself was imperiled. At the foot of the cross, remembering that for one sinner Christ would have laid down His life, you may estimate the value of a soul."[17]

Can you visualize the desperation here? Men and women in a lab, at two in the morning, exhausted but working with intensity, spinning out those stem cells, trying to save their friend's life. A young mother traveling across the oceans with her little boy, coming to City of Hope Medical Center, willing to make any sacrifice to rescue him. A Savior from heaven's highest courts, traveling down to the dust and the degradation of planet Earth, willing to submit to the cross if only to save me. Or you.

And our closing reflection is this: you and I, if we're in God's family, are also part of this great effort. Project Rick. Project Natasha. Project Kim. Project John and Jane Doe. From every lonely village and sprawling inner city. You and I have on the white coats in the laboratory, and we're commissioned to help the Good Shepherd go and get that one lost sheep. Ellen White concludes by sharing this invitation: "How many of the wandering ones have you, reader, sought for and brought back to the fold? When you turn from those who seem unpromising and unattractive, do you realize that you are neglecting the souls for whom Christ is seeking? At the very time when you turn from them, they may be in the greatest need of your compassion. In every assembly of worship, there are souls longing for rest and peace. They may appear to be living careless lives, but they are not insensible to the influence of the Holy Spirit. Many among them might be won for Christ."[18]

How about it? Do you want to help the Lord make this happen?

And all through the mountains, thunder riven
And up from the rocky steep,
There arose a glad cry to the gate of Heaven,
"Rejoice! I have found My sheep!"
And the angels echoed around the throne,
"Rejoice, for the Lord brings back His own!
Rejoice, for the Lord brings back His own!"

Chapter 8

I CAN'T AFFORD
Your Free Tuxedo

It happens fairly often when you stay in a downtown hotel. You're eating in the smallest coffee shop, trying to save a few dollars. Or maybe even hiking a couple of blocks to the nearest Wendy's. But there in the main ballroom of your hotel is a huge, gala, black-tie affair. They have punch-bowl fountains spraying out pink champagne; there's a dance band set up in one corner. The place is set with the finest china; bouquets are everywhere. And milling all around are eight hundred guests who are about to sit down to a fifty-five-dollar-a-plate dinner.

Of course, you're not invited, but you do notice all of the glitter and the gold as you go back to your room with your Wendy's french fry wrappers and little packs of ketchup.

In Philip Yancey's *What's So Amazing About Grace?* he shares an anecdote from the *Boston Globe* in June of 1990. A young lady had gone with her fiancé to the Hyatt Hotel there in town to order their wedding banquet. Both of them had Cadillac tastes, and before they'd finished picking this and that off the menu, they'd signed their names to a contract for a thirteen thousand dollar shindig. So they wrote a check for half that amount as a down payment, and went home to start licking the wedding envelopes.

Well, bad news. The very day the envelopes were supposed to go in the mail, the groom chickened out and got cold feet. "I'm not sure," he said. "Let's wait; let's postpone."

The young woman, angry of course, drove down to the Hyatt to try to call off the big black-tie party. But the events manager shook her head. "I'm sorry," she said. "But the way your contract is written, you're stuck. That's all there is to it. We could refund you ten percent—just thirteen hundred dollars—but the rest can't be returned."

So here's what this Boston socialite decided to do. Since she was going to lose 90 percent of her thirteen grand anyway, she decided to go ahead and have the party. Not a wedding party anymore, thanks to her gutless boyfriend, but a party nonetheless. So she dug in her purse, paid the rest of the bill, and then hosted the biggest, boldest, most boogie-ing party Boston had ever seen . . . for all of the down-and-outers in the city.

Here's how Yancey caps off this odd, wonderful story: "And so it was that in June of 1990 the Hyatt Hotel in downtown Boston hosted a party such as it had never seen before. The hostess changed the menu to boneless chicken—'in honor of the groom,' she said—and sent invitations to rescue missions and homeless shelters. That warm summer night, people who were used to peeling half-gnawed pizza off the cardboard dined instead on chicken cordon bleu. Hyatt waiters in tuxedos served *hors d'oeuvres* to senior citizens propped up by crutches and aluminum walkers. Bag ladies, vagrants, and addicts took one night off from the hard life on the sidewalks outside and instead sipped champagne, ate chocolate wedding cake, and danced to big-band melodies late into the night."[1]

Well, it's a sweet story, but really the first telling of this socially upside-down event comes from the mouth of Jesus Himself. In Matthew 22, Jesus is right in the middle of telling several quirky tales. And if you go back one chapter, you find that His main audience was none too friendly, made up mostly of priests and rabbis and the elders of the church. This was the religious establishment of the day, and we think of Pharisees and Sadducees and their hard, humorless faces, their eagerness to catch this Teacher from Galilee in a moment of heresy.

So Jesus begins to tell this story right from the Jerusalem Hyatt Hotel: "The kingdom of heaven is like a king who prepared a wedding banquet for his son. He sent his servants to those who had been invited to the banquet to tell them to come, but they refused to come" (verses 2, 3).

We're always tempted, when we read stories like these, to immediately assign the characters. The king represents God, of course, and so the son in this wedding story would be Jesus Himself. No wonder Christ used parables! The priests and Pharisees never would have stood still for it if Jesus openly told this story on Himself.

Notice that we have here two invitations. Already an earlier invitation had been given, and now the king's servants went from door to door to the selected, upper-crust guests, just as a reminder, a follow-up invitation. *The Seventh-day Adventist Bible Commentary* notes that, even today, it's common in Asian cultures to honor special guests by sending out personal envoys.[2] And it's at least hinted that these envoys were knocking on the doors of people who had previously agreed to come. They'd already sent RSVPs.

Who, then, would be the people on this first guest list? One might answer, "The children of Israel," because they were the original chosen people. All through the Old Testament God had invited them to be in a special relationship with Himself. Through the Old Testament prophets and sacred writings, this first invitation had been sent. And certainly this first list of potential honorees would include the religious people of Christ's day: the priests, the teachers of truth. So it might well be that some of those standing there in the crowd hearing this story noted that they, too, were in the narrative.

So this little note is odd: "But they refused to come." Israel, of course, had said Yes to God in a generic sense; we recall that famous line right after God gave them the Ten Commandments at Mount Sinai: "All that the LORD has said we will do" (Exodus 24:7, NKJV). Here in Jesus' day, they certainly considered that they were full-fledged members of the wedding party. They were the seed of Abraham! But when it came right down to honoring the Son of God, the Bridegroom, they said No. They couldn't make it, after all.

So the generous king sent out some more limousines and hired a more prestigious messenger service. "Please do come," these ambassadors begged. "The king has gone to a lot of trouble. And this is for his son! You wouldn't want to miss that, would you? Please? You said you'd come. And the king has already had the big dinner prepared; the steaks are sizzling and the Dom Pérignon is chilled just right." (Nonalcoholic, of course.) Again, as in the parable of the prodigal son, we find a God who "kills the fatted calf." He spares no expense to show His feelings for the subjects in His kingdom.

And as Jesus tells the story, the people on God's A list just give a big shrug. "I can't make it," they say. "*American Idol* is on that night, and I don't know how to set up my DVR." "I've got to go check my field to see if my radishes are growing." "I've got to attend to my business affairs." Even though these people offer a pretense of loyalty to the king and accept his protection and rulership, when it comes right down to it, they don't want to honor him or his son. In fact, verse 6 says that some of these people grabbed the messengers, dragged them out of the palace limos, and beat them up. In a couple of neighborhoods, they even killed them! So this is nearly a state of civil war.

Interestingly, verse 7 does have one moment, one display, of royal strength: "The king was enraged. He sent his army and destroyed those murderers and burned their city."

That sober message resonates right down to our own time. Yes, the King is loving and kind and eager to provide a banquet feast for His people. But when people give Him the ultimate brush-off, when they turn their backs on Heaven and say, "Sorry, not interested," that is a very serious thing. Especially when men and women pick up rocks or guns to drive away God's chosen prophet—or even just send him packing with words—that is a very serious thing. God certainly does want every citizen of this planet inside His banquet hall; the Bible says so many times. But it also teaches that those who blatantly and willfully defy this invitation and reject the messenger sent by the king will miss the wedding, the feast, and eventually life itself.

A party at 3:30 A.M.

However, it's good to notice what happens next. His majesty opens up the banquet hall to everybody in town. Here's the CNN proclamation from verses 8–10: " 'The wedding banquet is ready, but those I invited did not deserve to come. Go to the street corners and invite to the banquet anyone you find.' So the servants went out into the streets and gathered all the people they could find, both good and bad, and the wedding hall was filled with guests."

So this king throws open the banquet doors of that Hyatt Hotel. "Go get any-body!" he says. "Anybody, anywhere. Go into the back alleys. Go into the bars. Go into the brothels. Go from door to door, finding sick people, poor people, good people, bad people. Losers and lonely people. Go find the people who haven't darkened the door of a church in many years." This king cranks up his printing press and engraves invitations with everyone's names on them; he floods the Internet with e-vites. You get one; I get one. Our neighbors get them. The postman delivering them to our front doors gets one himself.

You've heard the expression "a blanket invitation." Here's the world's greatest example of exactly that. "Go get anybody," says the king. "I don't care who. Knock on doors everywhere. Get the street people. Get the gang members. Get the pool sharks and the hookers and the hustlers. My son's getting married, and I need a full banquet hall."

Maybe *you've* always been outside the hotel looking in as well-dressed couples went in. And you could hear the faint sounds of the orchestra, and just barely smell the hot buttered rolls, the salads, the desserts. But you never thought God's invitation was for you. Preachers get invited. People like Martin Luther and Billy Graham and the pope have an invitation. But not you. Until right now. Here as this story unfolds, you, friend . . . yes, *you* . . . are the guest of honor.

If you've ever felt left out, that feeling should end right here in verse 9. Because God sends out His limousines and His uniformed ambassadors to bring an invitation right to your door. It's an urgent invitation, because the feast is about to begin. The orchestra is about to play. And the king makes it perfectly clear that this invitation is sent out without regard to status or position or level of sinfulness or anything else.

So the message of this parable is wonderfully clear. God wants you! If you're in prison, He wants you. If you're on death row, He wants you. If you're a hardened criminal, He wants you. If you're a runaway. If you're broke or if you're rich. At this very moment, He's saying to you, "I want you; you're invited to My Son's banquet feast." And this is the message that needs to go out to every single lonely person in the world. "You've been invited to a great banquet for the Son of God, Jesus Christ."

And let's think together about weddings for a moment. At most functions like these, there are two kinds of guests: the casual drop-ins who don't really know the bride or the groom—and they sit in the back and get a free piece of wedding cake. Then there are those who really are connected with the two newlyweds: they sit up close. They bring a nice gift. They wear their best clothes. But more than that, they love the bride and the groom. They're there to show support, to show that they are connected with these people. They identify with them. They support them. They truly are "well-wishers" in the best sense of the word. And when the preacher begins, "Dearly beloved, we are gathered together . . ." these are the people he's talking about. "Dearly beloved" people—friends and relatives—who dearly love the bride and the groom.

So you've been invited to a big wedding. Who's it for? The son of the king. Who is that? Well, it's Jesus, of course. Wouldn't you like to go to a banquet where our Friend Jesus is being honored? Furthermore, wouldn't you like to be one of those who sits down close to the front, as if to say, "Yes, I'm a close friend. I really do love the Groom! I support Him and have for a long time. This moment of victory for Him is one that thrills me too." It's interesting and wonderful that

God invites everyone, even strangers—especially strangers. But as this parable unfolds, we'll encounter a thoughtless man who came to the wedding, but didn't show much interest in ever identifying with the Groom. He was there with his own agenda, his own pride and motives. But God invites people to the wedding who really want to be the friend of the Groom, the Son of the King.

As we realize that, we can find more than one interpretation for what this wedding feast really is. True, it reminds us of the second coming of Jesus, when there will be a great feast in heaven. What a banquet that will be—and yes, every citizen of this world is now being invited to attend.

But in a larger sense, the wedding feast is an ongoing experience with the King and His Son even right now. Do you believe that? The invitation is out there now, and has been for two thousand years. "Come in! Please come in! Wherever you are, whoever you are, come in and enjoy a relationship with the Groom; show your support for Him."

Again we peek ahead in the story and find that a man is eventually thrown out of this feast. Palace guards show him to the door, and we'll weigh the very sober reasons why that might happen. Of course, such an event would have to happen before the second coming of Jesus. Because in heaven, in God's kingdom where the real banquet begins, no one will ever leave or ever want to leave. All of the friends of the Groom will be eternally secure there.

There's a parallel story told by Jesus in Luke 14, and I don't intend to mix the two here. But in the second story, the invitation doesn't just go out to "everyone." Here the master specifies the following types of guests: "the poor, the crippled, the blind and the lame" (verse 21).

That's interesting, and perhaps from a spiritual perspective we find ourselves in one of those categories. Are you poor? In your soul, is the bank account empty? Have you felt distant from God? Have you felt that Jesus was far from you and you from Him? Then this is good news, because God has invited you to His wedding feast. Maybe you're blind—and the book of Revelation tells us that we all have some cataracts when it comes to the things of God. But here God specifically wants to invite people who have been blinded to His goodness. "Maybe you don't trust Me yet," reads the invitation . . . perhaps written in Braille. "Maybe you have never glimpsed the wonder of Calvary, the personal gift I made for you. You're groping around in the darkness of discouragement or the confusion of drugs. That's all right; I don't hate you. I have an invitation for you instead."

Or you're crippled and lame. Crippled in terms of walking daily with Jesus.

You haven't been doing it. Or you're emotionally crippled, too confused to really focus on the principles of God's kingdom. You read your Bible and it's a jumble, a confused mess to you. But right here God invites the cripples of the world to get into the limousine and ride directly over to the palace.

God longs for wedding guests who will become close friends of His Son. But He'll take us where we are right now! Because the wedding is right now! "Come this moment!" He says. "Dinner's about to be served. When you get here, I want you to meet My Son and learn to love Him, but first just come! Come just as you are."

In President Jimmy Carter's book *Living Faith,* he relates an anecdote he heard from evangelist Tony Campolo. Tony was suffering from jet lag in Hawaii one night, and because he couldn't sleep, went to an all-night diner. Lo and behold, in the next booth over was a little group of prostitutes. Down on their luck—women who obviously were having a very hard life. And one of them said to the others, "You know, tomorrow's my birthday."

"Really?" And they teased her a bit. "How old are you going to be?"

"Thirty-nine." And then this lonely hooker added, "You know, I've never once in my life had a birthday party."

Tony Campolo filed that away. Later, when the girls were gone, he got together with the manager of the diner, and arranged a party for that lonely hooker, that prostitute. The next evening when the same little group of "ladies of the evening" convened at that diner, he sprang the surprise on the birthday girl. Cake, ribbons, presents, flowers, everything. He went all out with this surprise birthday party. All of the women were just blown away, absolutely stunned and thrilled, of course, and Tony even had the opportunity to pray with all of them, especially that lonely thirty-nine-year-old hooker. Who knows? Maybe in his prayer, he was able to mention a loving God in heaven who was about to throw a surprise wedding banquet party of His own too.

But later, after all the cake was gone, and the girls were gone, and they were cleaning up, the owner of the diner said to Tony: "Man, what kind of church do you belong to anyway?" And Campolo looked at him and said very quietly: "I belong to the kind of church that throws birthday parties for whores at three-thirty in the morning." And Jimmy Carter adds, "This was Jesus' kind of church."[3]

In the classic Frank Capra holiday story *It's a Wonderful Life,* a young idealist named George Bailey is the spiritual core of Bedford Falls. When the corrupt banker, Mr. Potter, tries to take over the savings and loan, it's George who single-handedly saves the situation.

There's a run on the bank, and people are crowding around, demanding to get their money out. Old Potter is offering fifty cents on the dollar for anyone's shares, and George Bailey has to try to keep people from selling out to the evil empire. And so he stands there, just minutes away from leaving on his long-awaited honeymoon. And he's got two thousand dollars—his own money. His honeymoon money. But one by one, he says to his friends, "How much do you really need to tide you over? What could you make do on?" And twenty dollars at a time, he gives out his own money to all of these clamoring people, hoping to keep them afloat, keep their hopes and dreams alive.

Here in this parable of the wedding feast, we find a similar George Bailey moment. Actually, there are two such moments. First of all, an invitation is issued—and how much does it cost the recipients? Every four years here in the U.S., as candidates are lining up to be elected or reelected, many people will put on their mink coats and their cummerbunds and attend thousand-dollar-a-plate fundraising dinners. But in Matthew 22, the greatest banquet ever, there's no mention of a ticket price. In fact, it's very obvious, considering the ragtag clientele, the scandalous guest list, that this banquet is free. The king is simply throwing open the front doors and inviting everyone. "No charge! No two-drink minimum! No campaign pledges required!" All the riffraff of the world can simply walk into the chandeliered ballroom, sit down at a table with a damask tablecloth and candelabra, and be waited on by a maitre d' in a Pierre Cardin tuxedo.

Now, why does the invitation come to us free? Nothing in life is free, and if there's a banquet in a ballroom, surely a bill is presented to *someone,* and a person somewhere pays it. Never has that been so true as in this story. The price of this banquet was paid on Calvary. It was paid in full at the cross. Without the sacrifice of Jesus Christ on that Friday afternoon, without that greatest of ATM card swipes, God could not, would not, should not be able to morally let sinners into the great banquet hall of His kingdom. He couldn't do it!

But this is the foundation message of the Christian faith—our price of admission has already been paid. The Father and the Son themselves, the King and the Bridegroom in this story, pay the banquet charge for you and for me and for your neighbors and my neighbors. This is why the King can properly and justly say to His servants in verse 9: "Go to the street corners and invite to the banquet anyone you find."

Anyone! Anywhere! Good and bad alike. And there's no complaint from the hotel, because the price has already been paid for every place setting in the great hall. Jesus paid it all, and all to Him we owe. Just as George Bailey doled out money out of his own pocket, the Father sent us His beloved Son out of His own heart.

Which is why it's so wrenching when people spurn this invitation. This free invitation that was actually so very, very expensive. It comes free to us, but it cost God everything. And what a poignant, terrible moment recorded in verse 5: "But they [the original guests] paid no attention and went off—one to his field, another to his business."

"Ho-hum," they said to one another. "Big deal, another banquet. It's free; how much can it be worth?" And they shrugged off the most important invitation of their very existences. The most precious piece of engraved paper the post office has ever delivered, and they sent it spinning into the trash can and surfed over to another TV show.

Designer gowns for everyone

But now there's an important part two to this interesting story from our Lord. We now get to the part about the wedding garments. With a title like "I Can't Afford Your Free Tuxedo," we wonder what this is all about.

The Scriptures don't explicitly state this, but many good Bible scholars have determined, or at least suggested, that in a story like this one, the king most likely provided not only free invitations, but also sent out, at his own expense, the proper attire for the gala occasion. In other words, everyone who got this royal invitation, whether rich or poor, high or low, good or bad, also was given a custom-fit tuxedo or a sequined gown by Halston, Versace, or Armani. Especially if the king's ambassadors were looking for dinner guests on skid row and the bowery district, in trash Dumpsters and crack houses, this would be a necessity. In the New International Version text notes, the team of scholars makes this very suggestion: "It has been conjectured that it may have been the custom for the host to provide the guests with wedding garments. This would have been necessary for the guests at this banquet in particular, for they were brought in directly from the streets."

Admittedly, we enjoy debating what this person and that one represents in this parable. That's part of the fun, part of the puzzle. But this point is anything but light fun, because it's clear that this wedding garment, this tuxedo, is of vital importance. Having it on is so important that a man without it is shown to the fire exit and thrown back out into the street.

So we have to ask, what would be necessary for a person to enjoy fellowship with God forever at His wedding banquet? What does the Bible teach is the requirement or the standard to reach if a person wants to live in heaven?

That's really not hard to answer. All through the Old Testament and the New as well, we're taught that God is holy. He is righteous. He is sinless. In the Old Testament, the Ten Commandments describe the holiness and righteousness of God. In the Gospels, of course, we have the pure, sinless life of Jesus Christ. In the book of Romans, none other than Paul, the great preacher of the gospel of grace, tells us that our sins are what condemn us to death (Romans 6:23). So in order to be in this wedding banquet party, and especially in order to stay there, a person needs righteousness. He or she needs goodness. He or she needs a life of obedience.

Ah . . . and now the parable takes on a whole new light, an entirely different cast, with shades yet again of George Bailey and the gifts from his own wallet. Here's another word of explanation from the diligent Bible scholars for the NIV. "The wedding garment no doubt speaks of the righteousness that God, the gracious host, provides for all who accept His invitation. God issues an undeserved invitation to undeserving people, and in addition provides the righteousness the invitation demands."

He mails out to every would-be attendee a brand-new, custom-fitted tuxedo or two thousand dollar dress from the designers in Paris. And that gown is the righteousness of Jesus Christ. To be in the wedding hall, and in order to remain there in the presence of the king, every person in attendance absolutely must have on this robe of Christ's righteousness.

So we have here, not one, but two incredible gifts. First of all, an invitation that's absolutely and completely and totally free. It is! There's no price tag on it anywhere except for the one already paid at Calvary.

And then because heaven is a place where only righteous people can dwell, this gracious King goes the necessary second step. He provides a robe of righteousness—a free tuxedo, an Armani gown—to every man or woman who wants to be a part of His wedding party. Now, whose righteousness is it in these tuxes and gowns? It's the righteousness of our Lord and Savior Jesus Christ. He lived a perfect life. He died on the cross to pay the price for all of those invitations. And then He and His Father grant to each one of us the opportunity to put on the second gift, the robe of His righteousness.

We have to ask, what more can any good Host do? And all of us who stand in our new tuxedos and gowns in that resplendent banquet pavilion can only thank the King and say to each other: "It's a wonderful life."

Is Mr. T really good now?

Despite the generosity of the King, though, we have to do some studying about this *free* tuxedo. And let me borrow an illustration from a Hollywood actor who often sported tons of jewelry along with his black-tie attire at Oscar Award soirees. Maybe you remember Mr. T starring in *The A-Team*, or in WWF wrestling matches with his mohawk hair. Or maybe you remember the line he made famous in one of the *Rocky* movies where he vowed he would beat up on the Italian Stallion, Sylvester Stallone. "I pity the fool," he snarled—and it became his tagline. Why in the world would I mention a bad boy like Mr. T in conjunction with this Bible parable?

Again, this wedding garment provided by the king represents righteousness. Holiness. Obedience. Purity. Commandment keeping. And so it gets very disquieting when we get to the end of the story, and read what happens in verses 11 and 12: "But when the king came in [to the feast] to see the guests, he noticed a man there who was not wearing wedding clothes. 'Friend,' he asked, 'how did you get in here without wedding clothes?' The man was speechless." And what happens next? This is very sobering. "Then the king told the attendants, 'Tie him hand and foot, and throw him outside, into the darkness, where there will be weeping and gnashing of teeth.' For many are invited, but few are chosen" (verses 13, 14).

So we have a wedding that is free. Everyone is invited to attend with no up-front fee being charged. But once inside, this question is asked, Are you wearing the proper robe? Are you sufficiently dressed? Are you righteous? But there is one man who, for whatever reason, disdains the elegant wedding robe provided to him. "I don't need it," he must have said to himself. "What I've got on is fine." And he goes in the front door wearing his own clothes.

But now he stands there speechless when that question is asked. "How did you come in here without a wedding garment?" And he is unceremoniously thrown out into the back alleyway with the trash Dumpsters and the empty soda cans and the rats, where there is weeping and gnashing of teeth.

And we now head into a tunnel of bad news—good news. Christians read this Bible story and come to this part where the king comes in to see the guests. In fact, he's almost inspecting them, it seems. This is a kind of judgment scene. "Who is wearing a wedding garment, a robe of righteousness?" It's clear from this story that at least one stubborn—or perhaps ignorant—attendee isn't wearing the tuxedo, and is thrown out. And so we begin to say, "Wait a minute. If this story is true, then my assurance of salvation is shaken and shattered. How can I know if the King won't approve of what I'm wearing either? I'm certainly not as righteous as some of the others in my church, not as well-dressed, character-wise, as they are. This is bad news!"

Well, actually, it isn't bad news after all, is it? Because remember, the King provides the robe! It's given out free! You receive one; I receive one. We all receive one. In *The Seventh-day Adventist Bible Commentary,* the team of writers makes this suggestion: "The wedding garment represents 'the righteousness of Christ.' . . . Hence, the rejection of the garment represents the rejection of those traits of character that qualify [people] men to become sons and daughters of God. Like the guests in the parable, we have nothing suitable of our own to wear. We are acceptable in the presence of the great God only when clad in the perfect righteousness of Jesus Christ by virtue of His merits."[4]

So what sounded like bad news isn't bad news at all. Because when the King comes in to see His guests, and when He comes by your banquet table, where the white linen is so sparkling white and the candles are twinkling, and His eyes fall on you, what does He see? He sees the robe of Christ's perfect righteousness covering your sins. You appear in His eyes just as His own Son, Jesus, does. Perfect. Sinless. Loyal. Loving. Obedient. He looks at you and He sees Jesus' heart, Jesus' holiness. And He says, "Welcome to the feast for My Son. In fact, you look a lot like Him. I'm so glad you're here."

Back for a moment to big, bad, enemy-stomping Mr. T. *Los Angeles Times* columnist Mike Downey tells us something that perhaps we didn't know. Mr. T, it's been reported, has cancer. What's more, he's a born-again Christian. Along with the chemotherapy for skin cancer, he has on the robe of Jesus' righteousness at this very moment. He tells what happened when he heard the bad news: "I got down on my knees to pray. I said, 'Lord, give me the strength that You gave Abraham, that You gave Joseph, that You gave Moses, that You gave Job.' Because how would I know that my God is a healer, if I never got sick. My God would be a fair-weather God if He was only with me when I got millions of dollars from doing 'The A-Team' and commercials and whatnot. I don't want no fair-weather God. I want a God who will be with me through *everything*."

That's the testimony of Mr. T. He doesn't want to be covered by boxing trunks or by all his gold necklaces or his mohawk. He wants to be covered by the robe of Jesus' righteousness. But now what seems to be such good news, the very best, in fact, takes us into another area of deep Christian debate, especially within our Adventist community. We wear this robe of Christ's righteousness. It's beautiful; it's free. We join Mr. T in thanking God for such a wonderful free tuxedo or evening gown.

However, a disturbing question lingers. Is this robe simply and exclusively the righteousness and goodness and holiness of Jesus Christ that *covers over* our wickedness? Or is this robe a kind of righteousness that Christ gives to us . . . to the point where *we ourselves* grow to become good and holy? Does He in fact come in and actually make His people good?

Or put it this way. Will heaven's banquet hall be inhabited by people who are forever wicked and sin stained, but only covered up by someone else's million-dollar tuxedo? Some theologians refer to this as "legal fiction," in which the entire universe has to forever pretend that bad people are good. Other Bible scholars debate about whether the holy character of Jesus is "imputed" to believers—in other words, simply credited to us in a mathematical sense—or "imparted" to us, where His goodness is in reality given to His people, and they actually become people who love righteousness.

You can see how a person's insecurities might come surging back. If this robe of righteousness has to, in any way, be my own goodness, then I begin to worry. Because perhaps I don't see much progress in that department . . . and I hear the trumpet sounding as the Great King of the universe begins to wind His way through the banquet pavilion, about to inspect the wardrobes of His guests.

I take courage, though, from the touching story of mohawk-haired Mr. T. This snarling, scowling, "I pity the fool" sneering, bad boy of wrestling and TV. Now he's a Christian. Now he's got the robe of Jesus covering him. But lo and behold, something has actually happened to this man inside. That robe he is wearing has actually become *him*. He is now loving and tender, soft-spoken, and kind. And he tells Downey how he now spends his time in children's cancer wards, quoting the Bible to them, visiting with kids for hours. He talks about his mother, how she raised him and his eleven siblings. His dad was a junkman who preached on Sundays. "We were poor financially," he says, "but we were rich spiritually. Drugs and crime were all over me, under me and around me, but never in me. Why? Because I respected my mother. I'm a big, overgrown mama's boy. That's the problem with society. We don't have enough mama's boys. If we had more mama's boys, there wouldn't be so much disrespect for women."

Downey says to him: "It must have been hard telling your mom about your cancer." And here's the end of the column: "And for the next few minutes in the restaurant, without a word, the biggest, strongest, roughest, toughest, baddest dude you'd ever want to meet is crying his eyes out, while I hold his hand. You would want to meet him, believe me. I pity the fool who never gets the chance."[5]

It's a beautiful story of a man who is transformed from the inside. The righteousness of Christ has truly become his own.

So is this robe of Jesus something that covers up our wickedness, or is it a garment that actually makes us good? The answer is yes! Yes to both questions! Yes, the robe of Jesus is a pure and spotless garment that covers up our great sinfulness. It qualifies us for heaven because of Calvary. That is justification.

And yes, the robe of Jesus' righteousness is a miraculous gift that also gets inside a person and touches the heart—glorious sanctification. Just like a tuxedo on a homeless person or a vagrant bum seems to bring out that person's best qualities, the wedding robe in this story is Christ reaching down into our hearts and making us really good, truly good from the inside out. It is not "legal fiction" in which the whole universe has to forever pretend that wicked people are really OK after all.

So the free robe is both a covering *and* a growing reality within us. Furthermore, and this point is extremely important, in both interpretations the robe is a gift from God. As the robe covers us, that is God's gift. And the robe transforms us, that robe is also a gift. Ezekiel 36:26 demonstrates the internal working of this wedding present: "I will give you a new heart and put a new spirit in you; I will remove from you your heart of stone and give you a heart of flesh."

Jesus, speaking to His disciples in John 14:15, encouraged them with this motivation: "If you love Me, keep My commandments" (NKJV).

Paul, writing about the inner workings of this wonderful gift robe, says in Romans 12:2, "Do not conform any longer to the pattern of this world, but be transformed by the renewing of your mind."

And he goes on to emphasize the gift aspect of the robe, with this powerful promise in Philippians 2:13: "It is God who works in you to will and to act according to his good purpose."

So the incredible gift of this robe is free on both counts, as it covers and as it transforms. This amazing, generous King really does it all, doesn't He? In *Mere Christianity*, C. S. Lewis observes, "After the first few steps in the Christian life we realise that everything which really needs to be done in our souls can be done only by God."[6]

He goes on to say a word of encouragement for any person who may worry that this gift robe isn't doing what it's supposed to do—that it is covering, but not transforming. Ironically, this is from a chapter titled "Counting the Cost": "The practical upshot is this. On the one hand, God's demand for perfection need not discourage you in the least in your present attempts to be good, or even in your present failures. Each time you fall He will pick you up again. And He knows perfectly well that your own efforts are never going to bring you anywhere near perfection. On the other hand, you must realise from the outset that the goal towards which He is beginning to guide you is absolute perfection; and no power in the whole universe, except you yourself, can prevent Him from taking you to that goal. That is what you are in for."[7]

Happy with our own clothes

But what about the person who looks at himself in the mirror—without the robe of Christ—and says, "I think I'm all right as is. I look OK. I'm dressed for the feast with my own wardrobe"? The same book contains a word of warning as well: "If you are a nice person—if virtue comes easily to you—beware! . . . If you mistake for your own merits what are really God's gifts to you through nature, and if you are contented with simply being nice, you are still a rebel: and all those gifts will only make your fall more terrible, your corruption more complicated, your bad example more disastrous. The Devil was an archangel once; his natural gifts were as far above yours as yours are above those of a chimpanzee."[8]

Years ago, when I worked at the Voice of Prophecy radio ministry, we received an interesting letter describing a woman's spiritual journey. But a few paragraphs later, she stated that at the present time she was living a life that was free from sin. She was no longer sinning, she wrote. Now, to be honest, in the very same paragraph she did say that God had given her this gift. And she listed several sins that she simply did not commit—not once in a while, not ever. Soon she felt led by God, she wrote, to leave her church. Now she kept company only with other perfectionists like her who were having the experience of living a life completely free from sin. "Why should I associate," she asked, "with people making twenty grand a year when I can be in the million-dollar club?" As she looked at herself, she truly felt that she had attained perfection.

Now let me be careful here in concluding. God promises to give us the gift of Christ's righteousness. That's biblical truth. But when a person looks into his or her own soul and sees perfection there, what a temptation it might be to go to the wedding feast wearing one's own clothes. And so many of us in the church every single day have to fight the temptation of thinking our own wardrobe is good. This foolish man in Matthew 22 must have thought that. "I worked hard for these clothes," he said. "I've obeyed God my whole life. Why should I accept this gift outfit, which is the same as admitting I'm a naked wretch on my own? I won't do it."

In a way, that's like celebrating Memorial Day without wanting any connection with the sacrifice that made it possible. "Give me my barbecue and my swimming pool and my TV with the ball games. Give me the goodies of the American lifestyle. But I don't want to acknowledge my debt to the man who bled and died. I don't need him; I don't want him." And like the Christian who says, "I don't really need the Son and His robe. But I do want the free banquet."

How's it going to be with us? Morris Venden puts these two wedding RSVPs in front of us. One: "I pray Thee, let me be excused." That's what the majority will say.

Or how about this other one: "To the King of kings and Lord of lords: I have just received Your Majesty's urgent invitation to be present at the marriage supper of Your only-begotten Son. I hasten to reply. By Your grace, I'll be there. P.S. And thank You for the beautiful robe."9

Chapter 9

YEAR-END REPORT
of the Ten Mutual Funds

Have you had a chance recently to enjoy the thrills and adventures of an old-fashioned board game? Not Internet virtual reality, but the regular kind where you sit down with your kids or your spouse and roll the dice and actually move your little man around the board like in the old days and spend valuable game time rotting in jail? I've noticed recently that Parker Brothers, makers of Monopoly, have come out with some new editions of the game, where the streets aren't the familiar Marvin Gardens and Boardwalk, out of Atlantic City, of course. There's a Los Angeles version now, with Sunset Boulevard and some of those streets. There's a Hollywood version, and I imagine that one has Rodeo Drive and all of the Beverly Hills boulevards featured in the high-rent district. When I was a kid attending Andrews University Elementary School, it was fun to play a Dutch version with our friends David and Sera LaRondelle, and I remember that theirs had street names from downtown Amsterdam, and the money was in guilders. It was amusing recently to read how comedian Steven Wright had made the comment: "I think it's wrong that only one company makes the game Monopoly!"

In any case, there's a common motif for many of these board games. Every player starts out with a certain amount of money—in Monopoly, it's still fifteen hundred dollars—and the object is to make a lot more. As we all know, the goal in Monopoly is not only to keep all your own money, but to wipe out everyone else so that they don't have any. When everyone declares Chapter 11 except you, then you win.

As we continue with this tour of Jesus' most popular parables, we find in Matthew chapter 25 a kind of Monopoly game being set up . . . but with one huge difference. There are three players, and the master of the house sets up each of them with an initial fund and instructs them to see what they can do with the money. Let's pick up the story in verses 14, 15: "[The kingdom of heaven] will be like a man going on a journey, who called his servants and entrusted his property to them. To one he gave five talents of money, to another two talents, and to another one talent, each according to his ability. Then he went on his journey."

It's been a common theme in these parables thus far that the math of God's kingdom is poles apart from what we ever learned in grade school, or what we find printed inside the box of a Parker Brothers game. Because in this experiment, the master of the estate gives each of the men *different* amounts. When they pass "GO," they don't all collect two hundred dollars; in fact, one man—apparently the smartest of the three—starts the game with five times as much as the low man on the totem pole.

The Bible plainly tells us why the master does this. Notice: he gave them talents "each according to his ability." The man with the greatest potential got the most, and the servant with very limited investment skills received a rather small portfolio.

And how do we as humans feel about this kind of skewed, biased math? Here in Los Angeles, as a new baseball season approaches, fans all notice that often one player will be paid far more than any others. Some particular superstar will have a contract worth more than one hundred million over six or seven years. He makes thirty thousand dollars per swing of the bat; each time he catches a fly, more hundred-dollar bills fly into his offshore bank account. Many other players, on the other hand, get quite a bit less than that. A few of them have to scrape by almost on welfare, earning perhaps only a couple hundred thousand dollars a year. And those of us sitting in the stands, way up high in the cheap seats, just can't relate at all to these kinds of home-run numbers. But here are men who want to be paid "according to their abilities." And in the Bible, this master or team owner, who represents God, actually does hand out different sums to different people based on *His* assessment of abilities.

If we segue from thinking of "talents" as money to thinking of "talents" as abilities, or *talents,* of course, that's the point of this whole story. And any time you go to a church and sit down in a pew, you're immediately confronted with this reality. Some Christians simply have more abilities than other ones. Some preachers are better than others. Some believers barely have one gift, while others seem to do absolutely everything in the church, do it well, and drive up to the church parking lot in a Mercedes Benz to boot. They are the people, obviously, who started out the game with the five thousand dollars.

I still remember my freshman year at Far Eastern Academy in Singapore. My parents were missionaries in Bangkok, and I went to an Adventist boarding school where kids from all over the Far East gathered together for their four high-school years.

Our concert band had three trombones, and I was that "third of three." But the first-chair guy was one of those Matthew 25 characters who had it all. Dwight was a senior while I was a freshman. He was tall and good looking. He got top marks in every subject. He was witty and popular. He always had a gorgeous girl-friend. (Being five foot three and wearing braces and having an obnoxious sense of humor, I was lucky to have any dates at all.)

This Dwight kid went on from our missionary school, got a DMin in theology, and has been the senior pastor of Pioneer Memorial Church at Andrews University for the past three decades. It still doesn't seem fair, but when God looked down and handed out the talents, He chose to give that talented kid a very full basket.

The fact we all need to keep in mind every day of our lives is who the money belongs to. It belongs to the Master. It wasn't the servants' money; it was the Boss's. He entrusted it to them, but it was still His. And so it was entirely appropriate for Him to look hard at the résumés of His servants, and then place them in charge of different money market accounts according to His own wisdom about what they could handle.

So how is it when it comes to the Christian man or woman and the issue of talents? Whose talents are they? Well, perhaps you think that your abilities belong to you, but think again. Where did they come from? Who gave them to you? Who entrusted you with the talents you have today, right now?

In the Tyndale New Testament Commentaries for Matthew, Dr. Richard T. France makes this comment: "In the context of Jesus' ministry the sums of money entrusted to the slaves are more likely to represent not natural endowments given to men in general, but the specific privileges and opportunities of the kingdom of heaven."[1]

For example, you might be good with your hands. Or you might have a great singing voice, or be skilled at organizational matters. Those are your gifts; and to be sure, they came to you from God. But in the Christian faith, it's also true that when people commit their lives to God, they're also endowed with spiritual gifts that go beyond just talents and musical aptitude. Leadership turns into spiritual leadership; a compassionate personality is especially guided into the spiritual gift of giving a person spiritual comfort. And here, for sure, we can know that the gifts are God's ownership, and that they're simply entrusted to us for use in service to Him.

In the telling of this little story, Jesus gives us a clue as to the importance of these talents. In Bible times, we read in various commentaries, a talent of silver was a huge amount of money. A talent was equivalent to sixty minas, and a mina was a hundred drachmas. Well, that doesn't mean much until we learn that a drachma was basically a day's pay for the common person. That would make a talent—just one talent—the equivalent of six thousand days' pay. That's about twenty years' worth of salary for most of us, and this master gives out five talents, two talents, and one talent to these three men. So it's not just pocket change; this is a serious expression of trust and also a great spiritual challenge: "What will you do with this money?"

But let's reiterate again: this is God's money. Or in your case, these are the talents God entrusted to you or loaned to you. That line got a bad rap a few years ago when a certain Rush Limbaugh liked to boast on TV that he was "talent on loan from God." But in the best and humblest of senses, that's a true statement. Our money and our fortunes and our abilities are really God's resources entrusted to us.

This should give each of us two things for sure. One would be a quiet combination of humility and contentment. If you're a genius, it's because that's what God gave you. If you're a millionaire, that's God's blessings. True, you may have worked hard to use and fine-tune those gifts and turned them into a nice fortune. But who gave you the aptitude to be a hard worker, a success-minded person instead of a sleep-in-till-noon bum? That came from God too. So as we consider this human package called Self, and then as we look around at the other packages in the house or in the church, some of them bigger and better, some of them not quite as good, can we be content and humble because this is how God gave things out? It's so hard to do, isn't it? And don't we all spend a lot of time each day either complaining to God that we're on the short end, or patting ourselves on the back for being somewhere on the rich-and-pretty end of the spectrum?

Point two is this: if the money is God's, then shouldn't we be bold in investing for Him? He told us to go for it! He challenged us to double His portfolio! He went on an important trip and left us in charge of some pretty exciting missions down here. Are we taking a chance, investing here, looking over there for the best and brightest opportunities? Sometimes people bet scared with their own little bankroll, but God has invited us to do great things with the talents He loaned us. He wants two to turn into four, and five to turn into ten . . . and then twenty, and forty, and so on. It's His money; it's His game; in fact, it's His Wall Street.

Afraid to play the game

Quite a few years ago, my employer at the time had a disposable sum of money that needed to be invested somehow. Just a few thousand dollars. It wasn't tagged for immediate operations, and so the organization's treasurers needed to sort out the options and decide what to do.

Well, there were CDs, of course, and bank accounts and bond accounts and no-load mutual funds and all the rest. There also at this time were individual stocks, too, naturally. And one in particular seemed to hold real potential, but as the decision makers looked really hard at their options, they just couldn't see taking the risk. Investing with this certain company—and of course, I can't tell you its name, but it starts with *M* and is based in the Pacific Northwest—was just too much of a gamble.

Well, quite a few years went by, and that money invested down at the corner bank made a little bit of interest. But if it had been put into that certain *M* company that specializes in software, the fund would have been worth a cool million dollars by the time I heard the tale. And I guess we all know stories like that one.

Including this story in the Word of God! Even Jesus seemed to know about the topsy-turvy, high-flying dot-com market of recent years, and He describes these three fund managers who are given quite a pot of cash to play with while He was overseas checking out some hot tips and derivative deals in the Pacific Rim market.

So how did they do? The market was hot at the time, apparently, and trading was fast and furious in the pit. The story resumes in verses 16 and 17: "The man who had received the five talents went at once and put his money to work and gained five more. So also, the one with the two talents gained two more."

There's an intriguing Greek nuance hiding right here. In the King James Version, verse 15 sets up the story this way: "[He gave] to every man according to his several ability; and straightway took his journey."

Now here's the bit of trivia. The scholars now suggest that the word *straight-*

way might actually belong to verse 16, not verse 15. So that instead of the master going "straightway," or right away, on his journey, that word really applies to the first servant. So that this man who was entrusted with five talents got to work "straightway," or immediately, and began investing just as soon as he could.

I like that enthusiasm! Right away this man wants to score a victory for his Lord. He knows this is a huge sum of money, many years' worth of salary. And so he doesn't say, "I'll get started first thing tomorrow." Or, "I'll wait until after the holidays before investing." No, he begins making phone calls immediately; he calls the overseas markets; he rushes down to the corner and gets a copy of the *Wall Street Journal.* What are the rates right now? This first servant had a sense of urgency about him; he wanted to get that money working right away.

I can relate a sad little story on myself at exactly this point. Back in 1997, Lisa and I bought a new house, and, of course, you know how that goes. You are signing papers and writing endless checks for this fee and that due-diligence fund and some unexpected filing report over there. After a certain point, you feel like screaming, "One more check, and I'm going to just cancel the whole deal and move back in with Mother!" But we finally got to the end of the paper trail and were ready to close escrow and move in on a Friday morning. We rented a U-Haul and spent a fatiguing day toting boxes. We hauled the last one in humming "Day Is Dying in the West" and collapsed amidst the cardboard heap just as the Sabbath hours commenced.

Unfortunately, somebody slipped up, and just one little document didn't get signed and notarized correctly. No big deal, right? Well, it turned out to hurt quite a little bit because the mortgage loan didn't fund that Friday . . . it held over until the following Monday. And that wouldn't seem so bothersome either, except for the fact that because we moved in on Friday, the builder now wanted *three full days of RENT,* enough to make up for the fact that he didn't have the money-making power of those loan funds for just those three days. A hundred and fifty extra dollars just out of the blue, because money didn't get "into the game" on Friday. Ouch!

But we can learn a lesson here. God has given each of us gifts . . . and the stakes are high! Those gifts you have, whatever they are, need to get "into play" right away. That's one of the biblical lessons of this story. Whether it's financial blessings or the gift of witnessing or the ability to make friends and lead them to Christ or the talent for showing hospitality for people less fortunate, the time to begin investing is now. Immediately. In my years of pastoring—and of course, I have to lecture myself, too, on this same point—it was so painfully obvious how the church, the body of Christ, was often held back because spiritual gifts were buried in the ground. People had talents, and they simply were not being used. Again, I admit, sometimes it's been me who buried the talent. "I'll get started with this later," I say to myself. "I know I *could* do that, and I *should*. But not right now. Maybe when the kids go back to school." And a whole six months of investing opportunity for the Lord is wasted.

As we return to our story, one servant decides to just not get into the game at all. Verse 18: "But the man who had received the one talent went off, dug a hole in the ground and hid his master's money."

Well, Christian preachers have used that line a million times ever since: "Burying your talent in the ground." This verse is where that expression comes from.

I have another embarrassing story to share! As a boy in Bangkok, I took violin lessons for several years. I've learned to play a little bit on the piano, and I know a few chords on the guitar and a line or two on a bass guitar. I can even hold my own in a band or jazz ensemble playing the trombone. But all of my Friday afternoon violin lessons with Briquette Barrois simply did not take hold. I am not now, and I never have been, a very good violinist. In fact, I pretty much stink.

Many years after I had accepted this reality and put my violin in an attic, someone from a nearby Adventist church called me one day and asked me to play special music. And they specified, *on the violin*. I said, politely, "Are you nuts? Wouldn't you rather have a trombone solo or piano or kazoo? I could fill glasses with water and tap out, 'Jesus Loves Me.' Anything would be better than the violin." No, they said, they really wanted a violin solo. I must have spent twenty minutes trying to dissuade this person. You don't know what you're asking, I said. You will jeopardize the salvation of all your new members. People are going to quit; they'll write to the conference office. They'll leave the Adventist Church and join offshoot movements and cults. Your offerings may plunge and never recover. The pastor might be defrocked over this.

But the guy on the phone said, "No, it'll be wonderful. Please come." Finally I agreed, after making them sign an affidavit that I could not be sued for the results and promising to not have me play until they'd already picked up the offering that Sabbath and cashed all the checks.

So I got out my violin and practiced, and it sounded terrible. I went to the church to wait for armageddon. They announced my name and I went up. Now, there's a reality in violin playing. If you're bad and nervous, it's going to sound even worse because your jitters will make the bow bounce and skitter along the strings. So I began to play, and the skips made it sound like I was playing into a fan. I can still remember the looks on the faces of some of the people as this reedy performance slowly screeched toward the finish line.

I finally finished, the pastor tried to recover and still get through some semblance of a sermon, and finally it was over. I was out in the parking lot afterward, not expecting any congratulations and not receiving any, when finally Cleo Rusch, a friend of mine, came up to me. He took my hand and said very kindly: "David, there are some talents that *ought* to be buried in the ground!" True story.

But in the parable Jesus tells, the one buried talent represents a lost opportunity, a wasted asset. When you think of it, all of the "buried treasure" stories in the world and *Raiders of the Lost Ark* trilogies do have this stigma of waste. Resources that could have been in the game, in the market, building a future with the miracle of compound interest . . . but, instead, they're buried under a rock someplace or in an ancient tomb in Tibet.

And so we ask, "Why?" Why did this man not get in the game? And the excuses begin to fly, "Well, the Dow Jones was due for a crash, and the bond market is wobbly right now. And banks are only paying 1.78 percent with a puny deposit like this. So I cashed out your funds and kept the money in my sock drawer. Here."

So that could be one reason: the element of risk. The Dow Jones is sky high, and what goes up has to eventually come down, we think. And so we don't invest.

From a spiritual point of view, are there elements of risk to investing our God-given talents? Sure there are. Someone gets a call to the mission field, and right away people point out nine hundred bad things that can happen. A would-be preacher thinks about the cost of going to the seminary. Then what if he doesn't get a call? What if he and his family can't make it on a minister's salary? What if the congregation rejects him? There are a million reasons to stay in a poolside lounge chair instead of getting into the water.

The element of risk might also be linked with our feelings about the fact that other people received the big pile of talents while we received only one. Face it, people all around us are rolling in talents. Which makes it seem all the more dangerous if we timidly raise our hands and volunteer with our one little gift. What if people sniff at the very suggestion? What if we get the infamous "Don't call us; we'll call you"? And perhaps there's a bit of pouting as we go out back with our little shovel.

But probably the biggest reason for the hole-in-the-ground strategy is recorded right here in the Bible. We're skipping ahead in the story, but here's the excuse given by Investor three: " 'Master,' he said, 'I knew that you are a hard man, harvesting where you have not sown and gathering where you have not scattered seed. So I was afraid and went out and hid your talent in the ground. See, here is what belongs to you' " (verses 24, 25).

This sorry little speech reveals two enormous misunderstandings on the part of this man. First of all, he doesn't really understand whose money it is, and tragically, he especially doesn't understand the master himself. *The Living Bible* adds this insight to the speech: "Sir, I knew you were a hard man, and I was afraid you would rob me of what I earned, so I hid your money in the earth."

This servant gives himself away with that accusation. First of all, he thinks the master is a hard man. Sure, he works for the boss and accepts a paycheck. But he doesn't like him, doesn't trust him. He's seething with resentment, especially over the fact that he's the last man in the five-and-two-and-one assignment. And so he says, "You're a hard man; you expect to score off of other people's work."

And then this last giveaway line: "I was afraid you would rob *me* of what *I* earned." Again we must ask, whose money is this? Whose talents are these that are entrusted to the men? It's not their talents; it's the master's money! The original investment is his, and so the profits are his as well.

Think for just a moment about your best talent. Actually, God's talent or gift, which is on loan to you. Right? It's His, not yours. He takes the risk, not you. And yet He invites us to the victory party when the dividends roll in. Now, isn't that actually a pretty good Boss to work for?

Our study of this parable, though, wouldn't be complete without careful consideration of the temptation of *ambition*. Is it acceptable, in God's kingdom, to want to be that five-talent man? Should the man of God, the woman of God, eagerly seize extra responsibility and increased power? Is it good to pray the now-famous prayer of Jabez: "Lord, expand my territory"?

"Please pass me your pie"

It seems like about once a year now, a hot-selling writer named Bob Woodward comes out with a new book. As half of the famous Woodward and Bernstein team that broke the Watergate scandal, he seems to have a knack for getting the inside scoop, the hidden details that escape the attention of others.

One of his earlier books, *The Choice,* chronicled the early parts of the 1996 presidential race, right up to the point where the Republicans chose Bob Dole, and the Democrats, of course, stayed with the Clinton-Gore ticket. How did Dole, at his age, manage to fend off Lamar Alexander and Phil Gramm and Pat Buchanan and Steve Forbes and all the others? What about the Colin Powell factor—why didn't he run? And he certainly had all the juicy details on the Democrats as well.

On that side of the aisle, a certain element was a rather key factor. That certain element was the shadowy figure of one Dick Morris. Now a news analyst for FOX News, this political operative schemed and worked to exert more and more and more influence on the president of the United States. He formulated policy, what he called the scheme of "triangulation." He established fund-raising goals and plans. He faxed ideas up to the president when he was thirty-five thousand feet up in the sky on Air Force One. He even wrote many of Bill Clinton's speeches for him.

Understandably, the rest of the White House staff didn't think much of this steamroller who was taking over all of their jobs. So they quickly worked to minimize the influence of Mr. Dick Morris, to bar his access to the Oval Office. But this ambitious operative just kept on grabbing turf for himself, carving away out of other people's pies. If an agency got him officially banned, he quietly established what were called "back channels." He found ways to get his proposed TV spots and suggested State of the Union addresses smuggled into 1600 Pennsylvania Avenue and on to President Clinton's desk.[2]

So this parable told by Jesus poses the question, is there anything wrong with such ambition? Here's a man who wanted to rule the world, and he'd step on as many toes as he had to. In the tale Jesus told, two men were rather ambitious, and we find the master congratulating them for it. Here's the verbatim transcript: "After a long time the master of those servants returned and settled accounts with them. The man who had received the five talents brought the other five. 'Master,' he said, 'you entrusted me with five talents. See, I have gained five more.' His master replied, 'Well done, good and faithful servant! You have been faithful with a few things; I will put you in charge of many things. Come and share your master's happiness!' " (verses 19–21).

The exact same line is repeated with Investor two. He'd doubled his portfolio as well, and received the same words of praise and commendation. "Well done, good and faithful servant! You have been faithful with a few things; I will put *you* in charge of many things. Come and share your master's happiness!" (verse 23; emphasis added).

So are these two men a couple of first-century Dick Morrises? Aggressive, power driven, back biting, and back channeling, bruising egos in order to score big on the stock market? And is there anything wrong with wanting to enlarge your slice of the pie?

We could make several observations. First, the Bible clearly teaches in this story that God Himself acknowledges and even intends the disparity of gifts in the church. It was God who gave out the five, the two, and the one talent in this story. *The Seventh-day Adventist Bible Commentary* shared this insight in discussing the Matthew 25 parable: "The amount entrusted to each servant was no more than, in the estimation of his master, he could handle wisely; at the same time it was sufficient to challenge his ingenuity and skill and thus provide him with an opportunity to gain experience."[3]

So even in God's system of government, there's room for a man or woman to rise up to become secretary of state or for a person to hold down two cabinet posts, as Henry Kissinger used to do during the Nixon years. Some preachers are given authority over a huge conference or diocese, while another man or woman has a little country church with eighteen members. (That would be me!) Both are precious to God, and both are rewarded if they do their best with the circumstances and talents entrusted to them. And certainly both are encouraged to seek more influence and a wider scope of service if their motivation is right.

In his excellent book *Surprised by the Power of the Spirit,* Dr. Jack Deere shares four suggestions regarding the topic of spiritual gifts or talents. First, we should pray for such gifts. The Bible teaches that in 1 Corinthians 12. Two, we should attempt to regularly use the gifts that we do have. Of course, that's the very point made in this parable of the three servants. If you have five, use five. If you have two, use two. If you have one, for sure, don't go out in the woods and bury the one. The third suggestion: we should study the gifts, the doctrine of spiritual gifts. We should study how to use our gifts more effectively. Undoubtedly the two good servants in this story pored over all kinds of manuals and investment forms; they were on the Internet every day, tracking the market, looking for tips. They subscribed to the Charles Schwab newsletter. They made themselves experts on fund management. And then Deere's fourth suggestion: have friendships with people who are more advanced in the gifts than we are. Rub shoulders with others who are also active in working for God. Share strategies; exchange success stories; look for tips. Tell how God is blessing your efforts for Him.[4]

But as Jack Deere makes all these suggestions, he firmly and emphatically takes all of us back to a core Bible text found in 1 Corinthians 12:7: "Now to each one the manifestation of the Spirit is given for the common good."

Notice: "for the common good." Whatever successes come through our efforts are to be given to the Master's house. They're for the good of everyone. If one person doubles his money, everyone rejoices, because that's a success for the whole family. This is why the one servant was so wrong when he said to the boss: "I was afraid you'd rip off the profits *I'd* made." And second, this tells us what kind of aggressiveness is appropriate as we seek to serve. Eagerness and ambition and zeal and horizon expanding are all good traits as long as we are serving the Master and His kingdom. As long as we are working for the common good.

Someone once asked C. S. Lewis this pointed question: "Is it wrong for a Christian to be ambitious and strive for personal success?" And the answer Lewis gives is right in line with these principles laid down by Jesus: "Ambition! We must be careful what we mean by it. If it means the desire to get ahead of other people—which is what I think it does mean—then it is bad. If it means simply wanting to do a thing well, then it is good. It isn't wrong for an actor to want to act his part as well as it can possibly be acted, but the wish to have his name in bigger type than the other actors is a bad one."

The same questioner, after a moment's pause, came back with this query: "It's all right to be a General, but if it is one's ambition to be a General, then you shouldn't be one?" And the response is colored by the biblical idea here in 1 Corinthians regarding the common good. "The mere event of becoming a General isn't either right or wrong in itself. What matters morally is your attitude towards it. The man may be thinking about winning a war; he may be wanting to be a General because he honestly thinks he has a good plan and is glad of a chance to carry it out. That's all right. But if he is thinking: 'What can I get out of the job?' or 'How can I get on the front page of the *Illustrated News*?' then it is all wrong. And what we call 'ambition' usually means the wish to be more conspicuous or more successful than someone else."[5]

Speaking of politics makes me think of another man besides Dick Morris who often sat in the Oval Office and sent faxes to many presidents. Billy Graham certainly has to be a man we would think belongs in the "five talent" club. Look how God has blessed him! Many talents were bestowed upon this Southern Baptist preacher, and God also allowed many breaks to come his direction.

And he has been ambitious in his career. It takes a bit of boldness to start a huge soul-winning team and then allow it to have this name: the BGEA—the

Billy Graham Evangelistic Association. Without a doubt, there have been those who criticized the size and scope of his operations, suggesting that he had too much power and influence in God's kitchen cabinet.

And yet here's a line from the very first page of the preface to his autobiography, *Just as I Am:* "If anything has been accomplished through my life, it has been solely God's doing, not mine, and He—not I—must get the credit."

In fact, on the jacket cover of his book comes this additional disclaimer: "I have often said that the first thing I am going to do when I get to Heaven is to ask, 'Why me, Lord? Why did You choose a farmboy from North Carolina to preach to so many people, to have such a wonderful team of associates, and to have a part in what You were doing in the latter half of the twentieth century?' " Then he confesses, "I have thought about that question a great deal, but I know also that only God knows the answer."[6]

Maybe you look up at heaven every night, too, and say, "Why me?" Or maybe you're looking up there and saying to God, "Why *not* me?" That's OK. As long as our ambitions and our steps up the success ladder are motivated by a desire to lift Jesus higher and not ourselves.

Probably the most practical question we continue to deal with—and it bears a second look—is this one of jealousy, of comparisons. It seems so unfair when a "Dwight" plays the trombone better than you do and pastors a church with 4,982 more members than yours. How do we handle the fact that this man who was given five talents not only scored five more . . . but also was given the leftover *one* left behind by Investor three?

The radio preacher who has never once hit a hole-in-one

This takes us clear back to the first page of the book; Hobbes's friend Calvin complains to the world: "It's so unfair!" Why do others get more than we do? Why do we see preferential treatment happening all around us? Why do the rich become richer and the poor become poorer?

A number of years ago, a Los Angeles athlete named Mike Piazza was angling for a multiyear contract worth something like one hundred million dollars. Unfortunately, his comments about it ended up in most of the newspapers, causing him to be booed rather roundly whenever he came up to the plate. The irony was this: Piazza was born into wealth already! His father was a very successful businessman back East, and this baseball catcher was a millionaire in the bassinet, long before his home-run power made him a candidate for even more money.

Every now and then there's a story in the paper about a person who hits the lotto jackpot *twice*! I mean, the big prize. And why? Why does God let that happen? They don't need the money. But here they win twenty-five million dollars or so the first time around, and then later they match all six numbers a second time. And the rest of us look on with unmitigated envy.

This third example is the most irritating to me, and you'll soon see why. Not that long ago, a forty-nine-year-old woman named Jeanette Roberts didn't just shoot a hole in one in golf . . . she hit *three of them in the space of eight days*. She'd been playing the game for only four years, compared to several lifetimes for some of the rest of us. She's a thirty-five handicap, which is nothing to write home about. In fact, her scores on the three rounds where she hit these aces were as follows: 101, 91, and another 101. But there in those sky-high scores were three shots that just rolled right onto the green and went *plink* straight into the cup. To add insult to even more injury, these three fluke miracles are on top of a fourth hole-in-one that Jeanette had lucked out with earlier there at Granite Bay Country Club.

Like I say, the world isn't very fair. How many holes-in-one have I ever had? Zero. I've had drives that almost went into the cup on a wrong green, which I'm told does not count. I've had a few in miniature golf, which I understand is also disallowed in terms of bragging. And as we read through some of the stories that Jesus Christ told, it's clear that dealing with the element of unfairness is a common theme in the gospel message. There are ragamuffin people and hoodlums who get invited to banquets they have no business attending. The prodigal son for sure gets some blessings he doesn't deserve. And here in the parable of the three servants and the talents there's yet another occurrence of what we might call the bad math of the kingdom.

Notice what happens when this third investor—or, we should say *non*investor—comes slinking in with dirt all over his checkbook. He didn't make a penny for the master. And that's not good, especially considering that there was a bull market going on and the other men in the game had both had returns of 100 percent. So how does the boss respond to this chicken-hearted guy? "His master replied, 'You wicked, lazy servant! So you knew that I harvest where I have not sown and gather where I have not scattered seed? Well then, you should have put my money on deposit with the bankers, so that when I returned I would have received it back with interest'" (Matthew 25:26, 27).

Now here's the kicker to the story, where the unfair math pops up again:

"Take the talent from him and give it to the one who has the ten talents. For everyone who has will be given more, and he will have an abundance. . . . And throw that worthless servant outside, into the darkness, where there will be weeping and gnashing of teeth" (verses 28–30).

Isn't that quite a story? It's interesting that "gentle Jesus, meek and mild" seems to have quite a few anecdotes up His sleeve where someone is bodily tossed out into the darkness where the teeth begin to grind in sorrow. But even more important is the fact that the boss takes this one talent from the no-account man and hands it over to the person who's already prospering. Here in Matthew 25, the poor get poorer and the rich get richer and the player who's already gotten a hole-in-one gets three more in a week.

We have already gleaned so much from this colorful story, but it certainly seems that the most important thing is to understand the Master. That's God, of course. Two of these servants seemed to know the Boss quite well. They enjoyed working for Him. When He gave them a challenge, they got right to work. They invested with zest and enthusiasm. Interestingly, there seems to have been no resentment between them over the fact that one got five talents and the other only two. That's quite a spread, but they didn't mind because they knew and trusted the Master. It was His call; that was fine with them. They knew it was His money they were risking, but they also seemed to feel confident and secure that He would love them and accept them and be proud of them no matter how they scored in their stock-market forays.

Here's another interesting note. How were these two good guys rewarded? Notice how the Master pays them: "Well done, good and faithful servant!" [He said to both of them.] "You have been faithful with a few things; I will put you in charge of many things" (verses 21, 23).

Did you pick that up? He says to them, "You men did well with a little bit of work. So your reward is . . . *more* work!" They went from a small amount of service to a large amount. Is that a reward? Is that a lovely payoff? Most of us, if we turn in a good job and meet a little deadline, aren't really that thrilled when the big man in the corner office says to us, "Good job! Now here's a huge pile of work folders with even tighter deadlines!" And yet this is the reward for these two workers: increased responsibility. But then this P.S.: "Come and share your master's happiness!" The King James gives this spin to the line: "Enter thou into the joy of thy lord" (verse 21).

Which follows the "more work" announcement: "I will make thee ruler over many things" (KJV). Which, except for the politically minded among us, is usually not received as good news.

But for these two, it certainly was. They loved and appreciated this Master so much that to work for Him was a great reward. When He said to them, "I've got even bigger jobs for you now," that was by definition "entering into the joy of their lord."

Of course, to understand this Good Master helps render obsolete not only the "bad math" of the gospel, but the false charge of this wicked servant. It's interesting that to do nothing with what God has given us is described by Jesus as not just laziness but downright wickedness and sin. That's something to think about. But now let's examine this false accusation. Investor three says to the CEO, "Man, you're a hard boss. You expect to score every time, and off the sweat of others. You want to harvest where you didn't plant and to gather where you didn't put in any seeds."

But if in this parable God is the Master, is that a true statement? When we do well for the kingdom, is God gaining a benefit that really didn't come from His original generosity? A missionary like my own dad sweats in the jungles of Thailand for years, and a few people are baptized in a little mountain stream; they become new Christians. Is God capitalizing on the hard work of that missionary and getting a harvest where He didn't plant? Of course not! It was God who gave that villager a conscience; it was God who softened his heart; the saving Calvary message came from Him in the first place. Furthermore, it was God who gave the missionary the talents and the motivation and perhaps even the finances to make that mission trek. It's a dynamic, living partnership, and I don't know of many missionaries who have ever come home complaining that God was a hard and unfair Boss. For sure, the Smith family says—to a man—that it was the greatest reward of their lives to work for such a Master . . . and they thank God if He gives them ten cities to rule next time instead of only five.

By the same token, there's no such thing as "bad gospel math" in God's vineyard. I've been in Russia where faithful Christians behind the forbidding iron curtain labored in secrecy for decades, with very sparse results. Then here comes a big American TV evangelist like our own Mark Finley. He brings stacks of hundred dollar bills into the country, rents a huge Moscow Olympic stadium, erects billboards, buys ads on Soviet TV, has enormous crowds, and baptizes five thousand people. Do the workers there complain, or do they celebrate? The ones I've met rejoice and consider that they are all full partners working for the same miracle-working Savior.

I spent nearly a decade working in Christian radio, where there were many, many ministries bigger than ours. And I thanked God if He poured on and piled on the blessings for someone who comes on the air after we did. If some other preacher on the dial already had ten talents, and then got one more, we praised the Lord that those funds are still invested in the same growing bull market.

You know, I think I'm going to stop saying "bad math." It's starting to add up better and better all the time.

But as we draw this particular story to a close, let me invite you to simply do this: *picture the face of our Savior Jesus.* Picture Him in heaven, waiting, building mansions, blessing our work, overseeing the growth of the Christian church around the globe. And every time we use a talent or invest a dollar or help build a church or save a soul, do we grasp that all of it is for the kingdom of this wonderful Redeemer?

Ask not what Heaven can do for you

Probably the inaugural sound bite of all time goes back more than half a century now, to a frigid January 20, 1961. A young Massachusetts senator stood in the wintry cold at the presidential microphone, where he had just accepted the mantle of leadership from Dwight D. Eisenhower. The torch had just been passed to a new generation, he announced. And then he said this: "And so, my fellow Americans, ask not what your country can do for you. Ask what you can do for your country."

There's a special reason why I choose that famous sound bite echoing down through time. President John F. Kennedy's invitation to do something for a grand cause resonates powerfully with this very Bible story. The owner of the estate gives three men a clarion call to do something *for the kingdom.* They're not investing for themselves; they're not using their own money and feathering their own nests— well, one of them was—they're in service to their Lord. They're doing His work; they're working for the success of His organization.

God, as the landowner in this story, is the One who knows His servants; He's the One who determines who will receive what talents and in what amounts. He's the One who issues the challenge and who provides the resources for this grand project. And of course, ultimately, we all report to Him because we're all in this story, aren't we? You've got a mutual fund to manage and so do I.

And yet it might be well to amend our story a bit, or perhaps to grow in our understanding. Is it possible that Jesus Himself—who is also God, to be sure—

was representing Himself in this Matthew 25 parable? After all, in actual fact, He did depart this world and return to heaven, leaving behind men and women with the assignment to work hard in His absence. That adds some real dynamic urgency to the story if we think of this Leader as being our own Savior. If it's Jesus who has placed these talents, these gifts, in our hands, wouldn't we want to do our very best for Him?

There's one final lesson for us to ponder. In verse 15 of the story, the Bible says rather cryptically: "Then [after giving out the talents] he went on his journey."

In verse 19, the thought is concluded. "After a long time the master of those servants returned and settled accounts with them."

A fair question comes to mind. How long is "a long time"? We don't know. For how many months or years was this master away? We don't know. Did he ever call in, or give them a beeper number? We don't know. Did he stay away longer than they expected? We don't know. It must not have been too many years, or the servants' achievement of doubling their money wouldn't have been that impressive. But the Bible does say that it was a long and unspecified time.

Now, if we think of Jesus as being this Master, doesn't the parallel give us something to think about? He's been gone a long time. Far longer than most Christians ever thought it would be. My grandpa Venden was so sure he would live to see Him come back in the clouds—but he passed away in 1973. The early Christians were sure of it too. Something that the workers in the field were so positive would only be a few months or years or decades has now spread out to two thousand years.

So what's the lesson? Very simply this. The good servants just keep on working for their Master until He gets back. They don't become discouraged. They don't ever say, "Well, I've done enough"—and quit. They don't assume that the experiment has been canceled and cash in the funds for themselves. They simply keep on working with those talents, growing them, expanding them, adding to them. As long as there's breath in them to work, they work.

Which takes us to our second conclusion. What would it feel like to meet Jesus on that great homecoming day and have to report that we did absolutely nothing with the gifts He gave us? In all that time. How would that feel? Can you imagine the tragedy of having to do that?

Now, the thief on the cross came to the Lord at the last possible moment. But even he invested immediately in Jesus: confessing Him and them boldly shushing up his fellow inmate. He did what he could in those last few minutes of life. But you and I are here on a good playing field with a heaven-sent strategy and with talents in our possession. We don't have any excuse. And I ask again, while examining my own soul right here too—what would it feel like to face Jesus Christ, our wonderful, generous Savior, on that day, and have no report to give?

And He asks very gently: "I gave you seventy years of time. What did you do with it?" "Uh, nothing."

"I gave you the ability to earn money. What'd you do with that?"

"Uh, nothing there either, Lord."

"I put neighbors on both sides of your house and across the street. Did you share with them, help them, lift them up, introduce them to Me?"

"No, I guess I never did."

"I invited you to walk with Me and experience obedience and character growth? Did you do that?"

"No, I'm afraid I didn't do that either. I meant to, but . . ."

What a sad experience that would be. Not because Jesus is a harsh Judge, a cruel Boss with a miserly, forbidding scowl. But because He was so generous! "Ask not," He had said, "what the kingdom of heaven can do for you . . . although it's done so much. What can you do—what *have* you done—for My kingdom and My Father's kingdom?"

For sure there's one talent every single man and woman in the kingdom has been given. Others may have more, but we all do have that one gift: the ability to say something to someone about the wonderful Master we serve, our friend Jesus Christ.

As we leave Matthew 25 and the frantic pace of Wall Street, let me ask you the same question I ask myself. Have we been waiting on the sidelines? Have we invested zero so far? Have we dug a little hole in the dirt and put our gifts in there? Well, the good news is this: we can dig those talents up right now! Shovels can bury, but they can also dig up! We can start today. The investment game for Jesus Christ is still going on. Others may have already climbed higher than you, dreamed more, and achieved more. But it's not too late for you to begin right now.

Remember again that bit of Bible math, where even the man with just one talent had been given twenty years' salary to invest. It actually was a whole lot of money! Then God, the grateful Owner, says to the good workers: "Well done, good and faithful servant. You have been faithful with *small* things. Now I have some big things for you!" And we think to ourselves, *Small? An amount equal to six thousand days' salary is small?*

166

If that's true, can we possibly imagine the wonderful things God has in store for us then? His promise is that it will be bigger then, better then, more challenging and wonderful and abundant and rewarding *then*. Even Everest will seem like nothing compared to the mountain peaks our Lord will lead us to scale together with Him.

But your climb, and mine, can begin right now.

Chapter 10

A REALLY HIGH-PAYING
Temp Job

The story is told of a man who went out into his driveway one day and found out that his beautiful new car had been stolen. What? And he was really livid. How dare they? He hated being ripped off. Why couldn't the police control things? What was the matter with the mayor? And on and on. He was very frustrated, and rightly so, because he didn't deserve this.

Lo and behold, a little while later he went out again, and there was his car. Whoever had taken it had brought it back and attached was a note. Apparently, a man had run out of gas while rushing his wife to the delivery room at the hospital. Desperate, the husband had hotwired the nearest car and gotten his wife to the delivery room just in time. And there on the dashboard, the "thief" had taped a big thank-you card, along with expensive tickets to a sold-out play, gift card for dinner at a nice restaurant, et cetera.

Well! That was more like it! Now the man felt like the favors were rolling in *his* direction, and he felt much better. He didn't deserve this either, but bonuses and goodies were fine as long as he was the recipient.

So this man and his wife went to the restaurant and then out to the play, rejoicing all the while that they were getting such a marvelous deal, essentially for free. What good fortune! But it wasn't actually that fortunate after all, because when the couple got back home they found a house that had been stripped completely bare of every single thing they owned. Furniture, money, jewels, silverware, everything. And of course, it was the same thief who had taken the car; the whole thing was a setup, a scam designed to get this fellow out of his house for the evening. And our friend with the bare floors and the empty cupboards felt ripped off again.

One of the great truths of human experience is that we hate to be taken advantage of. The converse is also true; to be on the good end of a bargain is absolutely fine. Don't our eyes light up when the very thing we want in life is suddenly marked down to half price? We don't mind if an item is marked wrong on the low side! We know it's a mistake on the part of the store, but if they want to put a fifty dollar sticker on a five hundred dollar TV set, we're the first in line.

This may actually be one of the most baffling parables that Jesus ever told. Despite our title "A Really High-Paying Temp Job," the headings in most Bibles say very simply, "The Parable of the Workers in the Vineyard." You'll find this parable in Matthew 20, and sometimes when you're studying something in chapter 20, it's not a bad idea to drift back to chapter 19 and read the context of this parable.

Right before this story about the really great temp job, a rich young man has just turned away in sorrow because the Savior had told him that if he wanted to get into heaven, he needed, essentially, to liquidate his holdings, sell everything he had, give it all to the poor, and become a disciple. Well, the man wouldn't do it, couldn't do it. And even the disciples stood around saying, "Man, I guess it's really hard to be saved. Does anybody have a chance?" And our friend Peter, always one with the math-oriented questions, has this one for Jesus: "We have left everything to follow you! What then will there be for us?" (verse 27).

And that's a fair question. Peter and eleven other men really had given up everything: family, friends, fishing boats, job security. Just to tramp around in dusty Judea and Galilee with this itinerant Preacher who didn't have two shekels to rub together. So, of course, when Jesus says how very hard it is to qualify for heaven, Peter has to ask, "Well, are *we* going to get any reward? We've been with You a long while here; where's the payoff?" And then Jesus tells this story.

"The kingdom of heaven is like a landowner who went out early in the morning to hire men to work in his vineyard. He agreed to pay them a denarius for the day and sent them into his vineyard" (Matthew 20:1, 2).

It's a bit sobering that many of Jesus' stories begin with the line "the kingdom of heaven is like" such and such. Most of the stories contain this "upside-down math." All the "wrong" people win in the end; the parables rarely have politically correct Hollywood endings. And yet we have this clear teaching: "The kingdom of heaven follows the concepts of this story. What happens here in this vineyard is what's going to happen in the church. The morals of this story are also the morals of the kingdom." It certainly makes the stories worth reading, that's for sure. But it's sometimes disquieting that such revolutionary ideology is going to be how things are when King Jesus takes over. If the endings in these stories bother us *now,* are we going to spend ten thousand years, bright shining as the sun, grumbling to ourselves about the unfairness of this gracey, forgivey place?

Here are men who have agreed to work for the landowner. That's God, of course. These grape harvesters get a denarius for the day, which was the fair wage of that era. A decent paycheck for a long, hot twelve-hour day in the sun.

Along around nine o'clock, "the third hour," as Jesus tells the story, the landowner goes to the marketplace and hires some more men. Only this time he signs them up with this promise: "You also go and work in my vineyard, and I will pay you whatever is right" (verse 4).

Notice, he doesn't specify this time what the pay will be. But he promises it will be fair. And the workers mentally calculate down from one denarius for the whole day, and figure they'll get three-quarters of a denarius or whatever. Today the men would think, *The full-time guys were promised seventy-five bucks, so we'll get fifty-five. Or maybe fifty-two or fifty-seven. But this boss looks OK; he said he'd be fair. We'll trust him.*

Now the plot thickens. Around noon the boss man hires more men. "Go work and I'll pay you a fair wage for the rest of today." Three o'clock, he signs up even more men. In fact, around five o'clock, just an hour before quitting time, he goes back to the center of town where he finds guys hanging around swapping stories and sipping on diet Sprites, and he says, "Hey, why aren't you working?"

" 'Cause nobody hired us," the men say.

"Well, I'll hire you. Quick, get out there to my vineyard. You can still get in an hour." And the men figure, "Well, five or six bucks is better than nothing. At least we can buy ourselves some supper." And they hustle out there and pick grapes with the others until quitting time, which was at six o'clock.

So as the closing gong sounds, the men line up to get their pay for the day. It's interesting that in Bible times—and this is a clear instruction from God found in Deuteronomy 24:15—laborers were supposed to be paid every single day at quitting time, for their own protection and financial welfare.

So what happens? The paymaster hands out cold cash, first of all, to the men who had just barely gotten there. They'd been on the job only for an hour. And what do you know? They get paid for an entire day! They score a full denarius, or today maybe the seventy-five bucks or whatever the going rate might be. But after working one hour, the coolest, breeziest hour of the day when things are already winding down, they're handed an envelope bulging with cash for twelve hours of work.

How do you suppose they responded? They could probably decide, "Man, this guy's a nut. He can't do math." But if they say that, they say it very quietly. They don't try hard to correct him. Or they think, *He's the best boss in the world. Wow! What generosity! This is twelve times what we thought we would get.* Or they might think that it's just a flat-out mistake. Someone's computer has gone haywire and is spitting out erroneous paychecks. Again, if they think that, they only think it to themselves.

How about the next batch, the men who came in at three o'clock? They get the exact same pay: a denarius. Now, that's still a hugely terrific deal, a major-league bargain, but not quite as good a deal as the five o'clock guys. So these men are torn: Do they rejoice or complain? Are they being ripped off, or are they lucky?

The men hired at noon—one denarius. The men hired at nine in the morning—one denarius. And here's the killer: the men who worked the whole steaming day, who put in the full twelve hours, who sweat through their clothes and got only a half hour for lunch and got briars and thorns under all their fingernails . . . they receive exactly one denarius. The same pay as the men who showed up a few minutes before suppertime. As Jesus tells the story, the master pays every man who worked in the vineyard the exact same amount.

And all of a sudden, we have a mess—the kind of mess God's kingdom is built on. Here's a very blunt question: Is God . . . dare I say it? Is He a nut? Or as theologian F. W. Beare has dubbed our heavenly Father: "The Eccentric Employer"? Hold that thought!

In a previous chapter, I mentioned a Jimmy Carter joke about a man who was turned away from heaven because he only had a dollar's worth of good deeds to cash in. The anecdote is from a chapter entitled "Reaching Out," from *Living Faith,* in which the president asks a thought-provoking question: What good is our faith if it only expresses itself in a total of one dollar given away to needy and hurting people during a lifetime of selfish living?[1] And yet, as we read through this much less funny story found in Matthew 20, we have to post a large sign of warning around any joke or anecdote or story or sermon or book or *anything* that suggests that a man can arrive at the pearly gates of heaven and say, "I deserve to be here."

171

If we make this a story about a really high-paying temp job, we might envision a person who's brought in as a sub to type away at a computer keyboard and rearrange Web sites. And let's say he puts in a huge, frantic Wall Street kind of day—twelve hours. He's there staring at the screen until well after dark. But right close to quitting time, the owner of this little shop brings in a second computer nerd to work at the next terminal over. And he barely boots up his system and logs on before it's quitting time. Lo and behold, when the company issues them each a check, the new kid gets paid for an entire day! Unbelievable! A full day's pay at temp agency rates, when he worked only an hour. And the technician who's been there since 6:30 A.M. feels his heart beat faster as he rips open his envelope. Because he ought to get about twelve times that much if math proportions mean anything. But no . . . there on his check is the exact amount the agency had said he would get for the day: $113.79. And he notices that the one-hour worker has precisely that amount as well: $113.79. A one-hour worker and a twelve-hour worker make identical amounts.

So we ask again, as reverently as we can, is this boss crazy? There's no way this is fair! It may be legal—barely. Technically, it may not violate OSHA and the Division of Labor Standards Enforcement requirements. After all, he did pay the first man the promised amount. But when you throw away huge sums on the second worker, the one who had it the easiest, that makes for tremendous turmoil in the workplace. This CEO is really steering his ship into a storm.

Well, reverence is due to the Boss, because it's very clear that the landowner in this story is God Himself. And in the vineyard of Christian service, it's equally clear that the pay scales are completely mixed up, messed up, upside down, and in total chaos. What kind of a Boss is this? And how should those on the short end of the stick—or the long end, too, for that matter—respond?

It's interesting that most of us identify with and immediately resonate with the person who worked all day. And as we read this Bible parable in Matthew 20, we're instantly angry. The Boss says he'll pay you $113.79, and He does. So that should be fine. We work; we're paid. We're paid what we were promised we'd be paid. Everything is just really wonderful until we see that someone else is paid as much as we are for far less work. And instantly we are angry. Instantly! Why is that?

Well, one word, one human, world-centered word, tells us why. And that word is *deserved*. A person deserved a certain paycheck but received far more. He received more than he deserved, and the rest of the workforce was instantly angry about it. We don't mind getting what we don't deserve, but we sure don't want anyone else getting what *he or she* doesn't deserve.

Think about the story of Jonah, which essentially parallels this one. God told the wayward prophet to travel to Nineveh to warn the inhabitants that destruction was imminent. They deserved to be wiped out. They were sinful, naughty, wicked people, and they all deserved to die. That was the message, and after swimming with a big fish for about three days, Jonah actually went to Nineveh and told the people what they deserved.

The only problem is this: God ends up forgiving the entire population. He "changes His mind." Instead of paying the people zero, or paying them the hot flames they deserve, God gives them the huge paycheck of grace and forgiveness.

And how does Jonah react? He's boiling mad! "Jonah was greatly displeased and became angry. He prayed to the LORD, 'O LORD, is this not what I said when I was still at home? That is why I was so quick to flee to Tarshish. I knew that you are a gracious and compassionate God, slow to anger and abounding in love, a God who relents from sending calamity. Now, O LORD, take away my life, for it is better for me to die than to live' " (Jonah 4:1–3).

I can guarantee you that the residents of Nineveh were a lot happier about God's forgiveness than Jonah was. But, you see, he was God's twelve-hour man! (Except for the very long lunch break he took, where he ran off in the opposite direction.) He was a prophet; he'd been faithful and obedient. He deserved God's favor, and these Ninevites didn't. And so when the pay scale was tampered with, he was beside himself with frustration. "How can I trust You," he lamented to God, "if You're going to treat people with kindness and forgiveness? I worked so hard in Your vineyard, and You pay me back by making a fool of me."

Time and again, this same pattern is shown. A thief dying on the cross repents at the last possible moment. In *What's So Amazing About Grace?* Philip Yancey writes, "In one of his last acts before death, Jesus forgave a thief dangling on a cross, knowing full well the thief had converted out of plain fear. That thief would never study the Bible, never attend synagogue or church, and never make amends to all those he had wronged. He simply said 'Jesus, remember me,' and Jesus promised, 'Today you will be with Me in paradise.' It was another shocking reminder that grace does not depend on what we have done for God but rather what God has done for us."[2]

And here's another complaint. The new Christian church was beside itself with frustration over the fact that Gentiles were going to be allowed to slip in the back door. How could this be? They weren't the chosen people! They hadn't followed Jehovah in the wilderness for forty years. Why should they be so overpaid? And yet, as Jesus tells us this offbeat little vineyard story, this is the way of the kingdom of God.

The doctrine of grace has tons more to say to us on this vital topic, but I guess we should just return to Saint Peter at the gate. If you or I ever once think that we can approach God and God's kingdom with the thought that we deserve something, that concept has got to go. It must be destroyed or, better yet, crucified. Have you given away lots of money? Have you done a lot of good deeds? Especially in contrast to your neighbor down the street? Does that then mean that you deserve heaven, or at least a little bit more of heaven than the next guy? That thought has got to go. The word *deserve* has got to go. The word *paycheck* has got to go. The word *earn* has got to go.

Robert Farrar Capon once wrote, "If the world could have been saved by good bookkeeping, it would have been saved by Moses, not Jesus."[3]

And as Yancey discusses this very vineyard story, he hits the nail right on the head. "Grace cannot be reduced to generally accepted accounting principles. In the bottom-line realm of ungrace, some workers deserve more than others; in the realm of grace the word *deserve* does not even apply."[4]

There was a sorry little story some time ago about our prosperous friend, Mr. Bill Gates. I don't know what his personal net worth is just now, but according to these calculations, if he were to buy a $250,000 sports car—like a Lamborghini— for him it would be the equivalent of spending sixty-seven cents. That's how much it would hurt. Sixty-seven cents. This same little math vignette suggested that if Mr. Gates were to see a hundred-dollar bill lying on the sidewalk, it literally would not be worth the two seconds it would take to bend over and pick it up. It'd be like straining your back to pick up a penny. You just wouldn't bother.

What does Mr. Gates's stupendous personal worth have to do with the kingdom of heaven? Again, it's dangerous, maybe even fatal, to have the word *deserve* in the Christian vocabulary. "I *deserve* such-and-such pay." "I *deserve* a mansion in heaven." "I *deserve* a high position in God's government, a seat right next to Jesus at the Last Supper." As we stand in the shadow of the cross of Calvary, it's foolish to think that we deserve any kind of paycheck at all at the end of the day.

Yancey adds yet another principle regarding this parable: "We risk missing the story's point: that God dispenses gifts, not wages. None of us gets paid according to merit, for none of us comes close to satisfying God's requirements for a perfect life. If paid on the basis of fairness, we would all end up in hell."[5]

Ephesians 2:8, 9 screams this principle through a megaphone: "It is by grace you have been saved, through faith—and this not from yourselves, it is the gift of God—not by works, so that no one can boast."

So in one sense, at least, if the words *deserve* and *earn* and *paycheck* are deleted from our spiritual vocabularies, then what is the point of this story?

One thing we can learn is that Jesus is telling us to take our eyes off our fellow workers. It is as if He says, *"Don't look at what others are paid. Don't pay a lot of attention to how Bill Gates is being treated. Just focus on your own relationship with Me."* Because one thing is true in this story: not one of the vineyard workers was underpaid. No one was cheated. The owner did live up to every bargain; He fulfilled all promises. And people got into trouble and into a murmuring spirit only when they began to look around at the pay stubs of their peers.

There's a quiet little story right at the end of the gospels where no one less than Jesus Himself tells someone to just plain mind his own business. Christ has just had a bit of a loving confrontation with Peter, who had denied Him before the Crucifixion. And in John 21, He very kindly tells His restored disciple Peter that one day he's going to die a martyr's death, just like Jesus had. Which is all right with Peter. He accepts that tough news. But just a moment later, he looks around and sees John standing nearby. And, maybe instinctively, he asks Jesus, "OK, but what will happen to *him*?"

And Jesus tells him this: "If I want him to remain alive until I return, what is that to you? You must follow me" (verse 22).

In other words, that wasn't something Peter needed to know. How God was going to treat John wasn't a concern for Peter. The bottom line for Peter was that Christ was going to sustain him, see him through, empower his ministry, be with him when he picked up his own cross, and finally guarantee him a home in heaven. That was the package for Peter, and that's all Peter needed to know.

In an earlier chapter, I mentioned the prickly reality that on a major-league baseball team, there will be a Mr. Big, a superstar, who's getting 8 or 9 or 10 million. Then a couple who get 5, one or two who get perhaps 2.3 million, and then several players who just get 1 million. Maybe the batboy gets 1 million. Well, I'm kidding, but there are also players on that same team who are paid perhaps $250,000. And they're on the same team, playing on the same field, as a guy who is getting 10 million for playing the same game. And especially on a night where superstar Manny Ramirez, the trillionaire, makes two errors and strikes out five times, or gets busted for steroids and sits out for two months, there could be some rumbling in the clubhouse afterward. "Why is this man making so much more than I am? This is unfair! I want to renegotiate my salary!"

Way back in the very first book I wrote (on an Apple IIe computer!), *Bats, Balls & Altar Calls*, I explored this very parable about the salaries and the hurt feelings, and then applied them to a ball team that goes on to win the World Series. And I tried to make this point for Christians to consider: "The fact is, the harvest came in. The overriding goal was accomplished. The championship was won. And if some workers made more than others, or had better batting averages, so what? 'Don't worry so much about what's happening in the lives of others,' Jesus says. 'You keep your bargain with Me, and things will be all right for you. You may make a little more or a little less than others in this life. Perhaps you'll be famous; perhaps not. But if you labor in My vineyard, eternal life will be yours.' "[6]

I went on to the example of Peter. How long did Peter serve Jesus? His entire adult life—with beatings and trials and nights in jail and persecutions and then a crucifixion at the end. How long did the thief on the cross serve Jesus? A few minutes, perhaps an hour or so. What reward did they both receive? An eternal life in God's kingdom, living in mansions with the identical floor plans. Is that OK with the thief? Sure. Is it OK with Peter? I'm sure he'll be happy with that arrangement as well.

Here's the bottom line. Whether you live in relationship with Jesus Christ and serve Him for one day or for forty-five years in the mission field like my dad or Dr. Paul Brand, the reward is the same. You will get an eternity—not a hundred years, not a thousand, not a million, billion, or trillion—but an eternity of a life greater and richer and more abundant than you can imagine. It is impossible to describe that abundance. But you and I and that thief on the cross and the mass murderer on death row who has a deathbed conversion, are all going to get that same paycheck. We're all going to get mansions. And we're going to live in them for a very, very, very long time.

With that in mind, does the concept of a little bit more pay or a little bit less pay or a slight discrepancy in the scale down here, for these few years on this little planet really matter? No! It doesn't matter! This isn't the real game down here! Down here, this is nothing! And Jesus tells us this parable to remind us to keep our eyes on the real prize. If we get hung up comparing things down here, figuring out who deserves what—when that word *deserve* shouldn't even be in the lexicon— then we've missed the point.

For the mathematicians among us, we could well think of that sideways eight that indicates "infinity." And when your prize is "infinity" you can't get more than that. You can't add to infinity. It would be like giving Bill Gates a dollar. Or like Bill Gates becoming upset if you *didn't* give him a dollar. People who have as many billions as he does in the bank really do not worry about the dollar, or about the paycheck for one hour or even one long day in the vineyard. Their eyes are on bigger prizes than that.

This great parable by Jesus also teaches us quite a bit about loyalty, if you think about it. I remember reading about the thriving business of being a political consultant. These are the media pros who simply know how to run campaigns. And if you sign them up, they can make your TV ads, help coordinate your schedule, do what's called "oppo" work on the enemy candidates, tell you what to say and think, design position papers, and all the rest. Of course, many of these people are available to just about any candidate from the right, the left, the middle, Democrat, Republican, Tea, or Green Party. Especially any Green Party candidate who's got green money. That's the bottom line, of course. I already mentioned the infamous Dick Morris, who used to work with just conservative Republicans, it seemed, but all of a sudden was brought in—for a price—to save the Clinton presidency. After becoming disillusioned with both Bill and Hillary Clinton, he swung back to the far right yet again and embraced the FOX News culture for a price.

The dilemma happening more and more, these days, is that of switching horses halfway through. Candidates will hire consultants—and, of course, they must pretty much put their lives into the handlers' hands. They've got to confide secrets, reveal closet skeletons, bare their souls. And more than once, for whatever reason, a political consultant has jumped ship and gone over to the opposite camp where the grass is greener and the money too. This has provoked a thorny question of ethics: once this handler is armed with secrets from one side, is he or she free to share that dirt with the opposition, with the new boss?

It's a lively discussion, but, as we sit at the feet of Jesus and hear this story of the vineyard, we want to move in the direction of commitment instead. There comes a time in a person's life when he or she must simply pick a boss and stay with him. In a way, these consultants are like surfers in the Pacific Ocean who float on their surfboards, wearing their wet suits and waiting for the right wave. And when it looks like it's coming along, they paddle for all they're worth and hope to ride that winning wave all the way to the shore of victory. Any consultant who endlessly jumps around, going for a few more bucks here, a higher title there, betraying confidences right and left, is going to experience only limited, short-term success.

Here in Matthew 20, the boss pays people what he promised, but in a very strange way. Those who worked the least amount of time get the same pay as those who have been on the campaign from the beginning. A campaign worker who didn't sign on until the end of October gets the same pay as a David Axelrod, who has served the boss fourteen hours a day, seven days a week, since the boss was a skinny junior senator from Illinois.

And so the question is very important here: is this a Boss you can trust? If the pay scales seem messed up, and if certain people—never you, for some reason—are paid more than they deserve, and get invited to *Meet the Press* more often than you are, should you stay with this Leader? Or should you ride some other wave?

In the Bible parable itself, the first workers are told very plainly how much they'll be paid. "One denarius, a standard day's pay, for a day's work." But workers who come along later hear this plantation owner tell them: "Please come work for Me, *and I'll pay you what's fair.*" Well, who's to know how much that will be? Can this man pull out a four-dollar calculator from Staples and figure out a mathematical proportion? But these workers trust Him, and things work out very, very well for every single one of them. They're all paid way more than any of them expected or deserved.

Again I say, where the story bogs down, in human terms, is when the Owner pays *other* people too much money. The all-day workers don't think He's mistreated them; they just resent how the Boss has overpaid all the other campaign staffers. This is where most of us reveal by our whining that we simply do not understand or comprehend or accept what Calvary and grace are all about.

Philip Yancey describes how he went to the play *Amadeus,* which was also the Oscar-winning Best Picture in the year 1984. "[This] play . . . shows a composer in the seventeenth century seeking to understand the mind of God. The devout Antonio Salieri has the earnest desire, but not the aptitude, to create immortal music of praise. It infuriates him that God has instead lavished the greatest gift of musical genius ever known on an impish preadolescent named Wolfgang Amadeus Mozart."

And all through the story, this aching anger and jealousy just eat at the older man. Why, oh why, oh why? God, what is the matter with You? This . . . this . . . kid, this profane, foul-mouthed, promiscuous child whose high-pitched giggling laugh desecrates the halls of the great cathedrals and palaces of Europe, is just brimming over with God-given talent. It's so insufferably easy for Mozart! And Salieri, who is a humble and obedient and loyal servant, both to God and king, simply can't compete. He can't compose as well, play as well, create as effectively. It's just not there. It's a case of getting a smaller paycheck from heaven, and no matter how much he cries or howls or schemes, God doesn't fix the situation. It appears that the heavenly Father is truly a bad Boss. In an irony of ironies, as Yancey points out, the very name *Amadeus* actually means "beloved of God." Why in the world does God love this profane, powder-wigged prodigy?

And in your life and mine, we can see the same rip-off being played over and over a million times. Someone else out there is always doing better than we are. God is blessing them more, treating them better, giving them more favors. They received five talents; we received but one. We'd like to be able to preach or sing or write great Broadway plays, but no matter how tightly we grip that pencil or practice our oratory, it's just not there. Just like in the parable of the talents, God, the mysterious vineyard Owner, has messed up the pay scale again.

Yancey runs down a shrieking list from right in the Bible, because this just happens over and over: "Why would God choose Jacob the conniver over dutiful Esau? Why confer supernatural powers of strength on a Mozartian delinquent named Samson? Why groom a runty shepherd boy, David, to be Israel's king? And why bestow a sublime gift of wisdom on Solomon, the fruit of that king's adulterous liaison? Indeed, in each of these Old Testament stories the scandal of grace rumbles under the surface until finally, in Jesus' parables, it bursts forth in a dramatic upheaval to reshape the moral landscape."[7]

So this is Heaven's way. Once again, we find, the math of the kingdom of heaven is just plain upside down. Two and two is never four; it's five, and then ten, and a hundred and a thousand . . . especially when God is paying *other* people. For you, two and two is four, but not for all the Amadeuses all around you. And this is fixed; this is how it is.

In his *Matthew* commentary for the Tyndale New Testament Commentaries, Dr. Richard T. France reasserts that this is the unavoidable nature of heaven, folks. "The essential point of the parable is that God is like that; his generosity transcends human ideas of fairness. No one receives less than they deserve, but some receive far more."

France then goes on to hit us—Antonio Salieri and you and me—right where it hurts. Right between the eyes. Notice and wince along with me: "God's grace to the undeserving should be a cause for joy, not for jealousy."[8]

And you say, "I'm not ready for that." Well, maybe none of us are. It sticks in the throat when God blesses someone else, when the worst person you know gets a favor from heaven. When it looks like the number-one scoundrel of your city is going to be saved in heaven and have a mansion as big as yours. And at that point, as we feel our blood boiling, we have to stop and ask ourselves, "What has God done for me? Hasn't He saved me too? Am I not going to receive a full eternity in His kingdom? Don't I have the same abundant, overly generous paycheck as the others . . . in terms of the forever of His eternal government in heaven? Didn't God expend the full treasury, the bottomless well of Calvary's grace, for me just as He did for my neighbor?" And then, as we stand in the shadow of the Cross, maybe we'll quiet down a bit and praise God for being the kind of Boss He is.

Theologian R. H. Stein, in his book *An Introduction to the Parables of Jesus,* makes this probing point. "It is frightening to realize that our identification with the first workers, and hence with the opponents of Jesus, reveals how loveless and unmerciful we basically are. We may be more 'under law' in our thinking and less 'under grace' than we realize. God is good and compassionate far beyond his children's understanding!"[9]

Does that diagnosis hit home? Are we angry when God favors others? If so, is it possible that we haven't yet experienced grace? Dr. France makes this gentle suggestion: "Parables are characteristically open-ended, and a general rule for their interpretation is, 'If the cap fits, wear it!' "[10]

I'm afraid mine fits rather snugly. How about yours?

But let me close our discussion of this parable with one more mission tale. We already met Paul Brand, super doc to the teeming millions of India. This story happens in China instead.

We're still in Matthew 20, and there are many, many vineyard workers milling around at the paymaster's table. Some of them have put in a long, tiring twelve-hour day. They've got grape stains on their clothes, kinks in their backs, and blisters on their fingers. And I'd like for you to meet one of the workers who did indeed work that entire long hot shift in the sun and didn't say a single word of complaint.

Our vineyard worker is Harry. That's his real name, actually. Dr. Harry Miller. As soon as I say that, many of you recognize him: the famous "China Doctor." For many decades this genius of medicine worked for God in the exotic but steaming-hot, crowded cities of faraway China. He went out there in the year 1903 with his young bride, Maude. Groaning their way over the Pacific Ocean in a tiny state-room just over the propeller shaft of the ill-named freighter *Empress of India,* it was hardly a royal ride. By the time they got to China, Harry had been seasick for so long he vowed to just live in Asia for the rest of his life and never return to the United States.

If you get the opportunity, get a copy of the wonderful book *China Doctor,* by Raymond S. Moore. But this brilliant surgeon literally gave his life to the country of China. He spent decades there, but just two years after arriving, he buried his wife, who died of a mysterious foreign ailment at the age of twenty-five. He started many Adventist hospitals; he survived the wars and rebellions. He lived as a Chinese person, even dressing in the Asian robes and wearing his hair in a queue. He operated on peasants and royalty alike. In fact, he was finally awarded the coveted Blue Star of China, by none other than Generalissimo Chiang Kai-shek and Madame Chiang Kai-shek for all of his spiritual and humanitarian work in Taiwan, Republic of China.

But there's quite a bit more to this story of a quiet and faithful worker in the vineyard. Because Harry Miller, as renowned as he was, also served some brief stints in the United States, where his inventive surgical procedures made him famous. He served as an attending physician to Presidents Taft and Wilson. He treated William Jennings Bryan and Alexander Graham Bell. Many, many fabulously wealthy celebrities sought him out. But, in all that time, did he become wealthy? Did he increase his paycheck?

A hospital worker recalled once how a famous Florida millionaire came to the Washington Adventist Sanitarium, desperate to be made well. Top specialists hadn't been able to spot his troubles, but Miller quickly diagnosed the problem and cured him. Grateful beyond words, the man paid his hospital bill and then asked to see the China Doctor. Expressing his thanks, almost with tears coming down his cheeks, this recovered millionaire took out a brand-new, clean, starch-stiff thousand dollar bill—the first any of the employees had ever seen—and pressed it into Dr. Miller's hand. This was his personal gift of appreciation. And this was back in the 1920s. Dr. Miller, at that time, was receiving a salary of exactly forty-four dollars a week. But just moments later, the humble doctor turned and gave the bill to his assistant. "Here, Stan," he said. "Take this down to the cashier."

During his entire career, in both China and the United States, he often received huge gifts from Chinese royalty and wealthy patrons—friends estimate that he turned over to the mission work *personal gifts* totaling at least 2.5 million dollars. One wealthy ruler, the infamous "Young Marshal," who kicked an opium addiction under Miller's supervision, handed him a personal check for fifty thousand dollars. The China Doctor endorsed it immediately into a trust fund to build a Seventh-day Adventist hospital in Lanzhou. Over in China, while many doctors drove around in luxurious U.S. automobiles, or even had chauffeur-driven limousines, Dr. Miller could be seen rumbling through the narrow streets of Shanghai in an old, beat-up Dodge convertible that had the top missing.[11]

The anecdotes on this man seem endless. I was privileged, as a young boy living in Bangkok, to have Dr. Miller once have supper with our family, and we were all fascinated by this humble man of God. He practiced medicine until the age of ninety-three, lived to be ninety-seven, and was still in active service to his God right to the very end. Even in his eighties, he was traveling around the world, still starting hospitals, still witnessing for the Lord through his exceptional talents.

So what's the upshot of this kind of story? Here's a man who worked in the vineyard for the Owner for the full shift. In fact, this was no twelve-hour day; it was fifteen or sixteen. He gave a long, long lifetime of hot, sweating, standing-in-lines-for-Communist-interrogation service for his God. And at the end of the day, the paycheck was not very spectacular. This man who could have been a multi-multimillionaire died and was buried in a modest grave, without much of an estate to leave behind.

So we ask the question one final time: what's the reward? These workers in the vineyard all received a denarius, a penny, at the end of the day. And, yes, there's a larger reward out there called eternal life. There's heaven and golden streets and a beautiful river of life and a land that's fairer than day. And the China Doctor was a man who knew he was going there. He knew there was a place being prepared for him. He knew he would live and dwell with Jesus for all of eternity. So is that the reward?

Just a few verses earlier, before Jesus began to tell this story, He gave Peter an answer when this disciple asked Him, "What's our reward for having followed You so faithfully?" And Jesus told him: "Anyone who follows Me and leaves houses and lands and family and friends for My sake will receive a hundred times as much . . . *and* inherit eternal life." So is this the payoff? Is this what makes the story of the vineyard turn out all right?

Well, yes, it is. But I'd like to suggest something more. And if you've ever looked on with frustration at those who live a life of flowing money and debauchery and drugs, and then just jumped on the Jesus train at the last possible minute—just in time to get the same full paycheck as you—I'd like for us to think of the perspective of the China Doctor. He's sleeping in Jesus now, but what if you were to ask him: "Do you feel cheated? You could have been wealthy. You could have had so much. But you worked for God in China all those years"? How would he respond?

Morris Venden answers on behalf of Dr. Harry Miller, in his book *Parables of the Kingdom.* "So what is the reward? What is the penny [the denarius]? *It is Jesus Himself!* He can't give the twelve-hour workers more than the one-hour workers, because He can give neither more nor less than Himself. Why? Because in giving Himself He gives all the riches of the universe."[12]

Let's put it this way: which workers got to spend the whole day with Jesus? It was those who were there twelve hours. Which ones got the most fellowship? The ones who were there twelve hours. Which ones experienced the adventure of serving side by side with the most wonderful Savior? The ones who worked twelve hours. If they wanted just money, yes, maybe they were ripped off. But if you wanted Jesus, and closeness with Jesus, and fellowship with Jesus, and partnership with Jesus, then who were the luckiest guys in the world? The ones who worked twelve hours.

In her book *Steps to Christ,* Ellen White takes the same view: "God might have committed the message of the gospel, and all the work of loving ministry, to the heavenly angels." He doesn't really *need* Dr. Miller or you or me. She continues, "He might have employed other means for accomplishing His purpose. But in His infinite love He chose to make us co-workers with Himself, with Christ and the angels, that we might share the blessing, the joy, the spiritual uplifting, which results from this unselfish ministry."[13]

Are there frustrations out there in the vineyard? Is it hot? Sometimes messy? Almost always fatiguing? Yes to all of the above. But that's where Jesus is. And you know, there's no place I'd rather work.

Chapter 11

THE GOOD GUY
From the Bad Neighborhood

Frank was a senior citizen, a widower who'd lost his wife, Estelle, nearly three years before. Fixed income, retired, with Social Security and a very small pension. He had a little house, which had been in a not-too-bad neighborhood in the early seventies, but by now it had fallen into what people used to call "the wrong side of the railroad tracks." Gangs had moved in; crack had taken over. Street hookers were more and more open about their business. Police didn't come by very often, and when they did, it was a cursory visit. In and out quick.

Frank really would have liked to move out and into a better neighborhood, or perhaps even down to Florida. He didn't like the people who lived on his block anymore. They were noisy, they were careless and unemployed; they were a vastly different skin shade than he was. Everything they did seemed to kind of feed the various stereotypes he'd always carried around anyway. But like it or not, this was going to be his neighborhood until he died because he couldn't afford better. In fact, he didn't even have a car anymore; unless he pooled with someone, he couldn't even get to a grocery store in an upscale area. So he bought all of his necessities like milk and razor blades at the corner 7-Eleven. And sometimes his guts tightened as he passed by the tough kids who hung out there with their skateboards and their black tank tops and their bandannas and their muttered obscenities. He never said anything to them, but his mind was always racing with the things he'd like to say. It was always a relief to unlock his own front door, undo the second deadbolt, plop his little bag of groceries on the scarred Formica table, and lock things back up tight.

And then one day, the thing he'd always feared might happen actually did. He was out of bread and cooking oil, and Gary, his occasional car-loaning friend, was away to take care of his sister. So Frank, taking just the few dollars he knew he'd need, walked slowly to the 7-Eleven again, noticing the new batch of ugly graffiti, most of it unintelligible. "Stupid punks," he muttered to himself. "They write stuff . . . and nobody knows what it means." Then he realized that it was probably better that way, but it still made him boil inside. He was about half a block from the crowded parking lot of the convenience store when a huge black car came by real slow, with the back end jacked up about a foot and a half, and with all of its subwoofers blaring out rap music that went right through pedestrians.

Then a shot rang out. For just a second, the kids in the parking lot thought the car had backfired. And then they saw Frank, this aging, lonely, angry, beaten-up man crumpled next to the curb, blood oozing from a wound in his shoulder.

And everybody just froze. For about five seconds, they just stood there. The car was moving away from the store, and they watched as it picked up speed and kept going down the street. No motive, no message. Just a random act of violence, a drive-by shooting. That was all it was. And the kids and the customers just stood there.

A couple of the teenagers went over about halfway and got a closer look. "Man, he's bleeding bad," one of them said. But they didn't know if it was dangerous to touch him, or if the car might be coming back, or just what to do. So they kind of moved back, walking backward, until they were in the parking lot again. "Anybody call the cops?" a woman asked. "I think the guy in the store will," a nine-year-old boy said. "He usually does." He said it like—"Well, that's his job. This happens all the time around here, lady."

On the other side of the street, filling up his tank at the ARCO self-serve station, was a preacher. He'd pulled off the freeway because he was down to fumes. And he, too, heard the one shot ring out. He saw the senior citizen jerk once, then fall down on the pavement. And about fifteen seconds later, the gas pump clicked off, and the man of God stood there, transfixed.

What do I do? he wondered. He was supposed to meet a wealthy donor at a restaurant in forty minutes. This was a man who'd hinted he was about ready to contribute twenty-five thousand dollars to the church building program. And he didn't like to be kept waiting.

For just a moment, the preacher, out of habit, almost started to cross the street. Then he saw the gang members down at the 7-Eleven. He saw the blood oozing onto Frank's gray flannel shirt. He pictured in his mind the mess, the hot tar of the pavement getting on his pants, the blood on his hands, the smell of sweat and the odors of this rough ghetto neighborhood on his clothes. And very slowly, feeling only a quickly passing twinge of guilt, he put the nozzle back, twisted the gas cap into place, and pulled back onto the freeway. *Somebody will call 911,* he assured himself. *That's not my job; it's their job.* And he was less than a mile down the interstate before he'd completely forgotten it.

Another man heard the same gunshot and froze up morally too. He was a deacon of a church about eight blocks away, but he always came over here during his lunch break because there was a funky little used bookstore that sometimes had the great religious classics for a quarter or fifty cents. In fact, this very afternoon he'd scored an autographed copy of Billy Graham's book *Peace With God*! For just two bucks! And as he came out of the bookstore and stepped into the hot sunshine, he heard the muffled little *pop!* and saw Frank collapse.

And again there was that moment of wrestling. *Is this my problem? I'm just a visiting shopper here. This isn't my neighborhood.* He watched the teenagers in their own slow-motion reaction, some kids moving hesitantly toward the fallen man, others going into the store, others easing away. One boy, holding his skateboard in one hand, was cradling a cell phone with the other. *Is he calling for an ambulance?* The deacon couldn't tell. But he glanced at his watch and noticed with a bit of relief that he was late. There was no way he could stop and check. He'd be late getting back to Century 21, where he was the top salesman. And he had escrow papers from three big deals sitting there on his desk. One of them was a sale to a Hollywood couple, and he hoped he might even have a chance to say something to them about God the next time they got together to work on the financing. He better get back to that and trust that someone here, someone who belonged here and knew the ways and the rhythms of this neighborhood, would take care of things. So very quickly, glancing around to see if that ominous black car might be circling back, he punched in the numbers for his new keyless-entry leased car, and drove away without looking back.

And Frank lay there on the pavement. Five minutes went by. Six. Seven. He was still conscious, but feeling weaker by the second. The blood wasn't flowing quickly, but he could tell that it was still seeping through his shirt. It was all over his face, and the little granules of sand and concrete particles were pressing into the scarlet streaks on his cheek. "Somebody help me," he tried to say, but his voice was drowned out by the traffic. "Please. Somebody."

And then he heard a voice. "Hey, bro. You OK?"

He couldn't turn his head even, but he could barely make out the form of a teenager. One of the kids at the 7-Eleven. Blue jeans, a ratty white shirt with nothing but a picture of a fist on it. The boy had put down his skateboard and was kneeling next to him. "Man, you're hit bad," the boy said, his words softened by his accent. "Those guys nailed you in the shoulder, looks like."

"Please . . . don't hurt me." Frank felt his weakened pulse fluttering for a moment. Would this street punk finish him off, take the three dollars he had in his pocket? "Can you . . . call 911 for me?"

"I already did, man." The boy took off his bandanna and began to gently dab at the blood on Frank's face. "But they're slow. Really slow. 'Specially around here. By the time they get to us, bro, you'll die for sure. Or at least melt in this sun."

And all at once, Frank, this white senior citizen with a bullet in his shoulder, found himself in the back seat of a classic Ford Mustang. And this skateboarding boy from the 'hood, and his fellow gang member, were driving their human cargo a mile and a half to the emergency room of the county hospital. Helping the orderly get Frank onto a stretcher. Waiting for an hour and fifteen minutes while doctors took a look at him. And, wonder of wonders, when the clerk at ER said that they had to have a signature, or a Medicare card, or an insurance number, or *some* kind of co-pay before they could do anything at all, this kid from 7-Eleven dug into the pocket of his jeans and pulled out a twenty-dollar bill. "That's what I get pouring concrete every weekend," he told the clerk. "Take it. And if you need more, I can get it . . . but probably not till Sunday."

"Can't your friend pay?" the nursing clerk asked him, her voice suddenly soft with a bit of awe, like she was experiencing something right out of the Bible.

"My friend?" The kid laughed, his amusement bouncing off the block walls of the unair-conditioned waiting room. "Are you kidding? Man, I never saw that guy before in my life."

* * * * *

"And who *is* my neighbor?"

That little five-word question came from a man who plied Jesus with one in a seemingly endless flow of trick questions. But Christ had an answer for him, a story, a parable, which has resonated ever since, right down here to the twenty-first century. "Who is my neighbor? Who am I really supposed to love?"

Afraid to even say the *S* word

They say the world loves a story, but Hollywood's back alleys are filled with scripts that got rejected, sitcoms that got canceled, and film stories that went into turnaround and never got made. And the reason some stories don't work is that they don't apply to how people live. Well, if there was ever a parable from the Bible that still works big-time here in this selfish new millennium, nearly two thousand years after it was first told, this has to be the story. The parable of the good Samaritan that answers the question, "Who is my neighbor?"

The book of Luke contains two stories in which a man asks Jesus Christ, "What do I have to do to inherit eternal life?" In the Luke 18 passage, Jesus says to the man, "Well, keep all of the commandments."

"Oh, I already do that," the ruler replies with a confident smile. "Ever since I was a boy. Is there anything else?"

"Yes," Jesus tells him, "sell everything you have, give the money to the poor, and then come follow Me. Be My disciple." And the man goes away sad, because he's a millionaire.

Now here in Luke chapter 10, Jesus gives quite a different answer to what's essentially the same question. Consider this reply from Jesus and decide for yourself if this response is easier or harder.

Actually, Christ knows that this man is trying to catch him in a verbal trap. The Bible says this "expert in the law" stood up to test Jesus. In the King James: "Behold, a certain lawyer stood up, and tempted him" (verse 25).

Jesus sees the trap a mile off, of course, so He wisely lets the man answer his own question. I'm reminded of the Jewish rabbi who was asked by a frustrated student, "Why do you teachers always answer questions with another question?" And the aging wise one responds, "So what's wrong with a question?" But Jesus says to the man: "What is written in the Law?" . . . "How do you read it?" (verse 26).

And the man gives this answer: " 'Love the Lord your God with all your heart and with all your soul and with all your strength and with all your mind'; and, 'Love your neighbor as yourself' " (verse 27).

And that was a good answer, quoting directly from Deuteronomy 6 and Leviticus 19. So Jesus gives him an encouraging nod. " 'You have answered correctly,' Jesus replied. 'Do this and you will live' " (Luke 10:28).

But think for a moment about the difficulty of this requirement. Maybe it seems soft to us—softer, anyway, than having a huge garage sale during which you sell not only the things in your garage, but the garage itself and the house and the whole thing, so that you can give everything to the poor. But are you and I and this lawyer really capable of loving God with all of our hearts? And with all of our souls and our strength and our minds? Giving Heaven a 110 percent commitment, all day, every day? Is that something we can do? Are we coming close? And then to love our neighbor as ourselves? Jesus wasn't just handing out a Hallmark card here that suggests, "Love your neighbor and hug a tree." He was actually saying this, and meaning it. We have to love God with everything we've got, every fiber of emotion and heart and soul we have in us. And then we have to love our neighbor with that same intensity.

In *Living Faith,* President Carter describes how back in the 1960s he partnered up with a Cuban-American pastor named Eloy Cruz for a summer of witnessing. And this man had a passion for people: simple people, poor people, struggling people. He and Carter would sit in the kitchen of some home where the people had tremendous problems and challenges to face. And somehow Pastor Cruz knew just the words to share, the best way to explain his own love for them and for his Savior Jesus. Time after time, Jimmy Carter would see tears flow and people respond spiritually to that love. And this quiet, dynamic missionary pastor had a slogan that comes right out of this story. "You only have to have two loves in your life—for God," he would say, "and for the person in front of you."[1]

And in this dramatic Bible story, as the sharpie lawyer tries to jockey with Jesus a bit, pin Him down with debating points, he's at a stalemate. Because he and Jesus agree on this answer. "Love God with all your heart; love your neighbor with all your heart." Not that this man was accomplishing those twin objectives, you understand. But he knew how to give the textbook answer, and Jesus had given him an A. So where should he go next?

Well, the lawyer takes the easy way out. He asks another question, one which feeds right into the popular discussion of that era. "All right, then, Mr. Jesus, tell me this," he asks. "Just who is my neighbor? Whom do I have to be nice to? Whom do I have to love?"

And immediately, there was a buzz of interest and approval. Because this was a point of constant coffeehouse debate in Israel. Who was your neighbor? Just the two families living on either side of you? Or everyone in your entire cul-de-sac?

There were a couple of "givens" in society back then. If you were talking about the heathen . . . well, that wasn't even on the table. Nonbelievers weren't your neighbors; they weren't anything. Even Jesus called them "dogs"—or seemed to, on one occasion at least. They were of absolutely no account, no worth, no anything. Nobody who'd graduated from kindergarten would even discuss that.

And how about Samaritans? Could they possibly qualify as "neighbors"? Not a chance! Not if they lived in your own backyard, which wasn't about to happen. The New International Version text notes for the Bible give us this bit of illumination: "Jews viewed Samaritans as half-breeds, both physically and spiritually. . . . [Samaritans were] a mixed-blood race resulting from the intermarriage of Israelites left behind when the people of the northern kingdom exiled, and Gentiles brought into the land by the Assyrians."

Speaking of spiritually, the Samaritans accepted only the Pentateuch as their Bible, rejecting all of the other writings held so dear by the Jews. There was a debate where the Samaritans had their temple on the "wrong" mountain, Gerazim, instead of on Zion, which was, of course, the right and proper place to worship. And on and on it went. But no Jew with a brain in his head would consider that a Samaritan ten miles away or ten feet away was a neighbor worthy of decent treatment. They were the McCoys to Israel's Hatfields.

And now Jesus launches into His story. We pick up the action in verse 30: "A man was going down from Jerusalem to Jericho, when he fell into the hands of robbers. They stripped him of his clothes, beat him and went away, leaving him half dead."

This road is the famous, or infamous, *Wadi Qelt,* which ran seventeen miles from Jerusalem, twenty-five hundred feet above sea level, down to Jericho, at eight hundred feet below. So it was a rocky, down-down-down journey, with plenty of places for Jesse James's gang to hide out. And that's how it works out here for this anonymous crime victim. Then Jesus continues, "A priest happened to be going down the same road, and when he saw the man, he passed by on the other side. So too, a Levite, when he came to the place and saw him, passed by on the other side" (verses 31, 32).

These two men, obviously, were operating under the "neighbor policy" of the day. "If I don't know you, forget it. Let the next guy dial 911, while I look out for number one."

And now comes the punch line to the story. "But a Samaritan, as he traveled, came where the man was; and when he saw him, he took pity on him. He went to him and bandaged his wounds, pouring on oil and wine. Then he put the man on his own donkey, took him to an inn and took care of him. The next day he took out two silver coins and gave them to the innkeeper. 'Look after him,' he said, 'and when I return, I will reimburse you for any extra expense you may have' " (verses 33–35).

End of story. Jesus takes a deep breath. Everyone in the crowd, kind of mad about the ending, takes a breath, too, and then grumbles a bit to the person standing next to them. "Stupid story. What's He mean?" And then Jesus leans in a bit to this lawyer. "Which of these three do you think was a neighbor to the man who fell into the hands of robbers?" (verse 36).

And even there, the man couldn't bring himself to say the dreaded *S* word, "Samaritan." He just couldn't do it, even after a story like that. But he cleared his throat and reluctantly admitted, "Uh, well, you know, that last guy. The one who had mercy on him."

"You're right," Jesus said. And then these five archaic King James words that still ring with such power, twenty centuries later. "Go, and do thou likewise" (verse 37).

The surprise double twist ending

So is it easy or hard to obey what Jesus tells us to do here? If you ever thought you had a neighbor that even the best Christian shouldn't be expected to love, then I have a little story for you to think about. On June 10, back in the year 1942, Nazi troops stormed into a town belonging to their Czechoslovakian neighbors. The village of Lidice had something like five hundred inhabitants. And the Nazis lined up the men and executed, in cold blood, every single one of them. Just mowed them down. It was one of the worst atrocities of all of World War II. They burned down every house in the village, the Nazis did. And the women and children were sent to concentration camps. These many decades later, and always in the month of June, Lidice Memorial Day is observed in New Jersey, as people remember the rape of this innocent town.

If you could find a survivor still today, maybe an old woman who was just a pale-faced, frightened child there in Lidice, could you ask her, even now, to turn around and consider the Germans her neighbors? Can the people of God not only love the people who have historically not been our neighbors, but also go the second and third and fourth miles and learn to treat as neighbors those who have been decidedly unneighborly toward us?

Here in Luke 10 is a story that's not only hard because of its ending, but made even harder *because it turns into a call to action.* Just as this good Samaritan was a good neighbor, Jesus then looks into the face of the questioning lawyer, and through the pages of Scripture into my face and your face, and gives us this command, "Go, and do thou likewise."

But is this Nazi story, "The Rape of Lidice," a proper application? How wide does Jesus Christ draw this circle, when we ask, "Who is my neighbor"?

The animosity, the hatred, between Jews and Samaritans certainly did rise to this level of "Nazis versus Czechs." These two groups hated each other, despised each other. These emotions started, of course, with nationalistic pride, and then went downhill from there. In the Tyndale New Testament Commentaries for Luke, Leon Morris addresses this question of "who is my neighbor?" "There were different ideas among the Jews on this point, but they all seem to be confined to the nation Israel; the idea of love towards mankind had not reached them."[2]

The hated Samaritans, of course, were right there among them: always in their faces, always worshiping wrong, talking wrong, looking wrong, smelling wrong. Naturally, the Samaritans felt the same way coming back. This war ran on both sides of the street, to be sure. A New International Version text note explains that Samaritans would never give Jews any shelter during their three-day trips from Galilee to Jerusalem. So travelers would have to take the long way around, going on the east side of the Jordan to avoid going through what they honestly considered to be enemy territory.

And here in Luke 10, Jesus tells this parable, which takes His listeners right into the heart of their own very worst hatred and prejudices and fears.

By the way, if you've ever listened to a story and thought that you were one step ahead of the storyteller and could see where this thing was going, that was probably the experience of this listening crowd. These things have a kind of rhythm to them, a one, two, three building up of the plot. Leon Morris suggests that the crowd very likely began to look ahead as Jesus tells the story. *All right,* they think to themselves, *the priest doesn't stop to help. That pompous, overpaid windbag, that Pharisee. And the Levite—he's a temple servant, and he doesn't stop either. So the big-shot church men don't stop to help. But hey, just a regular guy, a common ordinary, blue-collar, fisherman Jew will probably come along next, and he'll be the man who stops to help. Ha! I've figured it out ahead of time.*

Actually that would have been a not half bad parable. We could probably study that ending and feel spiritually satisfied. But with the whole crowd thinking that a regular good guy is going to come along and save the day for Hollywood,

Jesus throws them the most unexpected curve in the world. It is totally and completely unanticipated when He says in verses 33 and 34: "But a Samaritan, as he traveled, came where the man was; and when he saw him, he took pity on him. He went to him and bandaged his wounds, pouring on oil and wine."

And that had to completely freak the crowd out. "What! A Samaritan?" That plot twist hit them right in the guts. "Jesus, what are You talking about? You lost us right there." Not one of them saw that as a possible ending to the story.

Some of the others in the crowd, also self-proclaimed experts at guessing the punch line, probably expected that after the priest and the Levite came by, a villain was going to be next. In fact, the *International Bible Commentary* with noted theologian F. F. Bruce, makes that very suggestion: "A surprising *dénouement* [or Hollywood ending] to the story; 'the hearers would assume that the villain of the piece had arrived on the scene.' "[3]

So, no, Jesus didn't give them the expected bad guy. And He didn't give them the good guy they had anticipated. To this crowd of Jews, He gave them a Samaritan. If it were citizens of Czechoslovakia, He'd have given them a Nazi. To a group of Ku Klux Klaners, a black businessman. To the Crips, a member of the Bloods. To a devout, family values kind of church leader, a gay activist. And as you think about this story and what it ought to mean in your life, think of the kind of person—or perhaps the very exact person—you would struggle most of all to consider as a neighbor. And then have that person come along as Traveler three in this story. Or turn it around: make that enemy the bleeding, half-dead victim . . . and *you* are Traveler three. Because Jesus Christ tells this story to punch holes in every prejudice we've ever held, every grudge we've ever nurtured.

Speaking of grudges, this story about neighbors actually springs from a biblical lesson on the bearing of grudges. When the young lawyer, back in verse 25, asks Jesus, "What must I do to inherit eternal life?" Jesus lets him answer his own question. And the questioner correctly quotes from Leviticus about loving your neighbor. But here's the full verse, in chapter 19, verse 18: "Do not seek revenge or bear a grudge against one of your people, but love your neighbor as yourself."

Isn't that interesting? Maybe a hard kind of interesting. Because Jesus is telling us here that not only do our racism and our prejudice have to go, but also our resentments and our grudges. That person whose behavior just bugs you to death is your neighbor. The man you've steamed about privately for years is your neighbor. That boss, that hypocrite in the church, that person who took you to court is your neighbor. And in this story, it's that very person who is lying by the side of the road bleeding and half dead, and you are Traveler three coming down from Jerusalem to Jericho.

Maybe you say, as I am very tempted to say as well: "I don't want that role. I could never love that person; no way. I could never be a neighbor to so-and-so." What's more, you might think in your heart—and be right about the fact—that if the tables were reversed and you were lying in the dust, that enemy would never help you. It's interesting to note that in *The Desire of Ages,* Ellen White makes the very same point about this exact story. The traveling Samaritan comes down the road and sees this wounded Jew. She observes, "He [the Samaritan] did not question whether the stranger was a Jew or a Gentile. If a Jew, the Samaritan well knew that, were their condition reversed, the man would spit in his face, and pass him by with contempt."[4]

And he still gets off his donkey and helps his worst enemy.

So this is where we are. Can we be neighbors to someone who not only doesn't treat us like neighbors, but never will? Can we repay evil with good, even when we keep getting evil thrown in our faces? Jesus submitted to the cross, and He prayed for the Roman soldiers who were driving nails through His hands. He prayed out loud for them. But when they heard that prayer, were their hearts touched? Did they repent? Did they pull out the nails and say they were sorry? No, they just kept on pounding those spikes. But Jesus continued to love them. He continued to demonstrate the most neighborly moment this universe has ever witnessed.

Aren't you glad for a Neighbor like that? And wouldn't you like to be one—a man or woman so secure in the kingdom of grace that you simply help *everyone* who has a need, regardless of whether or not they deserve it?

The best enemy I ever had

Here's one more slice of healthy perspective, courtesy of a church bulletin in Australia, which contributed the following litany to the delightful book *More Holy Humor,* compiled by Cal and Rose Samra. It's entitled "The Pit."

"A man fell into a pit and couldn't get himself out." That's the premise of this particular dilemma. OK, now here come all the helpers.

"A *subjective* person came along and said, 'I feel for you down there.'

"An *objective* person walked by and said, 'It's logical that someone would fall down there.'

"A *Pharisee* said, 'Only bad people fall into pits.'

"A *mathematician* calculated how he fell into the pit.

"A *news reporter* wanted the exclusive story on the pit.

"An *IRS agent* asked if he was paying taxes on the pit.

"A *self-pitying* person said, 'You haven't seen anything until you've seen my pit!'

"A *fire-and-brimstone preacher* said, 'You deserve your pit.'

"A *psychologist* noted, 'Your mother and father are to blame for your being in that pit.'

"A *self-esteem therapist* said, 'Believe in yourself and you can get out of that pit.'

"An *optimist* said, 'Things could be worse.'

"A *pessimist* claimed, 'Things *will* get worse.' "

But here's the final entry: "Jesus, seeing the man, took him by the hand and lifted him out of the pit."[5]

That's good, isn't it? But maybe we all saw ourselves elsewhere in this story, standing over the pit and calculating the trajectory of the person as he fell in, or a Sabbath School teacher charting how many bad words the victim said while he was down there, or a dietitian using a calorie chart to figure out how long before this poor guy starves to death. And then Jesus, without asking how he got there, or what mistakes he made to trip and fall in, or rolling His eyes and delivering a sarcastic lecture, just reaches down and pulls him out.

For about the past quarter century or so, there's been a sinister cloud out there we call AIDS. The HIV virus. And every time it's announced on television or on the *Huffington Post* that a certain celebrity is infected, the question comes up immediately, "But how'd he get it? What did he *do*? Tell us so we can know how much blame to assign." And there's this discussion and this pecking order of descending acceptability, starting with an innocent child who gets it from his mother. And the person who gets it from a blood transfusion. Down from there, there's the person who gets HIV from a spouse who cheated. Then the one who got it trading dirty needles. And then below that is the person who was promiscuous, but only in a heterosexual sense. And then last, and certainly least as well, the person who gets AIDS from rampant homosexual activity.

But here we see a Jesus, a Savior, who puts off discussions about who is worse than whom, and simply pulls the helpless person out of the pit.

In the parable of the good Samaritan, the helpless victim isn't in a pit; he's lying bleeding by the roadside. But he is equally helpless. He can't do anything to get himself to an inn or a hospital or an urgent care center. If he's going to be rescued, someone else is going to have to do it.

And if we ever had a lesson to learn in life, it's that *we are that helpless victim*. Maybe we traveled purposely down that road where we knew full well there were pitfalls. That seventeen-mile stretch between Jerusalem and Jericho, or for us it might be a moral Sodom and Gomorrah with the bars and brothels and bandits. We knew Satan and his band were down there in the rocks, but we took a chance. We went onto his territory. And sure enough, he attacked us and left us for dead.

There's not a one of us who can get to a hospital on our own. We haven't got money for the ambulance; we haven't even got a cell phone to dial 911, except for maybe the long-distance miracle of prayer. But in terms of sin and slavery to sin, every one of us is not just wounded on the road, but fatally wounded.

Maybe that statement doesn't seem real to you as you read. "Hey, I'm not helpless," you say. "I'm not even wounded. Not a scratch. I'm doing fine." Believe me when I say that the human experience demonstrates this: all of us, sooner or later, are going to run into that nest of thieves. In terms of sin and righteousness, the realization of the human race's condition may not have hit you yet like it has hit so many others . . . but it's coming. Without a Savior coming along, I'm a lost person, and you're a lost person. There's a tough little verse in Isaiah 41 that says, "You are less than nothing and your works are utterly worthless" (verse 24).

God doesn't say that to hurt our feelings or to drive us down, except onto our knees, but He does lovingly tell us how things are. We're wounded and we're bleeding and we're helpless. Unless the right person comes along after us, we're doomed.

And then comes this third Traveler. After the priest goes by and the Levite goes by, here comes the Samaritan. In this beautiful story, the life-saving assistance comes from the fallen man's worst enemy—the dreaded and despised Samaritan. Maybe you scratch your head to follow the logic . . . because you don't consider Jesus Christ to be your enemy. And yet in terms of the human race and its response to God and His Son Jesus, we certainly have treated Christ as an enemy. He was an outcast when He came here. "My kingdom is not of this world," He told people (John 18:36). And just as Jews of that era might have wanted to ignore and insult and push and shove and spit on and kill Samaritans, they did all of that and more to this third Traveler, this foreign Visitor, this Alien who had come to rescue them.

As we read through the details of this rescue, we get such a glimpse of the heart of Jesus. It says in Luke chapter 10, verse 33 about the Samaritan, "He took pity on him." It was for pity and love that Christ came down here. He may have been an enemy to us, but we were never that to Him. He was moved by pity then, and He's still moved by pity now. As you bleed by the road, perhaps at this very moment, He's moved by pity, and He's also moved to action.

Here's verse 34: "He went to him and bandaged his wounds, pouring on oil and wine. Then he put the man on his own donkey, took him to an inn and took care of him."

Notice that the bleeding man is placed on the rescuer's own donkey. The Samaritan walks while the victim rides. And when Jesus rescues, He gives us His own ride, so to speak. We get the benefits of His holiness while He walks the painful road to Calvary in our place.

The story continues in verse 35: "The next day he took out two silver coins and gave them to the innkeeper. 'Look after him,' he said, 'and when I return, I will reimburse you for any extra expense you may have.' "

Do we find any parallels even here? We certainly glimpse a picture of ongoing assistance, of continued relationship. This good Samaritan paid the bill for right then, and he also provided for the long-term care of this wounded man, this enemy. Two silver coins, two *denarii,* back in those Bible times, would have been two days' salary. Which gives us a picture of a substantial gift, especially offered on behalf of a stranger and an enemy. Today, it would be like paying maybe several hundred dollars' worth of someone's medical bills at the ER. According to the historian Polybius, those two silver coins, the average wages for two days, was sufficient, on the other hand, to provide for lodging in an inn like this for perhaps a couple of months. And we see here in the scriptural story that he says to the innkeeper: "Take care of this man for me. Do whatever it takes. And if necessary, there's more where it came from. I'll reimburse you in full when I return."

In the Christian faith, Jesus' providence for us doesn't end on a hill called Calvary. That was a magnificent, noble rescue, but then we also see those two coins come out of the purse. And we receive continued, continuous healing from our Savior. He continues to be, in every sense of the word, a Savior. As we continue to fall and as we sometimes fail to trust in Him, He picks us up. He forgives. He answers prayer. His arms are always open wide. He gives us, through the Holy Spirit, guidance in our daily life choices. He is our Intercessor, our continuous High Priest.

Through the ministry of the church, Christ continues to radiate an expression of the two coins. Maybe you were saved many years ago, when you prayed the sinner's prayer and accepted Jesus as your Savior. That was the day Christ came along that Jericho road and picked you up, bound up your wounds, and carried you to the inn. But now, as the months and years go by, as you keep on healing, keep on growing, He reaches out to you through weekly sermons and fellowship and good Sabbath School discussions; He gives you continued medical help. Medicine for the soul, that is.

Well, all the glory goes to Jesus, of course. And you know, thinking about this Enemy, this Samaritan, and who He represents, there's a line I've always wanted to twist around and use in a new way. Here it is: *With an Enemy like that, who needs friends?*

Let's finish by prayerfully considering the closing challenge by our Lord: "Go, and do thou likewise."

Any time we study a Bible parable, we always like to place ourselves in the proper role in the closing credits. Of course, every citizen of this planet—pastors and popes and prostitutes alike—is the wounded victim by the side of the road. We all need rescue. We've all received the tender ministrations of the Great Physician, the roadside Healer.

But then there's the application, which is actually primary in this story. Because Jesus is talking here about *being* a good neighbor. And in this parable, it was the good Samaritan who did that. The good Samaritan helped his enemy; he was the one who swept aside prejudices and ancient hatreds and grudges and took a wounded foe to the inn and cared for him all night. And in the final credits, as Jesus gives that surprise ending, He then takes in the whole crowd in His direct gaze as He addresses the lawyer: "Which of these three do you think was a neighbor to the man who fell into the hands of robbers?" (verse 36).

And when the lawyer replied, reluctantly, "The one who had mercy on him" (verse 37), Jesus very clearly places a responsibility on the shoulders of every single follower in His kingdom. "Go, and do thou likewise" (KJV).

In *The Living Bible:* "Yes, now go and do the same."

Most of us think of an excuse, a loophole. "But, Lord, I'm so busy."

"No," He says. "Go and do the same."

"But . . . but . . . that person mistreated me. I've got a record of it in a file drawer back home."

"That doesn't matter," Jesus says. "Go and do the same."

"But that's not my gift! I'm not a good people person. I'm shy. I'd rather contribute to the church and let the deacons and deaconesses help the hurting man in the street."

And our Savior says in response to every excuse—both yours and mine: "No, My child. This isn't a role for just a few. This isn't an elected position for the very elect. If you're part of My kingdom, My heavenly entourage, then this is how it's going to be. As the good Samaritan did in My story, go, and do thou likewise." There's nothing soft or vague about these parables; they're not children's bedtime stories, but real, gritty, do-it-now spiritual challenges.

In the text notes from the New International Version, the Bible scholars comment where Jesus asks the question, "Which of these three men was the good neighbor?" Here's their own query: "Who proves he is the good neighbor by his actions?"

The Word of God calls us to a faith that is active, a faith that is proven to be legitimate and real by its actions. Especially in the book of James, but here as well, we find a two-thousand-year-old expression of the old adage that "talk is cheap." "Do you really love your neighbor as yourself?" Jesus asks. "There's someone wounded and bleeding in your path. Maybe someone you don't like. Someone you've looked down on or resented or hated. Now is the time to show if you're a good neighbor, the kind of good neighbor who will be in God's kingdom." Maybe you recall this line from 1 John 2: "He that saith he abideth in him [Jesus] ought himself also so to walk, even as he walked" (verse 6, KJV).

But what do those King James words mean? How did Jesus walk? Well, He walked with a lot of pauses and stops. When someone was hurting, He stopped and helped. When someone was crying, He stopped and dried their tears. When even an enemy was shouting at Him from the sidewalk, Christ paused and reached out to reconcile, to forgive and heal. And if we want to walk as Jesus walked, we have to pause where He paused, and stop where He stopped.

In *The Desire of Ages,* Ellen White beautifully explores this very Bible story: the good Samaritan. Then she addresses the issue of "talk is cheap." "The lesson is no less needed in the world today than when it fell from the lips of Jesus. Selfishness and cold formality have well-nigh extinguished the fire of love, and dispelled the graces that should make fragrant the character. Many who profess His name have lost sight of the fact that Christians are to represent Christ. Unless there is practical self-sacrifice for the good of others, in the family circle, in the neighborhood, in the church, and wherever we may be, then whatever our profession, we are not Christians."[6]

I remember the first time I noticed that last line. Unless we practice self-sacrifice "for the good of others"—not just in our homes and in our own neighborhoods, and in our own home churches, but everywhere—then it doesn't really matter what we say with our lips. My three brothers and I can carry around ministerial credentials for the Seventh-day Adventist Church; I can write books and make sure my name is on the cover. But those are just words. If I don't sacrifice as the good Samaritan did, if I don't love people as this paragraph says, "wherever [I] may be," then my profession of the Christian faith means nothing.

So this is a big deal! If you're looking for the skid marks where the rubber is supposed to meet the road, then you've just found it and so have I. And if you want biblical proof for this concept, look no further than 1 John 4, which is about this topic from start to finish. Here it is nailed down in verse 20: "If anyone says, 'I love God,' yet hates his brother, he is a liar." And then the chapter concludes with this admonition: "And he [God] has given us this command: Whoever loves God must also love his brother" (verse 21).

So as we assign roles in this dramatic story, you and I are the victim. But we're also that good Samaritan . . . at least we are if we want to be a part of God's kingdom.

Can we even find a third role for ourselves? When the good Samaritan had bound up the wounds and lifted the man on to his own donkey, he took him to an inn and asked the innkeeper to care for him until he should return. He provided the innkeeper with resources—those two silver coins. "Take care of him," he instructed. "If you need more money later, I'll provide that too. But until I get back, I'm putting this man in your care."

Let me suggest that all of us in the Christian faith have now been made innkeepers as well! Because Jesus, the Great Rescuer, the greatest Samaritan of them all, has picked up many wounded and broken people. Where does He take them? To the church. Again let's affirm that the church is the hospital for desperate sinners, for those who are bleeding, with problems and pain. And He says to those in the church: "I have to leave for a while. But here are resources—spiritual gifts and talents and blessings. If you need more, My Holy Spirit will provide them too. But look after this friend of Mine until I return."

Owners of a hotel franchise

In 2003, I spent two weeks in the Philippines, sharing Jesus in a series of evangelistic meetings. I met heroic pastors who literally spent every waking hour on the road, riding a sputtering motorcycle from one little church to the next. One of them, a Virgilio Sabagai, was in charge of *seventeen* churches! Earning just $240 a month, he ministered tirelessly to hurting, lonely, poverty-stricken men and women. He dealt with starving kids, with homeless victims, with people beset by bad habits and false doctrines. In terms of this parable, he encountered both the crime victims *and* the robbers . . . many times. But he obediently followed the example of Jesus, of being this good Samaritan. And he and his fellow pastors could tell endless stories of how Christ brought victims to the church for healing.

Some of these victims He brings are lonely or sad or emotionally wounded. But sometimes they're just sinners: bad people who do bad things. Frankly, people need rescue from sin more than from any other disease. More than from bullet wounds caused by drive-by shootings. And the Good Samaritan says to the inn-keepers in the church: "Take care of this person. I'll be back soon, and in the meantime, I'll provide the resources."

In that same book, *The Desire of Ages,* is another jewel of a paragraph: "By faith and prayer press back the power of the enemy. Speak words of faith and courage that will be as a healing balsam to the bruised and wounded one. Many, many, have fainted and become discouraged in the great struggle of life, when one word of kindly cheer would have strengthened them to overcome. Never should we pass by one suffering soul without seeking to impart to him of the comfort wherewith we are comforted of God."[7]

And I can look back in my photo album from my Philippines trip and remember that motorcycle pastor, Virgilio Sabagai. I guess he's not just a country preacher, but now, Jesus says, the head of a great lodging chain with seventeen hotels. And the message on his letterhead, directed at you and at me: "Go, and do thou likewise."

Chapter 12

THE GIRLS
Who Missed the Wedding

It was the high-flying corporate opportunity of a lifetime, and J. B.—short for Jackson Bishop Silvestri—had swung into gear in a nanosecond. Parable Enterprises had a shot at landing two contracts totaling 118 million dollars with the British government, but the twin proposals had to be at 10 Downing Street by 10:00 A.M. the following morning. Delivered in person, of course. And this was a case of starting from scratch.

There was no time to lose. From his Paris suite at the Four Seasons Hotel George V, J. B. picked up his phone, and with one terse phone call, put the emergency plan into effect. Team A, five top company reps, was already at the home office in New York, and team B, based in Dallas, would link up with them there. The Terrific Ten, he always called them, would fly out that same evening, Kennedy to Heathrow nonstop—on Virgin Atlantic, of course—drafting the twin proposals as they went. Flight number 4 would land at 7:10 A.M., giving them time to freshen up, grab a jolt of caffeine, zip out the hundred or so pages on a laser printer for rent at Heathrow's business center, and catch a company limo over to Prime Minister David Cameron's offices. Nothing to it—and ten sky-high, last-minute plane tickets wagered against a possible payoff of 118 million dollar was a bet old J. B. would take any day of the week.

Well, the Terrific Ten, and these ladies were the best in the business, got on board, fastened their seat belts, put their tray tables and seat backs in the full and upright locked position, and waited impatiently for Virgin Atlantic to get ten minutes into its flight so that they could boot up their Pentium-powered, high-speed laptop computers. And as soon as the pilot gave them the go-ahead, their fingers began to fly. Ninety words a minute, proposals and flow charts and Microsoft PowerPoint visuals with little logos flying through the screen with screeching brake noises. They barely touched their dinners, they didn't watch the movie, and they didn't look out the windows—except for Windows 2007 and the 118 million dollar report taking shape on the ten screens.

Just as the plane began to dip down from its assigned flying altitude of thirty-three thousand feet, and with the morning sun barely breaking over the horizon of the Atlantic Ocean and the distant profile of the coast of Ireland, the batteries on the ten laptop computers began to beep. The juice was just about gone. Well, this was expected; the Terrific Ten knew full well how long a battery pack would last. And they also had known that once they got to Heathrow, they had about an hour and a half where they could plug in and finish up the report before jumping in the limo.

And then all at once they heard those dreaded words come crackling through the plane's speakers and through all the headsets as people were watching a SKY report from NBC News. "Ladies and gentlemen, we're experiencing some delay with Heathrow. There's quite a stack of planes below us with the morning traffic, and tower control is asking us to circle. It may be about forty-five minutes, perhaps even a bit longer. We'll keep you posted."

What? One of the ladies from Parable Enterprises, on the B team, looked down at her watch. Forty-five minutes? That was pretty much all of their cushion. They needed that time on the ground where there was juice flowing at 220 volts. How were they going to finish their reports and get them to the prime minister?

"Are you almost done with your section?" one of them asked her seatmate. "No," she said, shaking her head. "I've got to have at least another thirty, forty minutes to summarize."

"How much time left on your laptop?"

"It's out. I just put everything on my flash drive and shut down so I wouldn't lose my files."

"I'm out too." And the young lady, Deirdre, undid her seat belt so she could see across to the other side of the big wide-body jet where the other team was still working away, clicking along at ninety words a minute. "Hey! Aren't your batteries running out?"

Carol, the team leader for the New York group, gave a little shrug. "Yeah, they did. But we packed along spare batteries just in case we hit a delay up here. So it's no big deal."

"You did what?"

Carol hit the Save button on her document. "We brought along extra battery packs. We ordered them from Best Buy, and they pop right in. That way we can go eight hours instead of four. Don't you have them too?"

Deirdre felt her face going flush. "Uh . . . well, no. I guess we never thought of it." And then she kind of gulped. "Any chance you have a second spare? Otherwise, there's no way we'll finish our half." Right at that moment the captain came on again to let them know that a landing slot might open up, but for sure it was going to make them at least an hour late . . . and that traffic going into London was bumper to bumper. A big groan went up from the packed Virgin Atlantic plane.

Once they were on the ground, Parable Enterprises' special task force, the Terrific Ten, found itself now in two groups: the five with foresight, and the five foolish Virgin Atlantic passengers who were still looking for a wall outlet. And while they looked on wistfully, the A team, five women who had their reports complete, rendezvoused with the boss J. B., got into a long black limousine, sank into the genuine leather seats, and said to the driver, "To the prime minister's office, please."

"Jolly good," said the chauffeur as he pulled on to the M4 expressway.

* * * * *

That's how Jesus might have told that story here in the twenty-first century. The Matthew 25 version has a dustier flavor to it, with primitive oil lamps that go out and a wedding feast in a Judean village. But there's still a scene in which someone runs out of an important resource—in the Bible it's lamp oil—and misses the ride of their lifetime.

If you haven't heard Matthew's version for a while, it's well worth a review. It's in chapter 25, right in the middle of a three-chapter section in which Jesus is teaching about His own second coming and the importance of being ready. It starts the same way most of His parables do. "At that time the kingdom of heaven will be like ten virgins who took their lamps and went out to meet the bridegroom. Five of them were foolish and five were wise. The foolish ones took their lamps but did not take any oil with them. The wise, however, took oil in jars along with their lamps. The bridegroom was a long time in coming, and they all became drowsy and fell asleep" (verses 1–5).

Do we already see the parallels? Aside from the word *virgins* and my very subtle choice of airlines earlier? Ten young women are heading to a very important event, and there's a delay. They end up waiting longer than they had expected. And the group ends up being split into two groups, the wise and the foolish. What made the difference? One group planned ahead, the other didn't. It was a case of being prepared; it's as simple as that.

This important story is filled with fascinating nuances, but this much is clear: being ready for the coming of Jesus isn't an automatic thing. People may debate what kind of preparation is necessary, but Jesus teaches that some kind certainly is. You can be ready, or you can be not ready. And in many of these mysterious, flavor-filled, hidden-meaning stories we call the parables of Jesus, a common theme emerges—people who miss out. Not everyone gets into the wedding feast; some are left out. No wonder my two daughters used to sing at Pine Springs Ranch camp each summer: "Give me oil in my lamp; *keep* me burning. Give me oil in my lamp, I pray."

Back in the year 1807, something happened that had a major impact on a still virgin country called the United States of America. A U.S. frigate sailing about forty miles out of Chesapeake Bay—coincidentally, the ship was called the *Chesapeake*—was fired upon by the crew of a British man-of-war vessel, the *Leopard*. Troops from the enemy vessel boarded the *Chesapeake,* and won the day partly because the commander of the American ship, a Commodore James Barron, was unprepared for battle. He simply had not done the most elementary of tasks required of a leader, so he and his men weren't ready . . . and the English troops came aboard. That June 22 event, just a footnote in history today, is one of the key factors that eventually led to the War of 1812. Commodore Barron later faced a court-martial and was actually convicted for the crime of being unprepared. In parable terms, his lamp had gone out; his laptop computer was dead. And two nations went to war.

No wonder Jesus leans closer to us and shares this warning, which makes good sense whether you're flying Virgin Atlantic, or down here below waiting for the Second Coming: "Keep watch, because you do not know the day or the hour" (verse 13).

What else, though, can we glean from this warning tale about preparedness and a well-stocked pantry or laptop case?

An extra can of Os

They say that when you're huddled in a tent at Camp Four on Everest, you really don't need much by way of food. (Although extra batteries to warm up your electric socks might be nice.) Most would-be summiteers on the world's highest mountain, when they get up there in the death zone at twenty-six thousand feet, and are about ready to head out for that killer eighteen-hour climb to the peak and back, simply can't force down any more food. The human body is so thrashed, it just can't take in nourishment. You eat when you get back down—if you get back down.

So when you plan for an assault on Everest, you can go light on the menu. But there's one other area where expedition climbers always, always, always make sure they have plenty of supplies.

In his book *The Climb,* Russian climber Anatoli Boukreev describes the endless wrangling to line up a huge shipment, thirty thousand dollars' worth, of this precious commodity. And, of course, I'm talking about oxygen. He had a connection in Moscow who manufactured the very latest. These bottles, made by a company called Poisk, were almost a pound lighter in weight than anything the competition could come up with. So after a lot of politics and threatening and undercutting, the Mountain Madness expedition headed by Scott Fischer bought a total of fifty-five Poisk three-liter bottles, fifty-four Zvesda four-liter bottles, fourteen regulators, and fourteen masks. The state-of-the-art Poisk bottles, the ones the climbers would use near the top, cost an incredible 325 dollars *each.* Planning for three bottles per climber just on summit day . . . well, you can do the math for yourself. No wonder clients were paying sixty-five thousand dollars per person for this fun-filled excursion to the roof of the world.[1]

One thing was for sure: you didn't want to run out of oxygen, or Os, as the top climbers called the bottled air. Climbing survivor Jon Krakauer wrote a gripping bestseller, *Into Thin Air,* after the tragic 1996 season, and there are some hard spiritual lessons to be found at 29,035 feet. And this is one lesson many climbers have learned the hard way. Summiteers respectfully and sadly remember the late Scott Fischer, and now also the late Anatoli Boukreev. Both men are dead, their bodies frozen high on the Himalayas.

Jesus' story of the wise and foolish virgins happens in warmer climates, and there's more oxygen in the Galilean air, but the stakes are just as high. Five girls plan ahead and have the precious fuel. They have plenty and to spare. Five foolish ones don't.

But it might be well, first of all, to notice what the ten virgins all had in common. All ten girls are waiting with the same goal in mind. They all want to see the bridegroom. In spiritual terms, they all want to meet God. They all are seeking Him, looking for Jesus' soon return. At least as far as that goes, they are all wise, all ten of them. Jesus told some stories in which people couldn't even be bothered to show up for the wedding, but not here. All ten of these women have good motives.

All ten had lamps. And as many of us like to figure out what everything represents, right down to the flavor of the wedding cake, it's suggested that these lamps represent the Word of God. Actually, Psalm 119:105 uses that very metaphor: "Thy word is a lamp unto my feet, and a light unto my path" (KJV).

Is it possible, then, that a man or woman might actually be looking for Jesus to come, and also have a Bible on the coffee table . . . and still somehow be lost? Christ certainly tells the story with that warning in mind. But first, what else do all ten virgins have in common?

Interestingly, all ten of them go to sleep. Matthew chapter 25, verse 5: "The bridegroom was a long time in coming, and they all became drowsy and fell asleep."

The foolish five went to sleep, and finally, so did the wise ones too. And that's a hard point to apply. Do we want to conclude that it's all right for Christians, God's people who eagerly await His coming, to get discouraged and spiritually go to sleep? Well, no, we certainly don't want to say that. And the Bible shares a great abundance of verses that talk about not sleeping, about not dozing, about staying awake and alert. In a section of Luke 12 titled "Watchfulness," Jesus offers this warning: "Be dressed ready for service and keep your lamps burning, like men waiting for their master to return from a wedding banquet, so that when he comes and knocks they can immediately open the door for him. It will be good for those servants whose master finds them watching when he comes" (verses 35–37).

And certainly we remember that sad, real story—not a parable—in the Garden of Gethsemane, when Jesus begged and pleaded for just one disciple to stay awake with Him. But not one of His friends seemed to be able to do so.

And yet here in this story, even the good girls are asleep. There's a delay; midnight arrives. And they just can't stay awake.

Consider this question: has there been a delay in Jesus' coming? If your grandparents were Christians, did they expect our Lord's return many years ago? Of course, they did. My father never thought he'd be in his retirement years, but he's been resting in his grave for years now, and my own AARP card has already arrived in the mail. In the early 1950s, a young Billy Graham told reporters: "Two years and it's all going to be over." The disciples pretty much felt the same way. Five years, maybe ten. But there's been a long delay, and we're well into the twenty-first century. The spiritual Doomsday Clock is fast approaching midnight now, but no one knows for sure when it will strike midnight. That's one of the biggest lessons of this parable, and one Jesus explicitly states in Matthew 25, verse 13. "You do not know the day or the hour." How many times have people missed those nine plain words?

And as we weigh all of Jesus' stories and sort out the details and the interpretations, it's clear that He speaks of a kind of sleeping that is all right and a kind that's not. "Be alert!" Jesus says. "Stay awake!" But even the wise virgins did fall asleep when there was a delay.

In the Tyndale New Testament Commentaries for Matthew, Dr. Richard T. France provides this interpretation: "During the 'delay,' " he writes, and that's certainly where we are right now, "life must go on, and we cannot live on constant alert. The difference was whether they [the ten virgins] had already prepared for the summons, or had left preparation to the last minute, when it would be too late."[2]

It would be easy to go off track right here. None of us would want to conclude that we should not live on "constant alert." But we can't live forever in breathless expectancy, magnifying glasses held in trembling fingers poised over our Bibles. However, it's certainly true that a Christian can and should be prepared, with extra oil or Poisk oxygen tanks, whatever they represent in spiritual terms. And then this parable suggests that it's appropriate for that same Christian to continue life in calm but joyful readiness. When bedtimes come, it's all right to sleep. When witnessing opportunities present themselves, he takes them. His life isn't frantic; instead, it is faithful. Adequate oxygen or oil is at the ready.

Maybe you remember the old story, where Saint Francis of Assisi, that great and aged champion of God, was hoeing in his garden one day. And then a detractor hooted at him, "What would you do if your life were to end this evening?"

And as the story goes, the Christian saint straightened up and said with great calm, "Finish hoeing my garden." Because he was ready, because he was looking for his Savior's return, there was no need to panic.

I once had a workplace friend who typified the fearful watcher. In his younger years, he struggled mightily with the concept of being ready. He wasn't just awake; his whole body and soul were twitching with fear and anticipation. *Was he prepared for Jesus' return? Were there any unforgiven sins in his life?* In fact, he went to a private Bible college where people learned to focus constantly on their own characters, their holiness or lack of thereof. How good were they being, how obedient? My friend actually began to do without sleep. He would fast and skip meals, and then determine to stay awake all night in prayer. According to his interpretation of this story in Matthew 25, if he was to be ready to meet the Bridegroom, he had to be awake at all times. "Watch and pray," the Bible had said, and so this meant being up and alert twenty-four hours a day.

I thank God that the gospel of grace finally came flooding into this sincere man; today he's a powerful gospel preacher for Jesus, presenting a balanced message of watchfulness and joyful rest in Christ. He's prepared, with extra oil at his side and his lamp burning at all times.

So as we look at the similarities between these two groups, we see that they're all looking for the return of the Bridegroom. They all have a kind of religious life, a lamp, which might mean that they're holding onto Bibles, even reading them. When there's a delay, they all relax and sleep, which apparently can be all right, too, as long as alarm clocks work correctly.

But when the buzzer does go off, we come upon the one great difference. And what a deadly difference! What does it truly mean when half of those waiting for Jesus to come run out of oil?

A Quaker state of mind

Borrowing again from an old comedy going back many years, a young Billy Crystal and a couple of friends were on a Wild West vacation, pretending to be cowboys and driving a recalcitrant herd from one state to another one. And Curly, the crusty old cowhand who was leading the way—and also scaring the clients to death with his macho, rattlesnake demeanor—entered into a bit of one-syllable philosophizing with Crystal. "Life really boils down to one thing," he said at last, holding up one finger mysteriously. "Just one thing."

Well, what was the one thing? Despite his fears, Billy really wanted to know. And then the answer: "I'm not going to tell you."

"What?"

"You have to figure it out for yourself."

Here in this parable of Jesus, we kind of come to a similar situation, and it's a bit frustrating. In this story of the five foolish ones, the point is to teach about the concept of preparedness. The five smart ones have extra oil for their lamps, and the foolish ones don't. The five with oil go to the wedding feast, and the others are lost. So immediately we ask the obvious and important question: what does the oil represent? We need to know because those who have it are saved, and those who don't have it are lost. And yet, in all thirteen verses devoted to this anecdote, Jesus never mentions or even hints about what the all-important ingredient stands for. It's like a joke with the punch line missing.

The wise and patient Bible student can't help but notice that when a man or woman asks this question, "What must I do to be saved?" several different answers are given. Paul and Silas, talking to a jailor in Philippi, said very simply, "Believe on the Lord Jesus Christ" (Acts 16:31, KJV). A man asking Jesus got this answer instead: "Keep all the commandments, and also sell all your belongings in order to be able to follow Me." Another man who asked the same question of the same Teacher, Jesus, received a third, completely different answer: "Love God with all your heart, and your neighbor as yourself. Be a good neighbor." In the parable of the wedding feast, which we already explored, a man had to have on a certain wedding garment in order to attain salvation. And here in Matthew 25, hidden in the subliminal threads of this story, is a fifth message: "You have to have an extra supply of lamp oil—whatever lamp oil is—in order to get into the wedding feast."

So how do we solve the riddle of the oil? It might be helpful to work backward, as detectives sometimes do, and look for clues through the process of elimination. What is this story not telling us?

Again, these were ten virgins who did many things the same. What does it take to be saved? All ten of these girls professed a membership in the wedding party. All ten were planning to attend the wedding. All ten were out in the city square or in the street where the bridegroom would be coming. Could we say, then, that mere profession or church membership isn't enough? "Oh, I've been a Christian all my life," someone says. That statement, all by itself, doesn't indicate that a person is going to be saved.

It has been suggested that the women's lamps are significant, that they could represent the Word of God. And maybe that's true. Does having a Bible in your house or even in your hand prove that you're a saved person? Obviously not. Some of the greatest enemies of the Christian faith memorize huge portions of Scripture for the purpose of debate and destruction.

As it became late evening in this story, all ten women fell asleep. When it was midnight and the tambourines and flutes leading the bridegroom's procession sounded, all ten awakened. And the five foolish virgins, even at that crucial moment, were still very interested in going to the wedding. We could interpret this to mean that there will be people at the very end who look up in the clouds, see the King of kings returning, and honestly think they are going to be saved. They want to be saved; they scurry around to do whatever it takes at that moment. So their desires are good . . . and yet, for some reason, they are not saved. When the door to the banquet hall is shut, they're on the outside.

Well, we still haven't uncovered the truth, but we can prayerfully surmise here that church membership is not the answer. Carrying Bibles and even reading Bibles may not be the entire answer. Thinking that you are saved doesn't always prove that you are. This is very unsettling, and so we come back to that oil. Clearly the oil has something to do with preparedness, with having something in reserve. But what? And, of course, the stakes in finding the correct answer are as high as stakes can be. This is a life-and-death Bible study.

Fortunately, our Bibles do provide us with two wonderful clues, and one of them is right here in the story. But let's take the other one first. In the Old Testament book of Zechariah, the prophet of Israel has a dream. In fact, the entire book is basically a dream, but we will look at chapter 4. "[The angel] asked me, 'What do you see?' I answered, 'I see a solid gold lampstand with a bowl at the top and seven lights on it, with seven channels to the lights. Also there are two olive trees by it, one on the right of the bowl and the other on its left' " (verses 2, 3).

Just a bit later in this beautiful chapter, the Bible describes a flow of golden oil from those two olive trees. Then, in verse 4, Zechariah asks the angel, "What are these . . . [things]?"

"Do you not know . . . ?" the angel responds (verse 5). And then this magnificent testimony: " 'Not by might nor by power, but by my Spirit,' says the LORD Almighty" (verse 6).

And Bible scholars affirm that the oil in this great vision does indeed represent the power of the Holy Spirit.

Now as we move back across time to the New Testament and this story of warning by Jesus, what does it mean if we give the parable this application? Could the oil for these lamps similarly represent the Holy Spirit?

Consider again that here are ten women, all in the church. All watching for the coming of the Bridegroom. All of them sent RSVPs that they planned to attend the wedding. All of them carried Bibles. But only five of the ten have a spiritual relationship that's alive—because they have the Holy Spirit. Only five are living in daily connection with the Bridegroom. Only five are reading those Bibles in such a way that they are really becoming acquainted with its subject.

Let's go a step further. I'd suggest that only five of these ten are really, as we say nowadays, "walking the walk," instead of just "talking the talk." Their connection

211

to Christ, because of the Holy Spirit, the oil, is a faith in action. They not only claim the name of Christ, but they try to live as He lived. They follow His example in obedience and in doing good in the world around them; in fact, the rest of this chapter proves that very point with two more famous parables.

In *Christ's Object Lessons,* Ellen White talks about the oil for these lamps. "Into the hearts of all who are united to God by faith the golden oil of love flows freely, to shine out again in good works, in real, heartfelt service for God."[3] Those who have the oil, the presence of the Holy Spirit, have an active faith, shining "out again in good works, in real, heartfelt service." These five wise watchers and seekers don't just say the name of Jesus and carry around His dusty Book. They know Him intimately! The Holy Spirit has invigorated their religious experience; their faith is a real relationship in which they are trusting a Savior they actually know.

Let's be bold in identifying the oil. This oil, this reserve, *is* knowing Jesus. Period. True, the Bible may describe it as the presence of the Holy Spirit. But why did Jesus send the Holy Spirit after He returned to heaven? To keep us connected with Him! "I'll send the Holy Spirit in My place," He promised. The Holy Spirit illuminates our minds as we read Scripture looking for Jesus! The Holy Spirit fills us with the thoughts and the attitudes of Christ, giving us, as Paul describes it, "the mind of Christ" (1 Corinthians 2:16).

And our faith can be affirmed by this second clue in this parable regarding the oil. Is it indeed the Holy Spirit who makes our faith real and living, who gives us an intimate friendship with Christ instead of a dry, formal, theoretical shell of impersonal religion? Let's cut right to the finish line, where Christ wraps up the parable. Matthew 25:10–13: "The virgins who were ready [with their oil] went in with him [the bridegroom] to the wedding banquet. And the door was shut. Later the others also came. 'Sir! Sir!' they said. 'Open the door for us!' But he replied, 'I tell you the truth, *I don't know you.*' Therefore keep watch, because you do not know the day or the hour" (emphasis added).

So what is the oil? It is to know Jesus through the indwelling of the Holy Spirit. In this story, the ones who had it knew Jesus, and He knew them. That's the bottom line right there. The oil was the ingredient of relationship, of friendship, of trust, of biblical faith that is a constant "leaning on the everlasting arms" and not just a Greek word in a concordance.

So how much do we need the oil then? In this Bible story, it was everything! Knowing the Bridegroom was everything! And it's the same today. Like those climbers on Everest who absolutely must have oxygen and don't take one step toward the summit without it, we must have the oil: a Spirit-led, Spirit-strengthened friendship with Jesus.

Doing push-ups ahead of time

This biblical imagery of preparedness also brings to mind the discipline of readying our bodies and minds and souls for supreme conflict and competition. I'm going to wear you out and make you feel tired with an old football story from the archives. *Instant Replay* was written as a diary by Green Bay Packer Jerry Kramer to chronicle the 1967 season. And, of course, back in those glory days, there was a certain short, red-faced, shouting Italian coach in charge named Mr. Vincent Lombardi.

The tale really starts with the preseason practice session, which runs eight weeks. The Packers held their camps at St. Norbert College in West De Pere, Wisconsin, ten minutes away from Green Bay. Two players to a tiny dorm room—these hulking 270-pounders sleeping on short little beds built for fresh-man English majors.

But then there were the practice sessions themselves. And by the admission of everyone in the league, nobody practiced like the Packers. The team went through "two-a-days," double workout sessions to get in shape. As Kramer describes it, "the agony [was] beyond belief." There was a drill called "up-downs," where the whole team would be running in place, lifting their knees as high in the air as they could for twenty, thirty, sometimes forty seconds. Then the coach would shout, "Down!" And the whole team would flop down on the grass, their stomachs smacking the ground. "Up!" And they'd run in place. "Down!" "Up!" Sometimes they'd do that sixty or seventy times until everyone on the team was gasping in exhaustion. Of course, this is mid-July in Wisconsin, with high heat and humid-ity. And this just went on and on and on. Kramer tells how a big kid named Leon Crenshaw, a rookie, showed up at camp weighing 315 pounds. One day in the cafeteria, after doing about eighty of those "up-downs," Crenshaw just flat-out fainted. Passed out cold on the floor. He'd lost twenty-five pounds in two weeks.

Another kid came to Kramer, his tongue hanging out down to his toes. "How do you do it?" he asked. "I can't hack it."

"You've got to block out the pain," the veteran told him. "Just don't think about it. Don't stop for anything."

"Yeah," the rookie said, "but man, I see visions out there."

"What do you mean?" And the kid repeated, "Visions, man. I see people walking around in the air." He was literally hallucinating. And Kramer adds a little P.S. "He got cut from the team a few days later."

Here's a bit more pain, though. Jerry Kramer, being a right guard, was a huge guy, weighing in at around 260. But he usually liked to play more at about 245; it was a season-long struggle to get down to that weight. So he'd sit in the cafeteria with the other players, some of the tight ends eating huge steaks with gravy and butter and rolls and ice cream. And Kramer would eat the tiniest little piece of meat, and a small dish of peas, and one glass of iced tea, and eat it all as slowly as he could, to make it seem like more food.

The point is this. All of this discipline—the "up-downs," the grass sprints, the dieting—was for one purpose. Playing a better game. That added tenth of a second of speed off the line when the center snapped the ball. That little advantage of power, of raw linebacker strength for when he had to face his old archrival, Alex Karras of the Detroit Lions, or Jethro Pugh of the Dallas Cowboys. But who could know if all that training and dieting would ever pay off big? Green Bay might win or lose every game by three touchdowns. Would it ever happen that all the agony, the preparing, the sweating and the crying and the pushing and enduring Lombardi's shouting fits would ever culminate in one big play that made all the difference?

Well, some of you longtime football fans will know the answer. To this day they call it the Ice Bowl, when on December 31, 1967, they had to face the Cowboys for the NFC championship. It was thirteen degrees below zero there in Green Bay. And the game came down to the very last minute, with the Packers behind, 17–14, driving for a TD. They got down to the enemy one yard line, botched two plays, and had one last shot. No time-outs left. They could have tried for a field goal to tie, but decided to go for the win right there. The call was for a quarterback sneak, a 31-wedge, with Bart Starr carrying the ball.

And it was going to be Jerry Kramer who had to open up the hole. He simply had to get Jethro Pugh out of the way. So Kramer writes how he poured everything he had into that one block. All the up-downs, the exercising, the relentless grinding of practice, practice, practice . . . and all the dieting to keep in perfect shape . . . all the endless drills of blocking, pushing, moving your man out . . . it all went into that last block. He blocked Pugh outside and Bart Starr churned into the opening and fell across the finish line. The Green Bay Packers were the champs again, and on TV sets all around the world, on instant replay—that's also the title of his book—people saw that block by number 64, Jerry Kramer, over and over and over again. All the preparing had finally borne fruit in a classic and thrilling way.[4]

Well, there's football, which is a game . . . and then there's Christianity and the challenge of living in these last days. And this parable by Jesus seems to hint at "up-downs" and glasses of iced tea. Five wise girls are prepared for the big game, and five foolish girls aren't. Five have trained, and five haven't. "At midnight the cry rang out: 'Here's the bridegroom! Come out to meet him!' Then all the virgins woke up and trimmed their lamps. The foolish ones said to the wise, 'Give us some of your oil; our lamps are going out.' 'No,' they replied, 'there may not be enough for both us and you. Instead, go to those who sell oil and buy some for yourselves.' But while they were on their way to buy the oil, the bridegroom arrived. The virgins who were ready went in with him to the wedding banquet. And the door was shut" (verses 6–10).

We notice how the five girls ask the others for help. "Give us some of your oil." And it's not that the wise ones are selfish; it's just an impossible thing they're being asked to do. They have barely enough for themselves.

This question resonates both in the NFL and here in the church. Can one person prepare spiritually for another? Can someone else stock your oil? Or do all your push-ups in training for the Super Bowl? That's not possible. Each Christian must have his or her own walk with Jesus. Each believer has to nurture his or her own relationship with God. *The Seventh-day Adventist Bible Commentary* shares a salient point: "Character is not transferable. One Christian cannot do for another that which he must do for himself in preparation for the crisis that lies ahead."[5]

Consider this too. There's a time to get ready and do your exercises and stock up your oil. And that time is before the crisis, before the midnight hour. A good Green Bay Packer couldn't come up to December 31, five or six hours before the kickoff of that championship game with Dallas, and think to himself: *Oh my, I'd better do a few push-ups here, and jog a lap or two.* It's far, far too late by then. In this story, there was a time to buy oil, and that time had passed. It was suggested that the five foolish virgins might go buy oil. But at midnight? How many stores were open at that hour? The story does have these five girls showing up late at the banquet hall, but it doesn't specify where they found oil. But when midnight comes, when it's time for the Super Bowl, the hour for preparing has long passed. It's now time for the results of preparation to manifest themselves.

Thomas Fuller once opined, "In fair weather prepare for foul."

The ancient philosopher Syrus adds, "We should lay up in peace what we shall need in war."

What does this mean for Christians? Training camp is happening right now.

We need to get that oil, the Holy Spirit, flowing today, now. We need to know Christ today, have a living relationship with Him at this very moment.

While my family served in Thailand, Dr. Ralph Neall, our Adventist missionary friend, toiled in nearby Saigon during the Vietnam War. So he knows a few things about preparing for crisis ahead of time. In *How Long, O Lord?* he comments, "The reward for the wise is a place at the wedding banquet of the Lamb. The loss of the foolish is to be shut out with the tragic words, 'I don't know you.' If we want Him to know us then, we must know Him now!"

And then he adds, "The parable of the virgins tells us we should cultivate our devotional lives and keep our vessels full of oil every day. We never know when we may find ourselves thrown into a situation in which we won't have time to study and pray before making a decision or giving an answer."[6]

Our Blackberrys don't digitally inform us exactly when the big game is. "No man knows the day or the hour"; that's the punch line of this story. But we know who the Coach is, and when practice is too. Practice is right now. Grab your shoulder pads and let's get out there.

Always ready for a fire drill

But one final lesson from this midnight tale. Many years ago, when I was working with the Voice of Prophecy radio ministry, an amusing incident took place at a fund-raising weekend. A bunch of us were at a workshop at a Hyatt Regency hotel in Bellevue, Washington, enjoying a marvelous, funny, rollicking-good-time story being told by my friend Terry Johnson, a former member of President Reagan's Honor Guard. And all at once, while Johnson was entertaining us, a fire alarm went off and a female voice announced through the entire hotel PA system—all twenty-five stories—that the hotel should be evacuated. "Please move to the exits." Well, we started . . . but after just about a minute, someone waved the white flag and said that it was a false alarm.

Terry, of course, rolled with the punches, and, thinking on his feet, made a good joke or two about it. But that false alarm set me to thinking, because in this parable by Jesus, a big wedding is delayed until midnight. And there are a lot of false alarms. You know, "Hey, Jesus is coming! I've figured it out with my prophecy charts." I'm sure you've heard those and so have I. As the world crept toward the year 2000, all sorts of unwise bits of speculation swirled about. False alarms, every one of them. But this very story tells us clearly that no man, no woman, knows the day or the hour.

So our final issue is this. What if it isn't a false alarm? What if the hotel really had been on fire? And suppose Terry Johnson had just kept on talking and preaching? What if all of us sitting around the banquet tables with our half-eaten desserts had just stayed there, not budging out of our seats? What if the waiters had just kept on clearing off the silverware, taking out the food? The point is this: there's a time for sermons and for dessert and for waiters to do their jobs. Those are all good things. But there's also a time to head for the exits because the hotel is on fire. And what would normally be an activity that indicates wisdom is suddenly foolishness because the time of crisis has come.

The clearest demographic demarcation in the story of the ten virgins is this: wise . . . and foolish. Five of these women were wise, and five, foolish.

In the chapter right before this one, Matthew 24, is another story about wise and foolish. Here's the heart of it: "Who then is the faithful and *wise* servant, whom the master has put in charge of the servants in his household to give them their food at the proper time? It will be good for that servant whose master finds him doing so when he returns" (verses 45, 46; emphasis added).

We learn two lessons from this cryptic story. What makes a person wise in these last days? We're plainly told. Wisdom is doing what we're supposed to be doing at the appointed hour. This man was in charge of the house, in charge of feeding the staff. When the master comes back, that's what he's doing! And that's wisdom.

If you read down a bit further in this story, Jesus then paints a contrast between this servant and another one who decides that the master has been gone a long time. So he begins to beat up on other people and abuse them. He puts the master out of his mind, assuming that he's gone forever. So here's wisdom, parts one *and* two. Wisdom is to be doing what you're supposed to be doing, and it's also to be consistently remembering your relationship with the master.

Back in Old Testament times, the children of Israel had a crisis of faith when Moses went up on to Mount Sinai and didn't come back for forty days. And the Israelites gave up on both Moses and God. "Out of sight, out of mind." So they said to Aaron, "Build us a new god, one we can see. We think this God is gone." That was rank, shortsighted foolishness.

If you've been to Sabbath School very many times, you probably recall another story, going back to chapter 4 of this book, where you had "wise" on one side and "foolish" on the other side of the beach volleyball court. My granddaughter Kira can sing that song by heart and do all the motions. A wise man, Jesus said, built his house upon the rock. The foolish man built his on the sand. And when the storm came, guess which house was washed away?

Again let's point out that wisdom is doing the right thing. In this case, the right thing is building houses on rocks. That was wise. Now, there's nothing especially wicked about building a house on sand, except that when El Niños are coming, that's the wrong thing to be doing. That's foolish. And let's also notice what these two builders represent. Jesus says it very clearly; we can't miss it: "Everyone who hears these words of mine and puts them into practice is like a wise man who built his house on the rock" (Matthew 7:24).

So what is wisdom in these last days? Hearing Jesus' words *and* doing them. That's preparedness; that's wisdom. Richard France defines wise people in commenting on these two stories: "those who are engaged in action appropriate to their professed status." He then adds, "It is the crisis which will divide the ready from the unready."[7]

Isn't that painfully true? It would actually be all right to build a house on the sand; after all, the view of the beach from there would be terrific. And it's no problem to build there, as long as a storm never comes. It would be all right to never really train hard for football, as long as every game you were in was never close or crucial. It would be all right to not have extra oxygen on Everest as long as no storms came along and you didn't climb very high. You could do without extra oil while waiting for the Bridegroom, as long as He wasn't late. But if a crisis comes—and of course, the Bible tells us flat out that there will be one before the midnight hour—there are going to be wise people who have prepared, and foolish ones who haven't.

As we get ready to throw rice at the bride and Groom, let's get just as practical as we can. We talk about oil and oxygen and push-ups, and perhaps you begin wondering, "But what do I really *do*? I want to be wise, but what do I *do* each Sunday, Monday, Tuesday, Wednesday, Thursday, Friday, and Saturday?"

In *How Long, O Lord?* Ralph Neall discusses how the second coming of Jesus has certainly been delayed. So how can we be ready? According to him, the answer is right here, and it's here three times.

There are three parables in Matthew 25: the ten virgins, the three servants who all received different talents, and then the story of the sheep and goats. And this brief trilogy tells us exactly what we should be doing here as midnight approaches. In the story of the ten virgins, the message is clear: we need to know the Bridegroom and have the extra oil of the Holy Spirit empowering our lives. Day by day, wide awake or drowsy, we need to spend time knowing Jesus Christ.

Story number two: the talents. And here we need to be using our gifts for God. If we have five gifts, use them. If we have one, use the one. But again, we keep in mind that the Master of the house—our Friend and Savior Jesus—is coming back, and we want to be able to give Him a good report.

Story number three: those sheep and goats. And here the wise person is simply doing in the world what good he or she can do. Be kind to strangers. Care for the widows and orphans. Love your neighbor. Visit someone in prison. Be a Matthew 25 "sheep" instead of a self-serving goat.

I'm especially impressed by the "calm" of Ralph Neall's book. No fear, no pulse-pounding crisis, no panic, no screaming headlines. He does make it clear, as Jesus does, that last-minute preparing is impossible. There does come a time when you can't buy oil and when the door to the banquet hall is closed and locked. But Neall just quietly writes that if we're doing these three things—knowing Jesus, using our talents, being kind and loving to others—then whether Christ returns in fifty years or tomorrow night at midnight, we'll be ready.[8]

Let's close this story with a line from the very famous Tom Bodett. Do you remember? "We'll leave the light on for you." Jesus speaks to us about lamps and oil. What does that Motel 6 ad slogan imply, "We'll leave the light on for you"? Two things. First of all, the motel staff will be ready for us. It may be late, and yes, the front-desk person might doze off, but when you ring the bell, they'll be ready. Second, they'll have a welcoming spirit. They'll be glad to welcome us as guests.

Don't you really want to say the same to our Friend Jesus right now, "I'll have the light on for You"? "Jesus, I'll be ready. Whenever You come, I want to be doing the wise thing, the right thing, the thing appropriate to the time. And Jesus, with all my heart I say this too: You'll be welcome. Please come and check in soon."

Notes

Chapter 1

1. Bill Watterson, *Calvin and Hobbes* (Kansas City, Mo.: Andrews and McMeel, 1987), 73.

2. Morris Venden, *Parables of the Kingdom* (Nampa, Idaho: Pacific Press® Publishing Association, 1986), 6; italics in the original.

3. Jerry Adler, "Heaven's Gatekeepers," *Newsweek,* March 16, 1998.

4. Beck Weathers in Broughton Coburn, *Everest: Mountain Without Mercy* (Washington, D.C.: National Geographic Society and MacGillivray Freeman Films, 1997), 178, 179.

5. Philip Yancey, *What's So Amazing About Grace?* (Grand Rapids, Mich.: Zondervan Publishing, 1997), 49–51.

6. Venden, *Parables of the Kingdom,* 34.

7. Ibid., 35.

8. Paul Brand with Philip Yancey, *Pain: The Gift Nobody Wants* (New York: HarperCollins Publishers, 1993), 74–80.

Chapter 2

1. Mark Twain, *The Adventures of Tom Sawyer* (New York: Bantam Books, 1875), 164, 165.

2. Ibid., 212, 213.

3. Ibid., 217.

4. Richard T. France, *Matthew,* Tyndale New Testament Commentaries (Leicester, England: InterVarsity Press, 1985), 229.

5. Ellen G. White, *Christ's Object Lessons* (Hagerstown, Md.: Review and Herald® Publishing Association, 1941), 103, 104.

6. Jack J. Blanco, *The Clear Word* (Hagerstown, Md.: Review and Herald®, 1994); emphasis added.

7. Eugene H. Peterson, *The Message* (Colorado Springs, Colo.: NavPress, 2002).

8. Tim LaHaye and Jerry B. Jenkins, *Left Behind* (Wheaton, Ill.: Tyndale House Publishers), 144.

9. France, *Matthew,* Tyndale New Testament Commentaries, 229.

10. White, *Christ's Object Lessons,* 104.

11. Ibid., 104, 105.

12. Joy Swift, *They're All Dead, Aren't They?* (Nampa, Idaho: Pacific Press®, 1986)

13. White, *Christ's Object Lessons,* 105.

14. Ibid., 109.

Chapter 3

1. Chuck Colson and Nancy Pearcey, *How Now Shall We Live?* (Wheaton, Ill.: Tyndale House Publishers, 1999), 394, 395.

2. France, *Matthew,* Tyndale New Testament Commentaries, 354; emphasis added.

3. Jimmy Carter, *Living Faith* (New York: Times Books, 1996), 209.

4. Francis D. Nichol, ed., *The Seventh-day Adventist Bible Commentary,* vol. 5 (Washington, D.C.: Review and Herald® Publishing Association, 1956), 511.

5. France, *Matthew,* Tyndale New Testament Commentaries, 357.

6. Ralph Neall, *How Long, O Lord?* (Hagerstown, Md.: Review and Herald®, 1988), 128, 130, 131; emphasis added.

7. Carter, *Living Faith,* 218.

8. France, *Matthew,* Tyndale New Testament Commentaries, 355.

9. Carter, *Living Faith,* 175, 176.

10. Colson and Pearcey, *How Now Shall We Live?* 365.

11. France, *Matthew,* Tyndale New Testament Commentaries, 358.

Chapter 4

1. Bill Hybels and Rob Wilkins, *Descending Into Greatness* (Grand Rapids, Mich.: Zondervan Publishing House, 1993), 178.

2. Ellen G. White, *Testimonies for the Church* (Mountain View, Calif.: Pacific Press®, 1948), 5:129, 130.

3. Tony Evans, *The Victorious Christian Life* (Nashville, Tenn.: Thomas Nelson Publishers, 1994), 116, 120; emphasis added.

4. Garrie F. Williams, *How to Be Filled With the Holy Spirit—And Know It* (Hagerstown, Md.: Review and Herald®, 1991), 66.

5. C. S. Lewis, *Mere Christianity* (New York: Macmillan Publishing, 1943), 22.

6. Adrian Rogers, *Believe in Miracles but Trust in Jesus* (Wheaton, Ill.: Crossway Books, 1997), 70; emphasis added.

7. Donna Partow, *Walking in Total God-Confidence* (Minneapolis, Minn.: Bethany House Publishers, 1999), 18, 19, 169, 170; emphasis added.

8. John Stott, *The Contemporary Christian* (Downers Grove, Ill.: InterVarsity Press, 1992), 89.

9. Ibid., 90.

10. Ibid., 92, 93; emphasis added.

11. Colson and Pearcey, *How Now Shall We Live?* 21.

Chapter 5

1. France, *Matthew,* Tyndale New Testament Commentaries, 225.

2. Nichol, ed., *The Seventh-day Adventist Bible Commentary,* 5:408.

3. White, *Christ's Object Lessons,* 72, 73.

4. France, *Matthew,* Tyndale New Testament Commentaries, 224, 225.

5. Nichol, ed., *The Seventh-day Adventist Bible Commentary,* 5:403.

6. White, *Christ's Object Lessons,* 70, 71; emphasis added.

7. Richard W. Dortch, *Fatal Conceit* (Green Forest, Ark.: New Leaf Press, 1993), 89, 90.

Chapter 6

1. Nichol, ed., *The Seventh-day Adventist Bible Commentary,* 5:449.
2. France, *Matthew,* Tyndale New Testament Commentaries, 277.
3. Ibid.
4. Ibid.; emphasis added.
5. White, *Christ's Object Lessons,* 245–247.
6. Mario Puzo, *The Godfather* (New York: Penguin Group, 1978), 30–32, 60, 61.
7. France, *Matthew,* Tyndale New Testament Commentaries, 277.
8. Nichol, ed., *The Seventh-day Adventist Bible Commentary,* 5:450.
9. Yancey, *What's So Amazing About Grace?* 70; emphasis in the original.
10. White, *Christ's Object Lessons,* 250.
11. Ibid., 251; emphasis added.
12. Yancey, *What's So Amazing About Grace?* 97.
13. C. S. Lewis, *The Weight of Glory and Other Addresses* (New York: Macmillan, 1980), 125.

Chapter 7

1. Max Allan Collins, *Saving Private Ryan* (New York: Penguin Group, 1998), 128, 129, 228, 258, 259; screenplay by Robert Rodat.
2. Nichol, ed., *The Seventh-day Adventist Bible Commentary,* 5:815.
3. White, *Christ's Object Lessons,* 190, 191.
4. C. S. Lewis, *Surprised by Joy,* in *The Inspirational Writings of C. S. Lewis* (New York: Inspirational Press, 1994), 124, 125.
5. Nichol, ed., *The Seventh-day Adventist Bible Commentary,* 5:447.
6. Ibid., 815, 816.
7. White, *Christ's Object Lessons,* 187.
8. Ibid., 188.
9. Ibid.; emphasis added.
10. Ibid., 188, 189; emphasis in the original.
11. Steven Mosley, *A Tale of Three Virtues* (Sisters, Ore.: Questar Publishers, 1989), 74.
12. Nichol, ed., *The Seventh-day Adventist Bible Commentary,* 5:815.
13. Ibid., 816; emphasis added.
14. White, *Christ's Object Lessons,* 189.
15. Bill Hybels and Mark Mittelberg, *Becoming a Contagious Christian* (Grand Rapids, Mich.: Zondervan Publishing House, 1994), 22; emphasis in original.
16. White, *Christ's Object Lessons,* 187.
17. Ibid., 196.
18. Ibid., 191.

Chapter 8

1. Yancey, *What's So Amazing About Grace?* 48, 49.
2. Nichol, ed., *The Seventh-day Adventist Bible Commentary,* 5:478, 479.
3. Carter, *Living Faith,* 198, 199.
4. Nichol, ed., *The Seventh-day Adventist Bible Commentary,* 5:480.
5. Mike Downey, "A Mama's Boy's Biggest, Baddest, Toughest Battle," California and the

West, *Los Angeles Times,* March 22, 1998, 3.

6. Lewis, *Mere Christianity,* 165.

7. Ibid., 172.

8. Ibid., 181.

9. Morris Venden, *What Jesus Said About . . .* (Mountain View, Calif.: Pacific Press®, 1984), 88.

Chapter 9

1. France, *Matthew,* Tyndale New Testament Commentaries, 352.

2. Bob Woodward, *The Choice* (New York: Simon & Schuster, 1997).

3. Nichol, ed., *The Seventh-day Adventist Bible Commentary,* 5:510.

4. Jack Deere, *Surprised by the Power of the Spirit* (Grand Rapids, Mich.: Zondervan, 1993), 166, 167.

5. C. S. Lewis, "Answers to Questions on Christianity," in *God in the Dock,* in *The Collected Works of C. S. Lewis* (New York: Inspirational Press, 1996), 334, 335.

6. Billy Graham, *Just as I Am* (San Francisco: HarperCollins, 1997), xiii and back cover.

Chapter 10

1. Carter, *Living Faith,* 209.

2. Yancey, *What's So Amazing About Grace?* 54, 55.

3. Robert Farrar Capon, quoted in ibid., 62.

4. Ibid.; emphasis in original.

5. Ibid.

6. David B. Smith, *Bats, Balls & Altar Calls* (Nampa, Idaho: Pacific Press®, 1987), 32.

7. Yancey, *What's So Amazing About Grace?* 60, 61.

8. France, *Matthew,* Tyndale New Testament Commentaries, 289.

9. R. H. Stein, *An Introduction to the Parables of Jesus* (Philadelphia: Westminster Press, 1981), 128.

10. France, *Matthew,* Tyndale New Testament Commentaries, 289.

11. Raymond S. Moore, *China Doctor* (New York: Harper & Brothers, 1961), 117.

12. Venden, *Parables of the Kingdom,* 47; emphasis added.

13. Ellen White, *Steps to Christ* (Mountain View, Calif.: Pacific Press®, 1892), 79.

Chapter 11

1. Carter, *Living Faith,* 216–218.

2. Leon Morris, *Luke,* Tyndale New Testament Commentaries (Leicester, England: InterVarsity Press, 1974), 188.

3. F. F. Bruce, *The International Bible Commentary* (Grand Rapids, Mich.: Eerdmans Publishing, 1964).

4. Ellen G. White, *The Desire of Ages* (Mountain View, Calif.: Pacific Press®, 1940), 503.

5. Cal and Rose Samra, *More Holy Humor* (Nashville: Thomas Nelson Publishers, 1997), 66.

6. White, *The Desire of Ages,* 504.

7. Ibid., 504, 505.

Chapter 12

1. Anatoli Boukreev and G. Weston DeWalt, *The Climb* (New York: St. Martin's Press, 1997), 31–33.

2. France, *Matthew,* Tyndale New Testament Commentaries, 351.

3. White, *Christ's Object Lessons,* 419.

4. Jerry Kramer, *Instant Replay* (New York: Signet Books, 1968), 33, 216, 217.

5. Nichol, ed., *The Seventh-day Adventist Bible Commentary,* 5:509.

6. Neall, *How Long, O Lord?* 129–131.

7. France, *Matthew,* Tyndale New Testament Commentaries, 349, 350.

8. Neall, *How Long, O Lord?* 130, 131.